# NEW YORK GIANTS

## SEVENTY-FIVE YEARS

BY JERRY IZENBERG ▪ FOREWORD BY FRANK GIFFORD

TIME
LIFE
BOOKS

A TEHABI BOOK

## Captions

**Right:** The blue-collar roots of the New York Giants fan base runs deep into its history, as evidenced by these hard hats decorated in the Giants colors.

**Pages 6–7:** The cry went out: "DEE–fense—DEE–fense." And in the late 1950s and early '60s, the New York Giants had one of the greatest units ever assembled in the National Football League. Defenders descending en masse on rival ball-carriers was the cornerstone of Giants football. As linebacker Sam Huff (70) closes in on a trapped Cardinals back, linebacker Tom Scott (82), end Jim Katcavage (75), tackle Rosey Grier (76), end Andy Robustelli (81), and tackle Dick Modzelewski (77) form an unpenetrable wall.

**Pages 8–9:** Giants defenders, left end Henry Reed (80), right tackle John Mendenhall (64), and left linebacker Jim Flies, swiftly bury an Eagle ballcarrier into the turf.

**Pages 10–11:** The sight of outside linebacker Lawrence Taylor in full charge was enough to make a quarterback close his eyes in fear.

**Pages 12–13:** Season tickets are sold out years in advance, making a capacity crowd at Giants Stadium a common sight.

**Pages 14–15:** The Giants celebrate a Gary Brown (33) touchdown during a 28-7 victory over Kansas City on December 20, 1998, at Giants Stadium. Joining in the festivities are quarterback Kent Graham (10) and linemen Scott Gragg (74), Roman Oben (72), Lance Scott (53), and Derek Engler (69).

## TEHABI BOOKS

*New York Giants: Seventy-Five Years* was conceived and produced by Tehabi Books. *Tehabi*—symbolizing the spirit of teamwork—derives its name from the Hopi Indian tribe of the southwestern United States. As an award-winning book producer, Tehabi works with national and international publishers, corporations, institutions, and non-profit groups to identify, develop, and implement comprehensive publishing programs. Tehabi Books is located in Del Mar, California. www.tehabi.com

Chris Capen, President
Tom Lewis, Editorial and Design Director
Sharon Lewis, Controller
Nancy Cash, Managing Editor
Andy Lewis, Senior Art Director
Sarah Morgans, Associate Editor
Mo Latimer, Editorial Assistant
Maria Medina, Administrative Assistant
Steve Lux, Art Director
Kevin Giontzeneli, Production Artist
Sam Lewis, Webmaster
Ross Eberman, Director of Custom Publishing
Tim Connolly, Sales and Marketing Manager
Eric Smith, Marketing Assistant
Tiffany Smith, Executive Assistant
Laurie Gibson, Copy Editor
Gail Fink, Proofreader
Ken DellaPenta, Indexer
Doug Murphy, Photo Researcher

Time-Life Books is a division of Time Life Inc.

TIME LIFE INC.
George Artandi, President and CEO

TIME-LIFE CUSTOM PUBLISHING
Terry Newell, Vice President and Publisher
Neil Levin, Vice President of Sales and Marketing
Jennifer Pearce, Director of Acquisitions and Editorial Resources
Laura Ciccone McNeill, Director of Creative Services
Liz Ziehl, Director of Special Markets
Jennie Halfant, Project Manager
*Time Life is a trademark of Time Warner Inc. U.S.A.*

Tehabi Books offers special discounts for bulk purchases for sales promotions or premiums. Specific, large quantity needs can be met with special editions, including personalized covers, excerpts of existing materials, and corporate imprints.

For more information, contact Tehabi Books, 1201 Camino Del Mar, Suite 100, Del Mar, CA 92014, (800) 243-7259

Library of Congress Cataloging-in-Publication Data
Izenberg, Jerry.
     New York Giants : seventy-five years / by Jerry Izenberg ;
  foreword by Frank Gifford.
          p.    cm.
     Includes index.
     ISBN 0-7370-0068-X (hardcover) --ISBN 0-7370-0067-8 (softcover)
     --ISBN 1-887656-17-0 (leather) --ISBN 1-887656-18-9 (corporate hardcover)
     1. New York Giants (Football team)--History. I. Title.
GV956.N41978 1999
796.332'64'097471--dc21             99-28527
                        CIP

99 00 01 02 03 / TB 10 9 8 7 6 5 4 3 2 1
First printing. Printed in Korea through Dai Nippon Printing Co., Ltd.

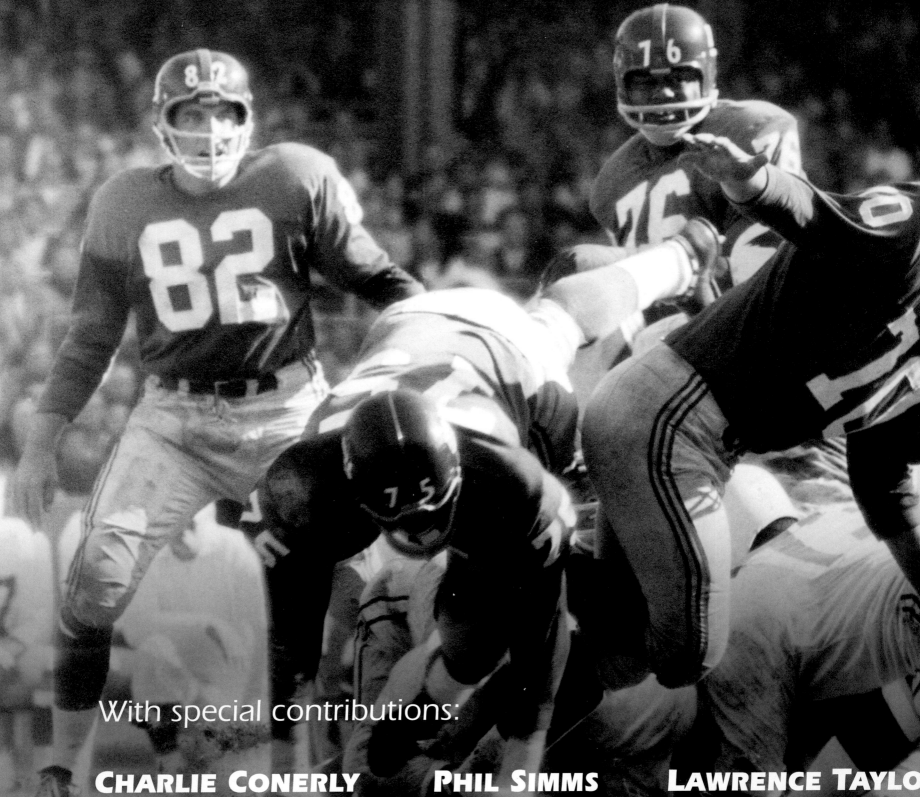

With special contributions:

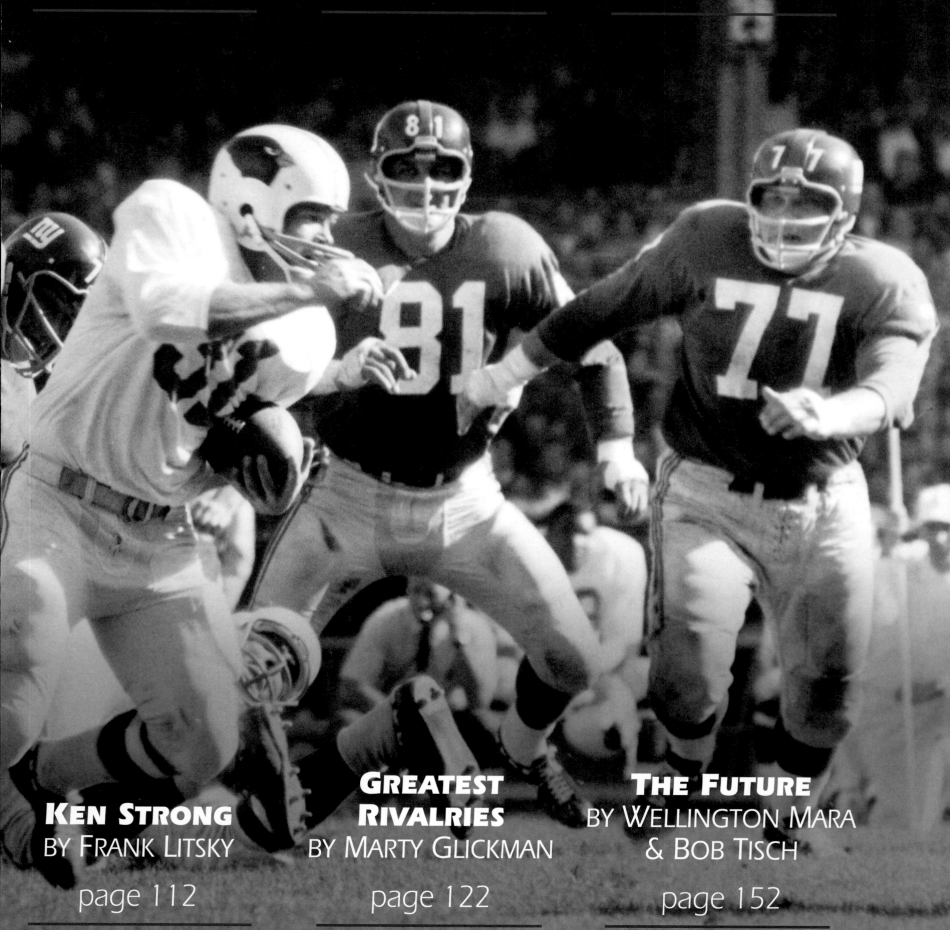

**W**riting a foreword to a historical review of the New York Giants is both an honor and a wonderful opportunity to relive some of the most memorable moments of my life.

Those moments began when I was scouted while at USC by owner Wellington Mara, and then drafted number one in 1952. Without question, one of the most memorable of those moments was being presented to the NFL Hall of Fame by that same Wellington Mara twenty-five years later in Canton, Ohio. In Wellington's presentation and my acceptance speech, we spoke openly and fondly of the "Giants family." And it is a family: a warm, wonderful family that has stuck together during tough times, lean times, and times of glory. Guys like Charlie Conerly, Y. A. Tittle, and Rosie Brown were truly my brothers during those years of frozen fields, broken bones, and championship triumphs.

When I recall the years of taking the field over and over before thousands of fans, my thoughts go equally to the members of my own family. For the first time in my pro football career, my dad was in the stands, watching me play in the historic 1958 championship game between the Giants and the Colts. It was a game in which I fumbled twice in the first half, perhaps paving the way for the Colts' sudden-death victory in overtime. Dad had spent the whole week before that game with me, accompanying me to practices, interviews, and Toots Shoor's saloon. And he was with me in the locker room after that devastating game when assistant coach Vince Lombardi came up to me, put his hand on my shoulder, and said, "Don't take it so hard, Frank, because we wouldn't have gotten here without you." There in that Giants locker room, my father and I fought back tears.

Another memory comes from the 1959 season, when the

# TIMES OF GLORY

## BY FRANK GIFFORD

Giants had really hit it big with the fans. I had an apartment at the Concourse Plaza, very near Yankee Stadium, where I lived with my wife and children during the football season. Those were heady times with rowdy fans so, to avoid a hyper postgame crowd, I would leave the locker room with my kids and take a shortcut through the dugout and out across the field. I loved that time almost as much as the game. My sons Jeff and Kyle would be racing around and, depending on the postgame condition of my body, I'd take a slow walk to the exit at center field, just savoring the pure joy and miracle of my being there.

I was with my eight-year-old son Cody for the thrilling 20-16 upset of the un-defeated Denver Broncos in week fifteen of the 1998 season, and it was yet another

wonderful moment for me. It was our first Giants game together and we took it all in. We watched the players warmup before the game, sat with my former teammate Y. A. Tittle in Ann Mara's box, and became part of the wildly cheering seventy-six thousand fans. When it was over, Cody and I visited the locker room, talked with the players and coaches, and then walked out onto the field where it had all taken place. It was strangely quiet by then, but the after-noon excitement was still with us. As we slowly walked around the empty arena with its many, almost ghostly memo-ries, Cody squeezed my hand, and looked up at me.

"You did that, didn't you Dad," he said. I looked at him and all I could do was smile and nod. I knew then that a new member of the Giants family was born.

**I**t was a gamble that only a bookmaker could take. So Tim Mara did. Think about it. Even in 1925, New York was the city that never slept. From Billy LaHiff's, a Manhattan speakeasy where fight managers, wise guys, and politicians swore they went for the cheesecake and not the illegal booze, to Harlem's lavish Cotton Club; from the elegant roof garden at the Hotel Pennsylvania, complete with dining and dancing to the sounds of the Nathan Abas Concert Orchestra, to what the New York *Times* advertised as "The Great White Way Revue-Cabaret-Night Club Sensation Earl Carroll's Vanities from 8 P.M. until unconscious": Cole Porter was right on the money when he wrote that when a Broadway baby said good night, it was, indeed, early in the morning.

This was the city that belonged to the baseball Giants and the Yankees and the Dodgers—to John McGraw and Babe Ruth—to Belmont Park racetrack and the old Madison Square Garden—to six-day bike races and world championship boxing.

Pro football? Who needed it? More to the point, who in the world's most exciting city even wanted it? It was a sport still shrouded in its artistic stone age, one that belonged in mill towns and hamlets where the only other entertainment options were eateries called Mom's Café and shot-and-a-beer pleasure palaces with names like The Shamrock Bar and Grill. Who wanted to be on an equal footing with them? Theirs was a game for Pennsylvania coal miners with massive Sunday morning hangovers.

Football? If the Great City wanted football, it could get more than enough from the college kids of NYU, Fordham, Columbia, and Manhattan, who hosted teams like Army, Nebraska, and St. Mary's, as well as each other, and drew crowds of as many as seventy thousand to Yankee Stadium and the Polo Grounds on autumn Saturdays.

# THE NEW YORK FOOTBALL GIANTS

**Upon acquiring his** National Football League franchise, Tim Mara struck a deal with baseball's Giants to share the Polo Grounds, opposite, as home. To distinguish the teams, Mara named his club the New York Football Giants. Both the football and the uniform have come a long way in seventy-five years. This 1929 ball was much slicker, wider, and less pointed than today's ball, making it much more difficult to throw. Giants back Hap Moran, below, who played from 1928 to 1934, had only a flimsy leather helmet and thin shoulder pads for protection.

---

Not only was professional football less sophisticated in New Yorkers' view, but look at the company it would put you in. Who in a city that considered itself the capital of the world could possibly work up any kind of emotion at all about Columbus, Ohio; Frankford, Pennsylvania; or teams like the Los Angeles Buccaneers, who never got any closer to Los Angeles than Chicago or Rochester because they had no home field, no home city, and the "Los Angeles" before their name was nothing more than a figment of a promoter's imagination?

In the face of that, who but a bookmaker would have the guts, the foresight, and the luck to buy such a franchise? The truth is that on August 1, 1925, Tim Mara had absolutely no intention of owning a football team. It was a fighter he wanted, and the particular fighter he had in mind was Gene Tunney, light heavyweight champion of the world and the man who would eventually win the heavyweight championship from Jack Dempsey.

"The biggest bet my father ever made was on Gene Tunney. He loved him. He also knew absolutely nothing about football," Wellington Mara said of his father. "He didn't even have a clue. I remember a game against Orange [New Jersey] a couple of years after he bought the team. One of our backs ran a sweep, then cut back to avoid a tackler, then reversed himself again, and ran in the original direction, and my father was on his feet, screaming and hollering through the whole thing. He then looked down at me and said, 'What a great run.'

"I had to explain to him that, after all of that, the runner only made three yards."

So it wasn't a deep and abiding knowledge of the game that led Tim Mara to bring pro football to New York. What it was, was his unshakable belief that whatever the game, if you could put "New York" on the jerseys, you would inspire love and loyalty at home and chauvinistic hatred on the road. Either way, he believed, the end result would add up to success at the box office. This was a belief rooted in his love of the city, his understanding of the collective psyche of its citizens who legally bet with him at the racetrack, and his close ties to the city's politicians and sports heroes.

Still, if truth be told, on that day he would rather have had a piece of Tunney, which was what had brought him to Billy Gibson's office. Gibson was Mara's friend and Tunney's manager. He was also a very stubborn man. By the time Mara arrived that morning, Gibson had made up his mind to keep Tunney, and no amount of arguing was going to change that. But when Mara came in, he found the fight manager visiting with a sportswriter from Ohio named Joe Carr and a retired army surgeon named Harry A. March.

March was a football fanatic and Carr was the recently named president of the fledgling National Football League. "These guys have been here all morning trying to get me to invest in their football league. I think it can work, but I blew $15,000 of my own money trying to finance one team in this town and I can't afford a second try. Maybe you and I could get together with March on this," Gibson told Mara.

**In the formative** years of the National Football League, the Giants were limited to twenty men; the starters played both offense and defense. The 1929 team that finished second in the NFL included Hall of Famers Ray Flaherty (1) and Steve Owen (55). Although the game was in its infancy, souvenirs like this pennant, right, were already a hot commodity.

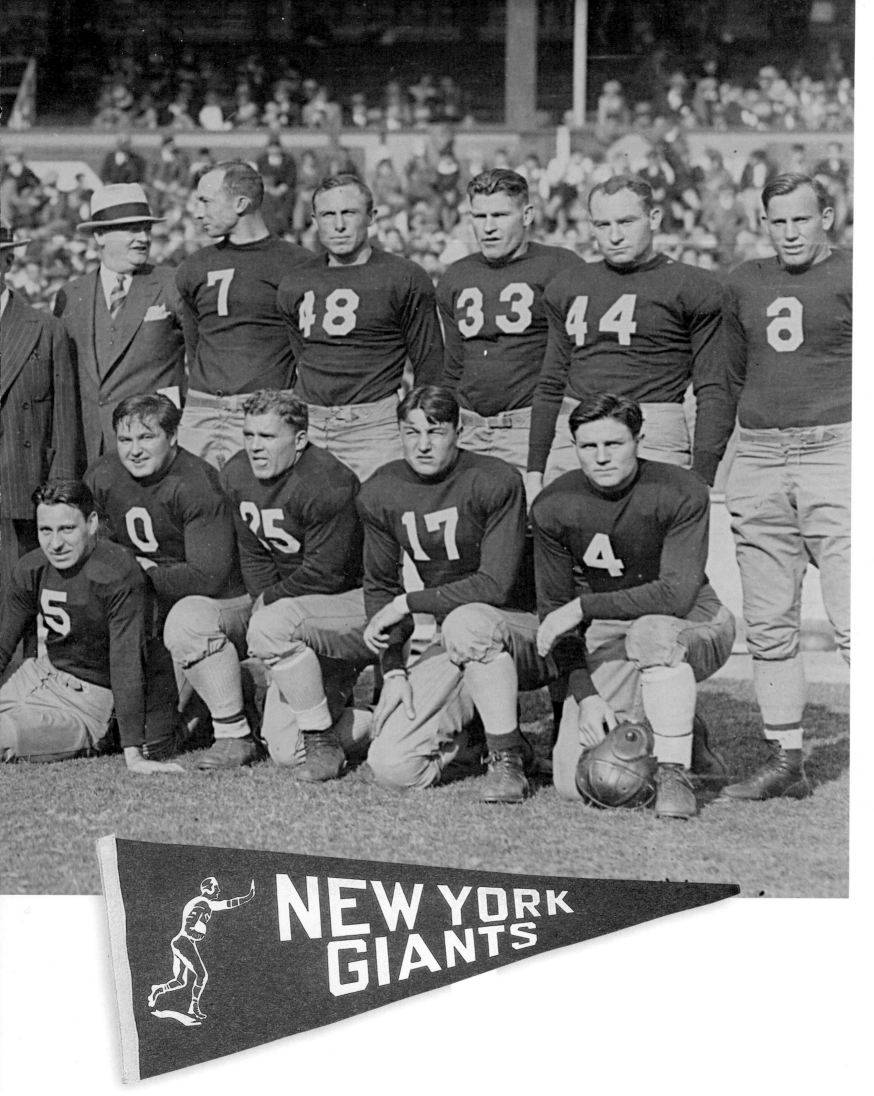

"It's a better deal than Tunney over the long haul," March said. "You might lose some money at first but you would have exclusivity in New York and down the road that could mean big money."

"How much for a franchise?" Tim Mara asked.

"Five hundred dollars," Carr said.

"Deal," Mara replied and stuck out his hand.

"I figured," he would tell a writer decades later, "that even an empty store in New York City was worth five hundred dollars."

In deference to the Polo Grounds, where they would play and which the baseball Giants called home, Tim named his team the New York Football Giants. From the very beginning, the New York Giants was very much a family operation.

"I didn't know anything about pro football," Wellington recalled, "but then neither did he. I was nine and I remember coming out of Sunday mass at Our Lady of Esperanza Church up on 156th and Riverside Drive, and he put his arm around me and told me that this was the day we were about to find out whether anyone else in this town cared about pro football. The whole family was going down to the Polo Grounds for the home opener against the Frankford Yellow Jackets."

The first thing Tim learned was that in order to get to pro football heaven you had to be willing to die a little. Seats were priced from 50 cents to $2.75 in an effort to attract customers by charging far less than NYU or Fordham did for their games in the same stadium. Because the Giants had already been beaten twice on the road, ticket sales were horrendous. Mara distributed five thousand free tickets—as he would do for every home game that year. Of the estimated twenty-five thousand who saw the Frankford Yellow Jackets beat the Giants 14-0 that day, fewer than half paid for their seats. Out of that day was to come the first Giants' slice of tradition and it was a direct result of a family member—one who had never even seen a pro football game or, quite possibly, any football game at all.

On that afternoon, Wellington's older brother Jack worked the first down chains while Wellington sat next to his father on the bench. Like with most teams, the home bench was

on the press box side of the field. It was a cold, windy day and by the second period, the home bench was covered in shadow. "I was always getting colds when I was a kid," Wellington recalled. "I even had bronchial pneumonia."

That night Wellington sneezed. When Wellington sneezed in the Mara household, Mrs. Mara paid close attention. And when Mrs. Mara spoke, Mr. Mara acted. "You will move that bench to the other side of the field where the sun is," she said, "or you will leave Wellington home."

The tradition stands even today. Four decades later, Bill Arnsparger approached Wellington and told him, "I want to move our bench to the other side of the field. The visiting team's assistant coaches can see our sideline signals from their seats in the press box."

"Get better signals," Wellington told him.

Tradition, thy name was, is, and obviously remains the Football Giants.

**Bennie Friedman, the** Giants' first star quarterback, struggles to get away from Green Bay tacklers in the 1929 game at the Polo Grounds that decided the NFL title, above. The Packers won 20-6 to finish with a 12-0-1 record to the Giants' 13-1-1 mark.

Opposite: The sight of Giants founder Tim Mara conferring with Steve Owen was a fixture for twenty-eight seasons. Owen played for the Giants from 1926 to 1936 and served as the head coach from 1930 to 1953. Right: The penalty flag wasn't introduced to the NFL until 1948. Before then, horns and whistles were used to signal infractions. The field judge, umpire, and linesman used horns to distinguish their calls from that of the referee, who used a whistle to signal the end of a play.

The Giants have survived and prospered for three-quarters of a century. But some of the teams they played along the way have since passed into history. All that remains are the scores in the record books and the programs in the Pro Football Hall of Fame archives.

PRICE, 10 CENTS

# NEW YORK GIANTS
## vs.
# BUFFALO BISONS

Sunday
October 25, 1925

PRICE 15 CENTS

# N. Y. FOOTBALL GIANTS
### vs.
# "RED" GRANGE'S YANKEES

"HINKIE" HAINES
Giants Scoring Ace

Sunday
December 4, 1927

PRICE 15 CENTS

# N. Y. FOOTBALL GIANTS
### vs.
# DETROIT WOLVERINES

STEVE OWEN
Captain and Tackle, New York Giants

Price 10 Cents

# NEW YORK GIANTS
## vs.
# BROOKLYN DODGERS

MEL HEIN
Who ends glorious career with Giants

POLO
GROUNDS

Sunday
December 6,

PRICE, 10 CENTS

# N. Y. FOOTBALL GIANTS
## vs.
# CLEVELAND BULLDOGS

Sunday
ber 11, 1928

Polo Grounds
New York

Sunday
November 1, 1925

PRICE 15 CENTS

# N. Y. FOOTBALL GIANTS
(National Football League)
## vs.
# PHILADELPHIA QUAKERS
(American Football League)

Captain JACK McBRIDE
Fullback
New York Football Giants

Sunday
December 12, 1926

Polo Grounds
New York

During the passions that led to the Giants' first Super Bowl appearance, the visitors locker room at San Francisco was rife with postgame yelling, hysteria, and elevated testosterone levels. Following the dramatic playoff victory that took them to the NFL's championship games, a player was heard to shriek over the growing madness:

"God is a Giants fan!"

For the record, nobody really can say with certainty from which direction the Giants' supernatural help has flowed over the past seventy-five years. After Bills kicker Scott Norwood missed a makable last-second Super Bowl field goal that would have stripped the '91 Giants' ring fingers bare and canceled a New Jersey victory celebration, he would have been more than willing to identify the source as coming from below rather than above.

Insert large ditto marks to that from the late Bears coach George Halas, who watched the 1934 world title slip away as the Giants donned basketball shoes while Chicago skidded and slipped on the frozen Polo Grounds turf. Add yet another set for the late George Preston Marshall, flamboyant owner of the Washington Redskins, who thought he knew everything about football while Tim Mara knew nothing, but still was beat out of signing Mel Hein, the greatest lineman of his era, who played fifteen seasons for Mara Tech until he retired in 1945.

"They gave me credit for a lot of signings when I took over personnel," Wellington said, "but I think my father made the biggest signing of all during that time when he got Mel Hein out of Washington State. Marshall was in a bidding war with us and my dad sent Hein a letter offering him the unheard-of figure of $5,000 for the 1931 season."

Hein had initially written to the Giants but they were slow in responding. In the meantime, Marshall, whose office was in Providence, sent him a contract. The day he sent the signed contract back to Marshall, the Giants' offer arrived. Hein immediately called Tim and asked if there was any possible way to break his contract with Marshall.

"Well, it seems to me," Old Tim said, "if I were you, I would call the postmaster in Providence, whoever he is, and tell him your problem, describe the envelope, and ask if it can be returned."

To Hein's amazement, Marshall's rage, and Tim Mara's delight, that's exactly what happened. What neither Marshall nor Hein knew, however, was that while Old Tim might not have known football, he sure as hell knew people. One of them was a man named Bill Halloran, a politician who loved football. He also happened to be the postmaster of Providence, Rhode Island.

Clearly, somebody or something, whether "up above" or "down below," has looked after this franchise since its inception.

They may not have the number of titles to match Dallas, Green Bay, or San Francisco, but the Giants' very survival was as much a triumph of happenstance as what came to be described by the late New York *Times* columnist Arthur Daley, and accepted around the Great Megalopolis, as "Mara Weather." No matter how deep the snow, how slippery the ice, or how heavy the rain on any given Saturday—time after time spelling sure disaster at the box office since there were precious few season ticket sales back then—the sun broke through on Sunday.

But it was a closely guarded secret that disaster for the football team that had planted the NFL flag in America's most important city was always just a bank note or a blizzard away for decades. Tim Mara enjoyed the role of owner but never really felt he would live to see the franchise become more than an unfulfilled promise. In the early days Al Smith, former governor of New York, presidential candidate, and close friend, advised him, "It's never going to work, Tim. Get rid of it."

---

**Among the pro** football "firsts" scored by Giants owner Tim Mara was the National Football League's inaugural luncheon. Right: The invitation for the September 9, 1925, gathering featured Giants head coach Robert Folwell. Above: The program from the Giants' second NFL Championship Game victory is a collector's item. On December 11, 1938, the Giants defeated Green Bay 23-17 at the Polo Grounds.

To which the patriarch of the Mara family replied, "I half-agree with you, but I can't do it. What would I tell my boys?"

Relief was not quick in coming. Right after World War II progress was measured by simply stayin' alive. Each week, Tim and Wellington, who ran the football end, and his brother Jack, who handled business matters, would meet. The topic always was, "Can we do this? Can we stay alive? Is it worth it?" And after each meeting they agreed, "Well, maybe something good will happen."

As late as 1948 a local bank held serious financial paper on this team. The Giants' debt originated with the huge sums of money they had to spend to fight off a 1926 incursion by the old All-America Conference. It must have been serious because insiders will tell you that it actually wasn't paid off until the early 1960s. Through this struggle the Giants didn't need a championship. What they needed was the kind of fan who would show up like clockwork each Sunday no matter who they were playing and no matter how well or poorly they played.

Once again this franchise of spectacularly beneficial accidents stumbled into the one that meant salvation. In 1955, the Giants had the nucleus of an interesting football team—offensive threats like Charlie Conerly, Frank Gifford, and Kyle Rote. The Maras' thinking was "Well, maybe we'll win something and then maybe season ticket sales will improve and then . . ."

It was just about then that Mara Tech stumbled into the happiest accident it had ever had: the one that turned the franchise's battle flag from a map of the Red Sea into the kind of mint green that will last longer than the team's artificial turf. Bert Bell, then the NFL's commissioner, called Tim Mara and told him that he had received a million-dollar offer from an unidentified Texas oilman to buy the Giants, contingent upon moving them out of the Polo Grounds and putting them in Yankee Stadium. The "oilionaire" was, in fact, Clint Murchison, who later bought the original Dallas Cowboys.

"A million dollars was an unheard sum of money for a football team back in those days," Wellington Mara remembered. "So the three of us [Tim, Jack, and Wellington] discussed it. How could we turn it down? We didn't want to sell, but a million dollars?

"We sat there sort of stunned, and then my dad looked at us and said, 'You know, if this franchise is worth nothing in the Polo Grounds and it's worth a million dollars in Yankee Stadium, then I say we better get to Yankee Stadium tomorrow.'

"And that saved us. We brought Alex Webster down from Canada and Mel Triplett became the fullback, and between them we had guys who could run the ball. Conerly was just becoming Conerly," Wellington recalled. "We moved to Yankee Stadium, we made money, we won the title."

That wasn't all they won that year. They won a huge cadre of fans and never gave them back. They won the kind of fans who came during that glorious season and stayed through some of the best and worst times any NFL franchise ever endured. They stayed even when the Giants crossed the Hudson River and received political asylum in the form of an incredible stadium built by the state of New Jersey on what had once been the kind of swampland that could rival the Okefenokee.

There was a rare moment in Canton, Ohio, when Wellington Mara came to stand for a lot more than the Giants with whom he had spent seventy-two years. On July 26, 1997, he was inducted into the Professional Football Hall of Fame. There, on a sunbaked afternoon in the same Middle America town where eleven men in an automobile showroom formed the first professional football league seventy-six years earlier, Mara was no longer simply the president and co-owner of the Giants.

He was the quintessential Lion in Winter, coming home to the valley of hundred yard history for a unique pairing of venue and man. Here, where you would have thought Wellington's sidewalks-of-New York accent might disqualify him as the main event, nobody blinked. There were six thousand fans in the bleachers, most of whom had come for the induction of Don Shula, who was a player in Ohio and later with the Colts long before he was a coach, and Mike Webster, the old Steeler center.

Fans of Webster, impatient for their man to take the podium, waved Steeler towels and all but booed the first two speakers off the stage. And then a strange thing happened. Wellington Mara was introduced, and as though some mystical hand had called for silence, you would have thought you were in church. It was as though Mara, then eighty-one years old, had caught their collective psyche and held it close to his heart.

They know their pro football in Canton. They knew that with his induction, he and his father, Tim, would form the only father-son combination in The Hall. They knew—because he told them—that he would have given whatever he had for his older brother Jack to have lived long enough to stand in his place with Wellington as the presenter.

And the silence held, a kind of punctuation mark to the bond between strangers who loved the same game.

Geography made it clear that these people did not much care whether his Giants won or lost. But they knew this game. And they had enormous respect for those who had bitten the financial bullet for years to make it happen.

In short, they did not need to be reminded that here was the National Football League's last battle-scarred patriarch. His father Tim and his brother Jack were gone—Art Rooney and George Halas were gone. So was George Preston Marshall. The man at the podium was the last living link between the old Polo Grounds and the Jersey Meadowlands, between the Pottsville Maroons in their leather helmets and the NFL's internet web site, between all the history they had heard and all the football they had seen.

So there he stood, with just a hint of sunlight reflecting off his gold Hall of Fame jacket. He spoke in measured tones. The accent might have been light years removed from Canton, but his thoughts went right to its soul.

And when he finished, the audience rose as one and gave him a standing ovation.

In that instant, they were telling him, "You are one of us."

# WELLINGTON MARA

**Wellington Mara was** nine years old and standing beside his father, Tim, on October 18, 1925, when the New York Giants were defeated by the Frankford Yellow Jackets 14-0 in their first home game at the Polo Grounds. Busts of Wellington (left) and Tim honor the only father-son duo in the Pro Football Hall of Fame.

**Pete Gogolak, shown** kicking off the infield dirt at Yankee Stadium,

became the Giants' first soccer-style kicker when he signed out of Cornell in 1966. Gogolak is the Giants' all-time scoring

leader with 646 points off 268 conversions and 126 field goals from 1966 to 1974. Opposite: Quarterback Y. A. Tittle (left)

and head coach Allie Sherman (second from left), shown with Alex Webster (third from the left) and Kyle Rote (right),

inherited the reins of the Giants in 1961. Together, they would lead the Giants to three straight Eastern Conference titles.

So 1956 became their benchmark year, the year New York City decided to embrace this team as it had never embraced it before. That year also became the benchmark for all of professional football. It was the year the Giants walked tall and a new cry was heard throughout the land:

"DEE-fense—DEE-fense—DEE-fense!"

Sure, that team could score points. It scored forty-seven of them against the Bears in the title game. But that ability seemed to pale when measured against what happened each time the Giants defensive unit buckled its chin straps and ran onto the field.

This was the reason for the passionate love affair that was taking root here: 1956 was the first year in Yankee Stadium and the huge season-ticket sales, which would be generated once the corporate expense account folks and the "in crowd" made the ballpark the place to be, were still to come. The walk-up crowds accepted the subways, the cold, and the hassle of buying tickets on game day because the defense that the Giants played was pure lunch-pail-thermos-bottle-put-strength-against-strength-and-let-weakness-go-to-hell. This was the city where the subway doors would slam in your face no matter who you were, but a mayor named Fiorello LaGuardia once went on the radio to read the Sunday comics to its children during a newspaper strike.

The new Giants fans, who could relate to the Giants' style of trench warfare, bellowed, "DEE-fense—DEE-fense—DEE-fense!" Not the sophomoric cry of "Hold that line" or even worse, "Push 'em back, push 'em back, WAAAY back." This was the heart and soul of a new constituency giving voice for the first

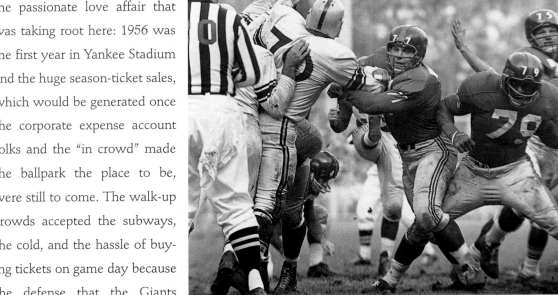

time to the kind of football that would—from the 1956 season on—grab it by its emotional jugular vein and hang on forever. This was so elementary to these new fans of pro football. To them, the emphasis was no longer on blocking schemes to analyze, but rather on thunder and lightning and goal line stands in the trenches.

Conerly threw the passes, Webster and Triplett made the tough yardage, but the collective heart of these huge crowds belonged to Sam Huff, the middle linebacker who, without pro football, would have spent the rest of his life in a West Virginia coal mine known as Jamison No. 9; to defensive tackles Rosey Grier and Dick Modzelewski; to defensive ends Andy Robustelli, for whom that position seemed to be made; and to draft choice Jim Katcavage. The secondary was outstanding but the front seven hammered out the kind of drumbeat to which the entire city could march.

Even when the more affluent, the celebrities, and the corporate types discovered the game and cornered the tickets, the tone had been set. And because a ticket to a Giants game had finally become a social symbol, these new elite fans just naturally followed the emotion barometer set by the blue collar ones who had come to Yankee Stadium before them.

"DEE-fense—DEE-fense—DEE-fense!"

From that moment on, mediocre Giants teams won games with it. Great Giants teams won Super Bowls with it. And Giants fans demanded it. By the 1960s the Giants rode that kind of defense to six out of eight divisional titles and one world championship. In the sports restaurant/bar joints like Toots Shor's, Mike Manuche's, and Gallagher's, the two-martini lunch

**All-Pros weren't** exempt from special teams' duties in the late '50s. Defensive tackle Dick Modzelewski (77) and defensive end Jim Katcavage (75) join forces blocking with offensive tackle Roosevelt Brown (79) as Ben Agajanian's kick soars toward the uprights.

**Sam Huff wore** No. 70 rather than a more traditional linebacker number because he was drafted by the Giants out of West Virginia in 1956 as an offensive lineman. He was shifted to middle linebacker during his rookie training camp. Huff's famed No. 70 jersey is now on display at the Hall of Fame.

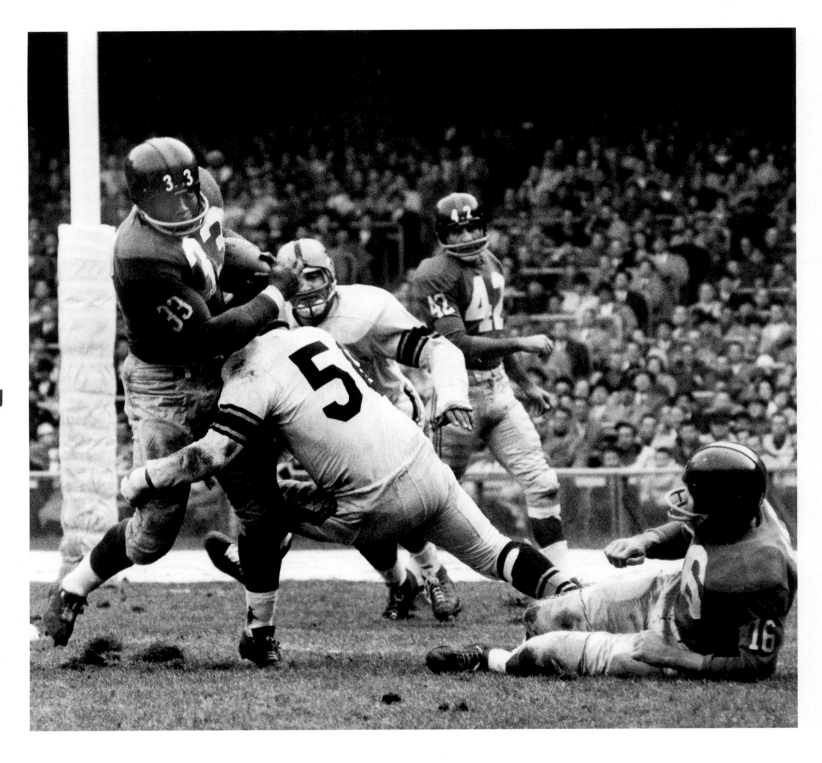

**Fullback Mel Triplett** (33), who excelled at blocking and gaining tough ground in short-yardage situations

for the 1956 NFL champions, tries to break a tackle as quarterback Charlie Conerly (42) and halfback Frank

Gifford (16) look on. Triplett led the Giants in rushing in 1960, his last of six seasons as a Giant.

**Fans fill every** seat at Giants Stadium, even those with views obstructed by the crowded sidelines, below. Few players in Giants history have been more proficient at their task than Pat Summerall, bottom photo, who doubled as an end and placekicker. From 1958 to 1961, Summerall was successful on all but two conversion tries in addition to kicking sixty-nine field goals. Following spread: Players change with time, but the grit and determination, evident in this profile of the Giants bench in the late 1960s, is unaltered over seventy seasons.

was replaced by the Monday multi-condiment recap. Here a salt shaker became Harland Svare blitzing. The water glasses were Emlen Tunnel and Dick Lynch double-covering the ketchup. The next day, the salt shakers became the backfield for next week's game.

In 1957, season tickets became the city's most prestigious status symbol. They remain so today. During a run of fifteen horrendous years on the field in the '60s and '70s after the Giants' move to New Jersey, nobody willingly turned back tickets. There are 76,891 seats in Giants Stadium. By 1989, just twelve years after the move to New Jersey, the waiting list was closing in on twenty thousand names. Put a kid on the list at age five and his grandchildren might actually get to see a Giants game.

Still, people are dying—sometimes more than once—to see them play. Aida had shorter and less passionate death scenes.

The calls come in every day to John Gorman, the Giants ticket manager. "Generally," he says, "it's things like 'My mother is dying. Her last wish is to see the Giants play. Help me. Please help me.' It is amazing how many dying people have this wish and how many times they die. If you didn't know better, you'd swear they were cats."

Well, it's worth a shot.

After all, they're Giants fans in cold, snow, rain, sleet, and anything else the Rust Belt can dump on them.

What's a little white lie between heroes and friends?

ny
42

In 1925, during the very first game the Giants ever played, Jack Mara moved along the sidelines at each snap, holding one of the first-down markers.

So it wasn't his father, Tim, the patriarch who shouldered that initial financial risk, and it wasn't his kid brother Wellington, the child who would go on to be the primary liaison with the players, who could first comprehend the true physical brutality of the sport. It was Jack Mara, who unlike his father, his brother—even the players on both teams—never got to sit down once that day.

The history of this franchise cannot be told without the story of Jack Mara. His autograph is written all over the Giants. All through the days leading up to his graduation from Fordham Law School, it was understood that Jack would become president of this team. Wellington had the football knowledge but pro football, even then, was very much a business. Jack Mara's lifetime business would become the New York Giants.

When it became imperative that the Giants move from the crumbling old Polo Grounds to Yankee Stadium, it was Jack who

# JACK MARA

made it happen. Jack went off to negotiate the deal with Yankee owner Dan Topping—who Tim could barely stomach dealing with since Topping had purchased a football franchise during the days of the insurgent All-America Conference—and he saved the financial future of the franchise. Jack was the one who put together one of the country's most lucrative radio packages, and when Pete Rozelle proposed all teams share their television revenue, Jack was a major force in lobbying for enough ownership votes to do it, even though Wellington was opposed.

"I thought we were giving too much away as the league's biggest market," Wellington explains. "But Jack was right. That deal enabled all of us

to stay in business."

But while Jack's business-minded pragmatism was vital in the Mara troika, it was often a compromise by the ever-faithful Old Tim that carried the day.

Once, during salary negotiations, Wellington came into the Mara meeting and laid out his needs:

"We have to give this guy an extra thousand dollars to keep him. And there's no doubt that we have to have him."

Jack, ever the cool businessman, would reply, "That's a lot of money. What if we have a bad year?"

But before Jack's thoughtful logic could be thoroughly mulled over, Old Tim broke in: "Will somebody please tell me how we could have a bad year?"

**Until his premature** death, Jack Mara (far left, with father Tim, center, and brother Wellington) was the steadying business hand that allowed the Giants to grow and prosper as a franchise. While Wellington oversaw the football end of the operations, it was Jack who helped develop a financial strategy for the Giants as well as the National Football League.

Over the course of seventy-five years, only two championship quarterbacks have come to embody significant eras in the history of the Giants franchise, and while both have had their numbers retired by the club, neither is in the NFL's Hall of Fame. Phil Simms, who still has time on his side, may make it to Canton some day, clear thinking permitting. But the same is not true for Charlie Conerly, the man who watched over the Giants from 1948 to 1961. Sadly, his legend may have been buried with him on February 13, 1996, in Clarksdale, Mississippi.

Conerly and Simms went through a strikingly similar initiation, one that was rude enough for them to fully appreciate what it meant to be the quarterback of the New York Giants. But they were also still around for the warm, tearful farewells.

By midseason 1953, Charlie Conerly qualified as an expert on the sequence of disagreeable sensations. First he would get flattened by a large man in an enemy uniform. Then, as his head cleared, he would hear the boos ringing in his ears. And finally, lying flat on his back, he would look up and see the banners hanging from the upper deck at

the Polo Grounds, anonymous attacks fluttering in the cold winds of autumn.

"BACK TO THE FARM, CONERLY," one message would read.

"CHARLIE MUST GO," a more personal note would suggest.

Then again, 1953 wouldn't have been a good year for anyone interested in playing quarterback for the Giants. They finished 3-9 that season, but only because they got to play the Chicago Cardinals twice. Those Giants were so bad they brought down Steve Owen, an institution who had been their head coach since 1930.

After the season was over, Conerly announced that he too had had enough, and that he was going home to Mississippi, back to the farm. And he would have stayed there if Jim Lee Howell hadn't come down and coaxed him into coming back to New York.

Howell, the new head coach the Giants had hired, was convinced he couldn't win without Conerly. So he tracked him down, found him loading fertilizer onto a freight train seventy-five miles outside of St. Louis. Conerly and his partner were all set to go into the fertilizer business, and as far as he was concerned, that beat getting knocked down by enormous strangers a dozen times or so every Sunday afternoon.

Then Howell made him a proposition: he would go out and get him some help, get him some protection, if Charlie would only come back and give it another try.

"If you try, I'll try," Conerly told him.

"The heaviest man they had on the offensive line then was 210 pounds," said Perian Conerly, who was married to Charlie for forty-seven years. "But he never really let it get to him. He wasn't that type."

To the sportswriters of that era, Conerly was always the strong, silent type. Reticent, that's how they put it. Lanky and reticent. The All-American from Ole Miss who quit school after his sophomore year, joined the Marines, and spent three years married to his rifle in the South Pacific. After the war he came home, finished school, and figured football was child's play compared to what he had lived through on Guam, while he was on scholarship at the University of

# CHARLIE CONERLY

## BY BILL HANDLEMAN

Semper Fi. So he signed a contract to play for the Giants, $62,500 spread over five years, with a $10,000 bonus.

In 1948, at age twenty-seven, he was the unanimous choice as NFL Rookie of the Year. He threw twenty-two touchdown passes that season, a rookie record that stood half a century, until another Mississippi boy—Peyton Manning—came along and broke it in 1998.

When Conerly returned from his brief retirement in 1954, things did start to get better. Jim Lee Howell had held up his end of the bargain and the quarterback was no longer getting mauled as a matter of routine every Sunday afternoon.

In 1956, their first season in Yankee Stadium, the Giants won the NFL championship, humbling the Chicago Bears 47-7 in front of 56,836 fans on a cold day in the Bronx. Conerly completed seven of ten passes for 195 yards that

afternoon and "called a near perfect game," according to the newspaper accounts of the day.

Conerly almost won another championship, in 1958, but the Baltimore Colts got in the way, winning the sudden-death game that secured the NFL's place on the landscape of American sport. But even though Charlie was the acknowledged leader of their high-powered offense, the Giants were forever looking for a successor.

"I always meant to try to list all the ones who came in looking to get his job," said Perian Conerly, who recorded her memories in BACKSEAT QUARTERBACK.

Travis Tidwell. Fred Benners. Bill Mackrides. Arnold Galiffa. Bob Clatterbuck. Don Heinrich. Jack Kemp. Tom Dubinski. George Shaw. Lee Grosscup. Frank Gifford.

Frank Gifford? Gifford was a halfback, a star halfback. Not only that, he was Conerly's roommate and one of his best friends.

"Frank came down to Mississippi that summer [1959] because he wanted to tell him himself," Perian Conerly remembered.

So they went out to play a round of golf, and Conerly didn't say anything, even though it had been in all the papers. Finally Gifford couldn't stand it anymore: "Charlie, you know I'm likely to take your job away from you this year, don't you?"

Without looking up, Conerly carefully lined up his putt, slowly hunched over the ball, and stroked it firmly. The ball dropped into the cup. Charlie then marked his card, turned to Gifford, and said "Giff, please, in the future, don't talk to me while I'm putting."

"Charlie said it didn't matter," said Perian Conerly. "Frank couldn't be the quarterback because then he wouldn't have had himself to throw to, for one thing."

Charlie Conerly led the NFL in passing in 1959 and was the near-

unanimous choice as the league's Most Valuable Player.

Y. A. Tittle finally got his job in 1961. Conerly was forty years old by then.

Also by then there were 63,053 voices chanting his name when he came off the bench to win a game against the Los Angeles Rams in October. There was a banner hanging from the upper deck too, a big banner that read "CONERLY FOR PRESIDENT."

Then, in December, when he came off the bench one last time and engineered a rally in a critical victory at Philadelphia, it was enough to bring tears to his wife's eyes.

After that game, when the writers went down to talk to him, this is what Charlie had to say: "When you win, you're an old pro. When you lose, you're an old man."

**A Marine who** saw World War II action in the South Pacific, Charlie Conerly was the NFL's Rookie of the Year in 1948 at the age of twenty-seven. But age was never a hindrance to the quarterback who was still throwing passes and winning games at age forty in 1961. Still ranked No. 2 on most Giants passing charts to Phil Simms, Conerly was the Most Valuable Player in the NFL in 1959.

CHUCK CONERLY
QUARTERBACK   NEW YORK GIANTS

**I**t goes beyond the money and beyond the celebrity. It can forever soften the dull post-career ache of cartilage strained too often and bruises that never seemed to heal. It is the one thing that makes a football player special beyond the all-star games and megabuck salaries.

It is called the championship ring.

Some of the greatest players in football have chased it. But despite the numbers they put on the board, when the hunt was over all they had to show for those years was a naked ring finger and a shattered dream.

Thousands pursue it but only a relative handful get to wear it. Whether earned during the leather-helmet, one-hundred-bucks-a-game era or during the glitz and glamour of a Super Bowl Sunday, the ring remains the ultimate certification of a champion.

Over a span of seventy-five years, the rings have belonged to the members of just six Giants championship teams. This is the story of how they won them.

1927—The NFL was just seven years old, the Giants only three. There were no divisions and no postseason, and in most towns there were very few spectators. But this team was on a mission. Tim Mara, the club president, was coming off a nightmare season—not in wins and losses but rather in a bottom line that was written in bright red ink. An outlaw league put together by a promoter named C. C. Pyle (his enemies said the initials stood for "cash and carry") had almost destroyed him.

Although the NFL won the war, Mara lost $60,000, a considerable sum of money back then. In a desperate effort to attract the fans he had been forced to share with Pyle's American League, Mara promised the city a championship. Toward that end, he fired his coach and added players like huge lineman Cal Hubbard, and put together a front line that was bigger, stronger, and tougher than the opposition.

# SEASONS OF VICTORY

And then back came Century.

Century Milstead, an All-American at Yale, had played for the Giants in 1925. Then he succumbed to the money offered by C. C. Pyle. Intensely loyal as Mara was to his friends, you would have thought he would have taken Milstead's defection personally. But he didn't. Not after his people convinced him that while Milstead might not be the best tackle around, his attitude and his fire were exactly what the Giants front line needed to dominate the league.

They were right. After a slow start without Milstead, Tim induced him to return and closed out the 1927 season with nine straight wins and the championship. They could have lost the title and the rings but for a spectacular defensive showing against the Bears, stopping them when Chicago had a first down on the Giants' five.

It was attitude that won them the title. Century Milstead was no small cog in that.

1934—This was the kind of championship of which legends are made. Here was a football team loaded with stars—Ken Strong, running back, placekicker, hero; Harry Newman, quarterback; Mel Hein, center/linebacker; and terrific rookies led by the Fordham tandem of quarterback Ed Danowski and guard Johnny Dell Isola.

A year earlier they had won the Eastern title and lost to the Bears in the league's first-ever postseason title game. Now it was the Giants versus the Bears again. George Halas was positive his team could handle Strong, Hein, and Newman.

What he failed to consider was whether it could handle Abe Cohen.

Abe probably couldn't tackle the biggest kid in a kindergarten class. He never caught a forward pass, blocked a linebacker, or kicked an extra point. But nobody from Strong on up to Phil Simms ever did more to bring the Giants a championship.

These were the Bears of Bronko Nagurski, the toughest power

runner in all of football; quarterback Gene Ronzani; and linemen like 265-pound George Musso. They had already beaten the Giants twice during the regular season. The Giants' chances were figured at very slim by Broadway bookmakers.

On Sunday, upon looking out of their windows that morning, the Giants saw their chances fall from slim to microscopic. The city shuddered in a massive frost. The Polo Grounds field had turned to ice. The protective tarp above it had frozen to the ground. And all coach Steve Owen wondered was how the Giants could even think of tackling a bulldozer like Nagurski on a field like this.

When Owen wondered aloud during breakfast at his midtown hotel about what kind of a battle plan he could formulate, Ray Flaherty, an end who was the team captain, said, "Basketball shoes."

"What did you say?" Owen responded with great irritation.

**Brothers Steve (55) and** Bill (36) Owen, shown here in 1934 with fellow tackle Len Grant (3) were part of the Giants story for more than a quarter century. Steve played from 1926 to 1936 and was the Giants head coach for twenty-three seasons, from 1930 to 1953. Bill played from 1929 to 1937 and was an assistant coach in 1941 and again from 1945 to 1948. Above: Harry Newman (12) was the quarterback of the first Giants team to win the National Football League championship. Newman led the Giants in both rushing and passing in 1933 and 1934.

"Basketball shoes. Back in college at Gonzaga we wore them against Montana on a frozen field and got much better traction."

"Why not?" Owen replied. "They won't let us use guns against Nagurski. This is better than any idea I have."

Enter Abe Cohen.

Cohen weighed 140 pounds and was just five feet tall. He had come to football as both a fan and a tailor—not necessarily in that order. He ran a tailor shop near the NYU campus and got himself the contract to make the school's football uniforms. When NYU coach Chick Meehan moved to Manhattan, Abe and his magic needle went too. On Sundays he helped out the Giants equipment manager.

Owen and Flaherty had tried calling every sporting goods store in Manhattan in the hope that one of them would be open on Sunday. The odds on that were longer than the odds on the Giants beating the Bears. But in the hotel lobby, he ran into Abe Cohen. "Listen," the coach said. "Don't go to the Polo Grounds. Get on the subway and go to NYU or CCNY or Manhattan. Get us some basketball shoes by any means necessary."

By halftime, the Bears had physically brutalized the Giants with a ferocity that seemed to border on criminal assault. Strong was limping with a bum knee. The score was 10-3 but the homeside players looked as though they were on the short end of a 50-0 count. Suddenly the dressing room door flew open and there stood five-foot-tall Abe Cohen, fresh from the equipment room of the Manhattan College gymnasium, under a small mountain of basketball shoes.

Actually, it was only nine pairs but then at Abe's height,

it must have looked as though he were carrying Mt. Everest. When George Halas, the tough coach of the Bears, saw the way the Giants were walking as they returned for the second half, he asked one of his players:

"What's wrong with them?"

"I think they're wearing basketball shoes."

"Good," the coach said. "Step on their toes."

It took the Giants an entire quarter to assert their new advantage but once they did, the Bears were left skidding and sliding while the Giants owned the fourth quarter. They took a 17-13 lead before a play that illustrated the footwear advantage Danowski hid the ball on his hip and then laid it into the pocket formed by Strong's hands as the running back cut behind him. In the cleats he wore earlier, Strong would have belly flopped into the line of scrimmage. But the added traction of basketball shoes allowed a scoring play that was good for eight yards and capped a fifty-yard march. Incredibly, in the final fifteen minutes they scored twenty-seven points to win it 30-13.

After an absence of seven years, the Giants were once again the champions of all of football. Owen was voted the coach of the year. And up at Manhattan College, a man named Neil Cohalan, who coached the basketball team, looked at what was left of the "shoes of victory" and remarked:

"I'm glad our shoes did the Giants some good. Now the question is, did the Giants do our shoes any good?"

**New York back** Ed Danowski is tackled by Chicago's Bill Hewitt late in the third quarter of the 1934 NFL Championship game in New York. With the temperature frozen at nine degrees and the Polo Grounds field covered with a sheet of ice, the New York Giants switched from football cleats to basketball sneakers while trailing 10-3 at halftime. The Giants scored twenty-seven points in the fourth quarter to win 30-13. (The streaks in the picture were caused by cracks in the glass negative.) Right: The 1934 Thorp Memorial trophy now sits in the Pro Football Hall of Fame.

**Ed Danowski tackles** Chicago fullback Bronko Nagurski in the second quarter of the 1934 NFL

Championship game as Giants Hall of Fame end Ray Flaherty (1) looks on. Nagurski scored on a

one-yard run to help the Bears to their 10-3 halftime lead.

1938—It was the Year of the Patchwork Heroes. The Giants had beaten the Washington Redskins 36-0 the week before to win the Eastern Division title, but the game had been brutal. The more points the Giants scored, the more physical the play became. The team that coach Steve Owen took into the title game with Green Bay looked more like survivors than contenders. Three key players—All-League guard Johnny Dell Isola, placekicker and versatile halfback Ward Cuff, and top blocker Leland Shaffer—couldn't even practice.

One by one in the pregame locker room they joined the other walking wounded for treatment and special taping. This was not a confident team. It limped and it hurt and the only sound to be heard was the strident voice of the team's physician, Dr. Francis Sweeney, hollering "Next!" Embalmers in ancient Egypt used fewer bandages on pharaohs. Assembled in their locker room, the Giants who would play Green Bay for the world championship that afternoon looked like candidates for the waiting room at a Saturday-night emergency room.

And as bad as they looked before the game, they looked even worse after it began.

The Packers were a big, strong team quarterbacked by Arnie Herber and coached by Curly Lambeau, the man who founded the team two decades earlier. They administered a fearful physical beating to New York's wounded warriors. Mel Hein, the team's best blocker and defender, had been forced out of the contest early with the sound of very large bells ringing inside his head. Hein had been an All-Pro six times and was the league's MVP that very year. But right from the start, with the courage few teams had exhibited all year, the Packers ran straight at him. For the first time in his professional career, Hein was carried off the field. So was Dell Isola. And yet the Giants miraculously managed to make it to halftime with a 16-14 edge.

The Giants had scored on Cuff's field goal set up by a run by Tuffy Leemans and a surprise pass to a rarely used end named Charles "Hap" Barnard. But it was a costly lead and coach Steve Owen knew it as he tried to pull together his walking wounded at halftime.

And as the battered group wearily listened to Owen's remarks, nobody sensed the gravity of the situation better than Johnny Gildea, the kicker who had missed the extra point after the Giants' first touchdown. Now, a field goal would put the Packers in front—and Gildea knew it.

Shortly after intermission, Green Bay kicker Tiny Engebretsen did just that. As Engebretsen booted one squarely between the uprights from fifteen yards out, Gildea slumped lower and lower, well aware that the Giants' two best linemen were out and points would be hard to come by.

"All I could think to myself," he would later say, "was about that missed kick. I thought it would cost us the championship."

The Giants had played magnificently in the face of their injuries. In the first half, Jim Lee Howell, destined to become the Giants coach one day, and Jim Poole each blocked punts that led to New York scores. But now—their energy spent, Hein still on the sidelines, and the Packers in front—New York's situation began to look hopeless.

For much of the season Owen had used his players in two separate units to wear down the enemy. Now he was running out of both players and time. Midway through the third quarter he picked his best eleven—at least those who could walk—and then sent them after the touchdown New York so desperately needed.

Hank Soar, later an American League umpire, carried the brunt of the attack. Green Bay had employed a sliding type of defense and Owen sent Soar on a series of cutbacks, in which he faked to one side and then rushed past the slanting opposition into a slender chunk of daylight. It was Soar who led the final assault and kept it alive with key gains of thirteen and eight yards.

The Green Bay defense suddenly stiffened. With fourth

and one on the Packer forty-four, Ed Danowski, the Giants quarterback and play caller, looked to the sidelines. On fourth and one, you punt—especially when you still have almost half the game left.

But Danowski knew the Giants were hurt and bruised and if they didn't score here, they might never muster the stamina for one last thrust. Owen gave Danowski the signal to go for it.

Once more the ball went to Soar, who dove straight ahead. When the officials brought the sticks out, the nose of the ball had barely cleared the chain—but the gain was enough for a vital first down.

Five plays later, Danowski threw for twenty-five yards to Soar for the winning touchdown. On that afternoon of brutal hand-to-hand combat, neither team scored again. The Giants won, 23-17.

1956—This was the year that defense really came of age. Playing their first season in Yankee Stadium, the Giants seemed to spring out of the darkness and into the light of a championship season without warning.

But it wasn't like that. This was a team that was a number of years in the growing. Eight years earlier, the rights to a rookie quarterback from Mississippi named Charlie Conerly were obtained from the Washington Redskins. That same year, unheralded and uninvited, Emlen Tunnell walked into Jack Mara's office, introduced himself as a former Iowa back, and guaranteed that, if given a chance, he could make the team. He was, he did, and he became an all-time Giants great.

In 1951 a marvelous athlete named Kyle Rote was drafted out of SMU and became a superb pass receiver. The following year, Frank Gifford was drafted out of USC. That year, Gifford made All-Pro on defense. A year after that, All-Pro on offense. He was ultimately one of the greatest that Mara Tech ever had.

By bits and pieces the Giants of the future were coming together. Jim Lee Howell, a former Giants player, replaced Owen as head coach in 1954. Little by little they came: Roosevelt Brown, a spectacular offensive lineman; quarterback Don Heinrich, who would alternate for a time with Conerly; linebackers Bill Svoboda, Cliff Livingston, Harland Svare, and Alex Webster, the best running back in the Canadian Football League; and Jim Katcavage, a defensive end out of Dayton.

And then Wellington traded for defensive tackle Dick Modzelewski and defensive end Andy Robustelli. The fitting of all these pieces into a championship jigsaw puzzle was a slow, steady process. It was as though they were all waiting for the catalyst. He arrived in 1956. They won in 1956. The man's name was Sam Huff. He was a ferocious middle linebacker. And because of him and those around him, the emphasis shifted to stopping the other team instead of scoring points.

As the unofficial Poet Laureate of Montclair, New Jersey, Yogi Berra would say that playing against the Bears was "déjà vu all over again." Chicago, New York, another frozen field. And the Giants in basketball shoes one more time. But there the similarities end. The defense dominated the Bears. It was 34-7 at halftime. The Giants won it 47-7.

This was a team of sheer brute force—right down to the placekicker, an ex-Redskin named Ben Agajanian who had lost all the toes on his kicking foot in an industrial accident as a young man. When a writer asked him the secret of his success, Agajanian didn't even blink:

"Well, first you find an open elevator shaft, then you put your foot inside and wait."

From lineman to placekicker, this was a team that asked no quarter.

**Allie Sherman, shown** above discussing strategy with quarterback George Shaw (15) and wide receiver Kyle Rote (44), served two terms as a Gaints assistant before being named the team's eighth head coach in 1961. Sherman had a 57-51-4 record in eight seasons as head coach and led the Giants to three NFL Eastern Conference titles. Right: The game program from New York's 1956 victory over Chicago.

**Jim Lee Howell succeeded** Steve Owen as the Giants head coach in 1954 and led the team to a 53-27-4 record in seven seasons. Under Howell, the Giants were champions of the National Football League in 1956 and won three Eastern Conference championships. An end as a player, Howell played nine seasons with the Giants (1937 to 1942 and 1946 to 1948) and later was an assistant coach during Owen's last three seasons. Following spread: The cornerstone of the Giants' 1956 NFL championship was the defense. And the foundation of that unit was the line of end Andy Robustelli (81), tackle Dick Modzelewski (77), end Jim Katcavage (75), and tackle Rosey Grier (76).

It wasn't simply a championship game. What it was, was history. The Giants didn't defeat the Colts on the frigid afternoon of December 28, 1958. But in the manner of their losing, they changed the face of professional football forever. Decades later, every Giant and every Colt who played in this spectacular sudden-death football game could look back and say with total honesty, "We played one for the ages . . . we played one for the league . . . we played one for the day that pro football finally grabbed an entire nation."

Actually, when you look at the whole picture, there were compelling reasons why most people doubted that the Giants could even get to this game. From training camp onward they did not figure to be there at the finish. For openers, they had all the team speed of a gang of herniated snails. Because of that, yards never seemed to come in

twin digits. Quarterback Charlie Conerly was thirty-seven years old. The tough-yardage running back, Alex Webster, was banged up, and Frank Gifford, who may go down as the most versatile player in Giants history, limped so badly that you could say with certainty his greatest asset all season was courage.

Shortly before this championship game, Vince Lombardi, who was then the Giants offensive coordinator, met with his quarterbacks and, at the

conclusion of that briefing, shook his head in amazement of how far this team had come.

"If anyone had told me two months ago that we'd be here today I'd have asked him where he got his opium. Us in the championship game? It seemed ridiculous."

Even after this team had established itself as a late-season contender, it was still chasing the Browns for the Eastern Division title. These were the Browns of Jim Brown and to reach the NFL

title game, the Giants would first have to beat them in the final game of the regular season and then beat them again in a special playoff to earn the right to face Baltimore for the title.

All the Browns needed in their first meeting was a tie and the second game would have been unnecessary. With 4:30 left in the game, they had it at 10-10. Pat Summerall, playing with a badly swollen knee, limped out and, as the snow swirled around him, tried a forty-eight-yard field goal—and missed. "I wanted to go anywhere except back to the bench," Summerall would later say. But as he walked slowly off the field, four or five players ran forward to meet him.

"It ain't over yet," one of them said. "We'll get the ball back for you, and you'll make it next time."

And they did, stopping the Browns cold and setting the stage for Summerall to try again. The clock had run down to 2:07.

# THE GREATEST GAME EVER PLAYED

**Pursued by a** Baltimore defender, Frank Gifford looks upfield for an opening early in the 1958 Championship game. In the fourth quarter, Gifford caught a fifteen-yard touchdown pass from Charlie Conerly to give the Giants a 17-14 lead.

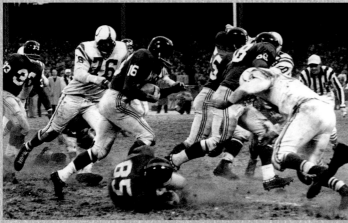

**For the Giants,** the highs and lows of "The Greatest Game Ever Played" were captured in two runs. Top: Colt fullback Alan Ameche's one-yard scoring plunge capped a thirteen-play drive and ended the game and the season after 8:25 of sudden-death overtime. Above: Late in the fourth quarter, Frank Gifford, running behind the block of center Ray Wietecha (55), was stopped inches short of a first down by Baltimore's Big Daddy Lipscomb (76). Had Gifford gained the first down, the Giants would have run out the clock and won the title. But the Giants could only wonder "What if?"

Above, right: The game ball and a piece of the goalpost are on display at the Pro Football Hall of Fame in Canton, Ohio.

Snow had obscured the yard markers. No one knew how long the kick was, but it was longer than the one he had missed. Now, with the falling snow creating a haze over the goalposts, Summerall waited for the snap and the hold. As he waited he recalled that he had kicked the first one to the left, depending on the Yankee Stadium wind to carry it to the right and through the uprights, but he had misfigured that wind. This time he kicked it straight ahead and drilled it through.

After the game Conerly, who was the holder, told a reporter that as he looked toward the goalposts, he thought to himself:

"Thank God. There was a lot of guilt riding on this one."

Risen like a Lazarus in shoulder pads, the Giants went out the following week and beat the Browns again, this time 10-0. They had no way of knowing it at the time, but in so winning they had just earned a ticket to ride into one of the most historic games that would ever be played in the National Football League.

The Colts were a multi-talented football team. There was John Unitas, football's ultimate Cinderella story. Three years earlier, he was playing quarterback for a semipro team just outside Pittsburgh called the Rams. He was paid six dollars a game. Finally, he was signed by the Colts. After Johnny U became a superstar for the ages, somebody asked the old Baltimore general manager why he had signed him in the first place. "When you get a quarterback for nothing," Don Kellett replied with undeniable logic, "you sign him."

Unitas was the trigger man but his offense was loaded with weapons: fullback Alan Ameche; outstanding receivers like Raymond Berry, Jim Mutscheller, and Lenny

Moorel; and a spectacular offensive line. On defense their rush line was awesome—Don Joyce, Big Daddy Lipscomb, Art Donovan, and Gino Marchetti.

The Giants could only hope that the strange run of luck that had protected them over and over all season would hold together for one last game.

It didn't.

Outstanding protection for Unitas and two fumbles by Frank Gifford gave the Colts a 14-3 halftime edge. Things seemed to tear apart even further in the third quarter when the Colts picked up a first down on the Giants' three. By now the field was frozen and the slippery footing served as a twelfth

man for the Giants' defense. Ameche could not get the traction he needed and Unitas's receivers could not make the cuts they wanted. The Giants held. Now they would make their move.

Three plays later Conerly hit Kyle Rote, who made an over-the-shoulder catch. Once a great freewheeling runner and receiver at SMU, Rote had been plagued by damaged knees ever since he turned pro. He was caught from behind and fumbled at the Baltimore twenty-five.

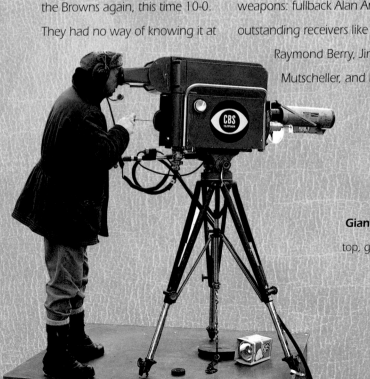
**Giants kickers played** a major role in the televised 1958 NFL Championship game. Pat Summerall, top, gave the Giants an early 3-0 lead with a thirty-six-yard field goal, and Don Chandler, above, kept the favored Colts pinned deep in their end of the field with his punts.

But then that strange—almost mystical—force that had protected this team all year surfaced again. Like a greased pig at a county fair, the bouncing ball eluded everyone. Then, suddenly, Webster scooped it up and raced toward the goal. Webster was stopped there but on the very next play, Mel Triplett hurdled the Colt defense for the score that brought the Giants within four points.

Now the huge crowd finally became a factor. The noise rose in a steady crescendo. When Conerly threw fifteen yards to Gifford for the go-ahead touchdown, the stadium girders seemed to vibrate. The Baltimore fans, with their long, blue, foghorn noisemakers, were silenced. All the Giants had to do was hang on—and it seemed as though they would. Time and again as the final quarter ticked away, Dick Modzelewski, Sam Huff, and Andy Robustelli led a ferocious defensive charge.

The action turned to a physical confrontation bordering on the vindictive. During one play, Huff slammed into Berry out of bounds, and Weeb Ewbank,

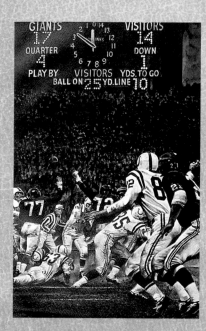

the Colts head coach, punched the Giants linebacker in the neck. Huff hit him back. In the heat of emotion, the game had turned almost primitive.

With time running out, all the Giants really needed was one first down to lock it away. With just 2:30 left and the Giants up by three, they sent Gifford to inside tackle. All he needed was three yards to earn a first down and enable the Giants to run out the clock. But Marchetti grabbed Gifford and Lipscomb fell on top of both of them.

It was Gifford's contention that he had made the necessary yardage. But Marchetti had broken one of his legs on the

tackle and Gifford believed that by attending to him and not spotting the ball first, official Charlie Berry had accidentally spotted the ball inches short of where Gifford believed it blonged. And by inches, the Giants failed to make their first.

So, late in the game and with the second-best punter in the league in Don Chandler, the Giants elected to punt the ball away. Chandler did his part. His kick gave the ball to the Colts on their own fourteen. In fewer than two minutes, Unitas drove them to the Giants' thirteen and Steve Myhra kicked a field goal, tying the game and sending it into the first overtime in the history of the NFL.

Once again the Giants came within a foot of the first down in the extra period's first sequence. But now they had no options. The punt was mandatory because they were on their own twenty-nine. In thirteen plays, Unitas moved the Colts eighty yards. Ameche covered the last yard to give the Colts a 23-17 overtime victory.

It was the game pro football so desperately needed to establish itself among fans who couldn't tell

a football from an egg. The television audience was massive. But of more importance was the overtime period because pro football had never had one. Now on the evening news in cities where no NFL team would ever play, local sportscasters dwelled on the game's extra period. The following morning, newspapers across America featured multiple-story coverage simply because these two championship contenders played longer and more dramatically than anyone else before them could claim.

Until the game, Unitas was just another quarterback; Ameche, a running back of skills that were impressive but not unique. After the game, everybody knew their names. And in years to come, sportswriters would claim over and over that this was the greatest pro football game ever played.

Years later, the late NFL Commissioner Pete Rozelle would tell a reporter:

"We didn't know it at the time, but it was the beginning for us. From that game forward, our fan base grew and grew. We owe both franchises a huge debt."

ny
63

**The Giants kept** pressure on Hall of Fame quarterback Johnny Unitas throughout the long afternoon. But the Colt managed to throw one touchdown pass and engineer two late-scoring drives: one at the end of regulation that resulted in a game-tying field goal and the long march to Alan Ameche's winning touchdown in overtime, above.

1986—Giants fans had waited three decades for this one. They had survived the emotional trauma of losing five world championships over a six-year span, between 1958 and 1963. They had survived a nightmare run of only three winning seasons and five different coaches in nineteen years. Over that time, twenty different quarterbacks came and went. The Giants seemed destined to suffer forever. Their team found ways to lose games that nobody else could imagine in their worst nightmares. Week after week, the customers never wavered. They were no longer fans— they had become emotionally indentured servants to a dream deferred for so long that they had trouble remembering what it was.

And then they got yet another coach. His name was Bill Parcells. And on January 25, 1987, in Pasadena, California, as the

booed by Giants fans more than they dare remember today, Phil Simms played quarterback in Super Bowl XXI the way no Super Bowl quarterback before him had ever played.

He completed twenty-two of twenty-five passes for 268 yards and three touchdowns. He was superb. But the rest of what the Giants threw against Denver wasn't exactly chopped liver— which was just as well for them because historically, for the pre-Parcells Giants, staying close at halftime was never enough.

They struggled through a first half that gave Denver a 10-9 edge. But the difference this time was a strong message to the Broncos. It was plain and simple, in the tradition of the late Satchel Paige:

"Don't look over your shoulder. We are coming."

Their delivery came in a goal-line stand that denied

sun set behind the Rose Bowl, nobody even considered calling him a coach. To the fans, what he had become was The Exorcist.

Every demon, every ghost, every poltergeist that generated the worst run of football failures in Giants history was hunted down and sent back to Football Purgatory by the man who grew up an easy ride from the stadium the Giants call home. He did it mercilessly against the Denver Broncos with a blue-collar offensive line that laughingly called itself "the Surburbanites," with a running back named Joe Morris who had heard all his life that he was too small but who rushed for 1,516 regular-season yards that year, and with a brutal defense keyed by Lawrence Taylor's twenty-and-a-half sacks.

But most of all on that day in California, he did it with a quarterback named Phil Simms, who stepped out of the shadows forever. Cursed by injuries, selected in the draft as a total unknown,

Denver a score after it had registered a first and goal on the Giants' one, and a predatory grab of John Elway by Leonard Marshall for a safety. At the start of the second half with the ball on their own forty-seven on a fourth-and-one, the Giants lined up in punt formation. They had the best punter in the league in Sean Landeta, but he never got the ball. Instead, it was snapped to substitute quarterback Jeff Rutledge, who was in the game to block as an "up back." Rutledge ran easily for the first down that proved to be the silver stake through the Broncos' collective heart.

From then on the Giants were golden. The final score was 39-20, but those are only numbers. The Giants were near perfect in the second half.

---

**Quarterback Phil Simms,** left, was Super Bowl XXI's Most Valuable Player for his record twenty-two-for-twenty-five passing. Above: Leonard Marshall (70) celebrates with Erik Howard (74) and Lawrence Taylor (56) after sacking Denver quarterback John Elway for a safety; George Martin (75) pressures Elway; and Mark Bavaro and Karl Nelson (63) try to free Maurice Carthon (44) from the clutches of the Broncos. Phil McConkey, right, proved an invaluable part of the Giants team. On a third and goal in the fourth quarter he miraculously scooped up a deflected pass off Mark Bavaro, the intended receiver. Following spread: Try as they might, Denver's blockers were unable to keep defensive end Leonard Marshall away from the Broncos all afternoon.

**Tight end Mark** Bavaro offers thanks in the Denver end zone after catching a thirteen-yard touchdown pass from Phil Simms in the third quarter. The score put the Giants ahead 16-10 en route to their first Super Bowl victory. Harry Carson, above, douses head coach Bill Parcells with the traditional Gatorade shower in the final seconds of Super Bowl XXI.

As right tackle John Elliott (76) and running back Ottis Anderson (24) take on the charge of Buffalo's Bruce Smith, quarterback Jeff Hostetler sets to throw in Super Bowl XXV. Subbing for the injured Phil Simms, Hostetler completed twenty of thirty-two attempts for 222 yards and a touchdown in the Giants' 20-19 victory. The Giants' detailed play diagrams and mid-game pictures, left, helped New York achieve a Super Bowl possession record.

1990—Bill Parcells was back in Super Bowl contention. Of course he wasn't supposed to be there—not with this team and not with the chattel mortgage that the San Francisco 49ers were supposed to have on all things postseason. Here were the 'Niners, virtually granted an automatic Super Bowl trip and their third consecutive set of Super Bowl rings. They had beaten the Giants during the regular season, 7-3, in a fierce defensive struggle. That was out in Candlestick Park and the Giants would have to come into their house again for the NFC title game. Nobody gave Mara Tech much of a chance against Joe Montana Magic. Moreover, Phil Simms, the hero of the Giants' season of redemption back in 1986, was finished for the year with a broken foot. Jeff Hostetler, a backup quarterback, whom the Giants viewed more as a scrambler than a passer, was pressed into service.

Nobody took this Giants' bid for a Super Bowl berth seriously.

Nobody except the Giants.

The 'Niners were the team for whom the Giants defensive coordinator, Bill Belichick, held a serious emotional grudge. Just the year before, the 'Niners had sent the Giants' Lawrence Taylor to the sidelines with a broken ankle on what Belichick believed to be an illegal block. Now those same 'Niners were standing in the way of his team's return to the Super Bowl. Driven by Belichick's reminders and defensive scheme, the Giants defensive unit carried the day during a brutally physical 15-13 victory.

The burden certainly landed squarely on its shoulders. The offense did not score a touchdown. All the points came on Matt Bahr's five field goals, which ranged in distance from twenty-eight to forty-seven yards. But the road to the Super Bowl in Tampa was hammered out by three other players—two from Belichick's defense and one from special teams.

Defensive end Leonard Marshall had two quarterback sacks and forced two fumbles with a pair of crushing tackles, one of which knocked Montana out of the game. Erik Howard made yet another ferocious hit on running back Roger Craig when the game appeared lost with just 2:36 left. Taylor gained a measure of revenge by recovering the loose ball, which led to Bahr's winning forty-two-yarder with no time left on the clock.

Now it was Tampa time. This was the strangest Super Bowl setting ever. The Gulf War had started. Each spectator was searched on the way in, and the lines seemed to stretch halfway to Texas.

The Buffalo Bills, who made something of a career out of getting to and then losing Super Bowls, would provide the opposition. Incredibly, they would fail because of yet another heroic performance by Bahr and two other players nobody thought much about. Hostetler had become the quarterback by default for the entire playoffs. Now on this day, the scrambler suddenly became the passer. He hit twenty of thirty-two attempts for 222 yards.

Bahr's field goal provided the winning 20-19 margin. But it was Ottis Anderson with 102 yards rushing and one touchdown who would provide the spark. Anderson was a resurrected veteran who had come over from St. Louis, played on special teams, and finally earned his way into the lineup as a goal-line situation runner. On

**Ottis Anderson's running** was a major reason why New York controlled the ball during Super Bowl XXV. Anderson, below, rushed for 102 yards and a touchdown and was voted the Most Valuable Player. Opposite: Head coach Bill Parcells is raised on the shoulders of linebackers Lawrence Taylor (56) and Carl Banks (58) seconds after the final gun sounded on New York's 20-19 victory over Buffalo in Super Bowl XXV on January 27, 1991, in Tampa, Florida. Joining in the celebration is defensive end John Washington (73).

this day, however, with their regular quarterback and starting running back, Joe Morris, out—and the team's offensive weapons far more limited than the ones that had brought the Giants their first Super Bowl victory over Denver—coach Bill Parcells went to a possession-type offense that featured the thirty-two-year old Anderson. Because of him, the Giants set an all-time Super Bowl record with a possession time of forty minutes and thirty-three seconds. The theory of course was that you can't win without the ball. And yard by yard, the Giants battled to keep it. Buffalo's Bruce Smith, the best pass rusher in the American Football Conference, was neutralized by a coterie of Giants blockers led by heavyweight tackle Jumbo Elliott. But sooner or later, you have to loan the other team the ball. With 2:16 left, the Giants were clinging to a 20-19 edge that Bahr had provided with a fourth-quarter twenty-one-yard field goal.

Starting from their own ten, Buffalo moved the ball as they knew they would once it was clear that the Giants were going into a "prevent" defense. Football purists are split on this kind of strategy, which essentially means you give up your short gains—particularly the short passes—and play your secondary deep so no receiver can get behind with a clear path to the goal line.

The Giants bent and the Giants gave but they did not break. The clock continued to tick. Buffalo was moving, but with eight seconds left, the Bills had no option but to try a forty-nine-yard field goal. On each sideline, grown men closed their eyes, afraid to watch. Some even kneeled in prayer. Scott Norwood—a solitary figure with the pressure

of the entire game squarely on his shoulders—paced off his kicking lane.

Frank Reich, the Bills backup quarterback, took the snap. His hold was true. Norwood saw nothing but his aiming point. The kick was solid. The crowd inhaled sharply as the ball soared into the eerie flood-lit darkness. And then—without warning—it shanked to the right, curving just outside of the up-rights as the clock ran down to zero.

Norwood was inconsolable. His head jerked abruptly downward like a man who had just been hit with a vicious left hook to the solar plexus. Nobody had to tell him how history was going to remember him.

The Giants were once again champions of pro football's hundred-yard world.

**Linebacker Gary Reasons,** opposite, escorts son Ryan from the field at Tampa Stadium after the Giants defeated
the Bills 20-19 to win the Super Bowl on January 27, 1991. Above: National Football League Commissioner
Paul Tagliabue presents Giants President Wellington Mara the Vince Lombardi Trophy moments after the
Giants' victory at Buffalo. With microphone is television commentator Brent Musberger. Right: The official game
ball of Super Bowl XXV is a prized Giants' trophy.

Phil Simms threw 1,814 more passes than anyone else in Giants history. He has 1,158 more completions than his nearest competitor, 13,974 more passing yards, and 26 more touchdown passes.

Some statistics lie. Those speak an obvious truth: Simms is the greatest quarterback to ever play for the Giants.

The Giants have had some good ones. Y. A. Tittle and Fran Tarkenton, who spent just parts of their careers in New York, are in the Hall of Fame. Charlie Conerly, a Giant from 1948 to 1961, should be.

But for sustained excellence, for an unshakable perseverance and an indomitable will to succeed, for overcoming hardships and deflecting criticism, and yes, for those brilliant statistics, no one can touch Simms.

Along with Hall of Fame linebacker Lawrence Taylor, he was the guiding light as the Giants rose from perennial doormats to regular

playoff participants and two-time Super Bowl champions. Simms was a leader on the field and in the locker room, a player who thrived under enormous pressure from coach Bill Parcells, the media, and the fans. Even when he was ruthlessly criticized, Simms carried himself with an uncommon grace and dignity, using his intelligence and sense of humor to keep everything in perspective. His great performances blunted criticism.

Simms played 164 regular-season games for the Giants, his only team. He threw 4,647 passes, completing 2,576 (55.4 percent) for 33,462 yards, 199 touchdowns and 157 interceptions. In 10 postseason games Simms completed 56.3 percent of his throws and threw 10 touchdowns and 6 interceptions.

As a starting quarterback, Simms was 101-68, a .590 combined winning percentage in regular-season and postseason games. Of the twenty-eight passing categories in the Giants'

record book, Simms sits at the top fifteen times. He is second in seven others. His No. 11 jersey was retired in 1995.

What makes Simms' success more remarkable is that his career had neither an auspicious beginning nor an uninterrupted ascent. Indeed, after five years it seemed he might be forced into an early retirement without ever having an opportunity to tap into his vast potential.

The Giants had suffered through six consecutive losing seasons and had not played a postseason game in fifteen years when Simms joined the team as a first-round draft choice in 1979. New general manager George Young needed a centerpiece for his rebuilding program, so he selected a relatively unknown quarterback from Morehead State in Kentucky. The New York tabloids greeted Simms with "Phil Who?" headlines.

They found out soon enough. Simms made his first

professional appearance in relief in the season's fifth game. The following week he became the starter for the rest of the season. He wasn't great—he threw more interceptions (fourteen) than touchdown passes (thirteen). But he was 6-5 as a starter and runnerup to Ottis Anderson in the Rookie of the Year voting. More important, Simms gave the Giants their first glimmer of hope for a bright future in more than a decade.

It didn't take long to dim. In 1980 the Giants won just four games. Simms threw nineteen interceptions in thirteen games and was forced to sit out the final three contests with a shoulder injury.

The next year Simms started in ten games, but was on injured reserve with a separated shoulder when the Giants clinched their first playoff berth in eighteen seasons. In 1982, he missed the entire season after suffering a knee injury in a preseason game against the New York Jets.

# PHIL SIMMS
## BY MICHAEL EISEN

But even that wasn't Simms' professional nadir. The following season Parcells chose the mediocre Scott Brunner to be his starting

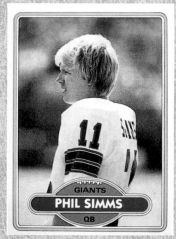

quarterback, a decision he rues to this day. Simms, livid and unable to see a future for himself with the Giants, demanded a trade. The Giants refused and in his second relief appearance of the season, Simms suffered a compound fracture and dislocated thumb that ended his season.

That once-bright future looked bleak for both the Giants and Simms after the 1983 season. The Giants were coming off a dismal 3-12-1 campaign. And Simms had finished a season on

the sidelines with an injury for the fourth consecutive year.

Simms' career had taken a sour turn. He couldn't stay on the field. When he did, the fans in New York took their frustrations out on the former golden boy, booing him unmercifully. It appeared Young had made a big mistake with his first draft choice back in '79. Some reporters even speculated that Simms' career might be finished.

But instead of retreating, Simms fought harder. He punished himself physically to get in the best possible condition. And Simms would be in Giants Stadium from early in the morning until well into the evening, studying game tapes and learning all the nuances of the Giants offense.

Parcells, whose head coaching career was in danger of being terminated after one embarrassing season, decided Simms was the man to lead the Giants to the promised land.

This time, he was right. From 1984 to 1986, Simms' career took off with the best three-year stretch any Giants quarterback has ever enjoyed. The once injury-prone quarterback did not miss a game. In those three years he led the Giants to three playoff berths and a Super Bowl title while throwing for 11,360 yards and 65 touchdowns.

Simms was extraordinary in 1984, setting single-season team records for passing attempts (533), completions (286), and yards (4,044). The boos that had once rained down on Simms from the upper reaches of Giants Stadium were now cheers. Simms, finally happy and healthy, led the Giants to a 9-7 record and a playoff victory.

The 1985 season brought more of the same. In one game at Cincinnati, Simms completed forty passes, including thirteen in a row, and threw for 513 yards, all team records. He was the NFC starter and the MVP of the Pro

Bowl, where he threw for three touchdowns. The Giants were 10-6 and again advanced to the second round of the playoffs before falling for the second year in a row to the eventual Super Bowl champions. This time it was Chicago.

Those disappointments, and Simms' consistently excellent play, were preludes to the magical 1986 season, probably the greatest in Giants history. The Giants finished 17-2 (including the playoffs) and won their last twelve games, including a 39-20 rout of the Denver Broncos in Super Bowl XXI. Simms was magnificent all season, and he was at his best when the Giants needed him the most.

In a game at Minnesota, the Giants trailed late in the fourth quarter and faced a seemingly impossible fourth-and-seventeen. Simms instructed wide receiver Bobby Johnson to run to a spot near the right sideline, then hit him with a pinpoint pass in the

**Phil Simms went** from "Phil Who?" when plucked out of Morehead State in the first round of the 1979 draft to the greatest quarterback in Giants history. The naive-looking youth pictured on his rookie card matured into the Most Valuable Player of Super Bowl XXI. On January 25, 1987, Simms completed twenty-two of his twenty-five pass attempts—a Super Bowl record 88 percent—for 268 yards and three touchdowns in the Giants' 39-20 victory over Denver.

face of a fierce rush for an incredible twenty-one-yard gain. That set up the winning field goal in a dramatic 22-20 triumph.

Two months later, Simms had absolute confidence that both he and the Giants would have big games against the Broncos in the Super Bowl. But not even Simms could have predicted how great both would be. Simms completed a Super Bowl record 88 percent of his passes (twenty-two of twenty-five) for 268 yards and three touchdowns and was named MVP in the Giants' first Super Bowl victory.

After a long, painful journey slowed by several setbacks, Simms was at last on top of the world.

His stay there would be fleeting. Simms never had it as good as he did in his wondrous three-year stretch.

In the strike-gutted 1987 season, his streak of fifty-nine consecutive starts ended when he sprained his knee and was forced to miss three games. The Giants missed the playoffs that season and again in 1988. They won the

National Football Conference East with a 12-4 record in 1989, but Simms threw only fourteen touchdown passes in a ground-oriented offense and the Giants suffered a bitter overtime playoff loss at home to the Rams.

Simms was back on top of his game in 1990, winning his first NFC passing title with a quarterback rating of 92.7. But after leading the Giants to an 11-3 record, Simms suffered a season-ending foot injury and was forced to watch in street clothes as Jeff Hostetler stepped in for him and led the Giants to their second Super Bowl title.

It got worse for Simms the following year, when new coach Ray Handley selected Hostetler to be his starting quarterback. Simms saw action in just one of the first

eleven games before Hostetler sustained a neck injury. Simms started the last five games of that season and the first four games in 1992. Then the injury bug bit again as Simms suffered an elbow injury that sidelined him for the rest of the season.

At age thirty-seven, and with fourteen years in the league, it appeared that Simms was finished. But he defied the skeptics, just as he had done almost a decade earlier. Dan Reeves became the Giants coach in 1993 and quickly anointed Simms as his quarterback. Suddenly, Simms looked and played as if he were twenty-nine again. He started all eighteen games, completed a career-best 61.8 percent of his passes, and threw only nine interceptions in four hundred attempts as the

Giants advanced to the second round of the playoffs.

Simms believes he could have been as effective the following year. But he never got the chance. Because he was slow to heal after off-season shoulder surgery, the Giants were uncertain if he would be ready to play in 1994 and unwilling to pay his $2.5 million salary if he couldn't. The Giants management thought it was too big a risk to assume in the first year of the salary cap. So on June 16, 1994, Simms was unceremoniously released.

He never played another game. Today, Simms still has a quick smile and his recognizable Kentucky drawl. He lives a short distance from Giants Stadium and has become one of the best and most popular NFL analysts on network television. The longer Simms is away from the game, the more his stature grows.

And as the new millennium approaches, the Giants are still trying to replace him.

**Phil Simms says** farewell, above, to a packed Giants Stadium upon the retirement of his No. 11 jersey on September 4, 1995. Simms was to the Giants offense what teammate and friend Lawrence Taylor, opposite, was to the Giants defense. Only Simms and the legendary Mel Hein played fifteen seasons for the Giants. Simms holds almost every Giants passing record, including career marks for attempts (4,647), completions (2,576), yards (33,462), and touchdowns (199). Twenty-one times in his career he passed for more than 300 yards in a game.

**Y**ou cannot begin to think of Giants' Super Bowl championships without conjuring up the image of Hall of Famer Lawrence Taylor zeroing in on the quarterback or Phil Simms throwing the ball on a brilliant California day as no Super Bowl passer before him ever had. You cannot recall that spectacular championship of 1956 without visualizing Charlie Conerly, his face forever lined by the pain of war in the South Pacific, standing tall and without so much as a hint of fear in the pocket while linemen and linebackers came at him in waves and Charlie seemed to be telling them:

"Go ahead. Take your best shot. You can't scare me after the things I've seen and survived."

You cannot remember the Polo Grounds without recalling the heroics of Ken Strong, the local boy out of NYU, who stamped his deeds in large letters across the emotional face of this franchise.

The ones you will read about here distinguished themselves in various ways, but the one common thread that bound them close to the hearts of generation after generation of Giants fans was the fact that each in his own way was a hero of his times.

Some of them played on losing teams. That doesn't matter. What matters is that each, whether lineman, back, kicker, or even a sixty-minute player under the old rules before free substitution, satisfied a need for the Faithful who were there rain, snow, icicles, or shine.

There are players who genuinely belong with the pantheon of Giants greats, men who truly were giants among Giants. These are some of their stories.

# GIANTS AMONG GIANTS

# 14 Ward Cuff

**When Ward Cuff** played for the Giants (1937–45), there was much more foot in football. And Cuff was one of the game's top kickers. In addition to kicking twenty-two field goals and seventy point after touchdowns, or PATs, over a six-year span, Cuff played in both the offensive and defensive backfield.

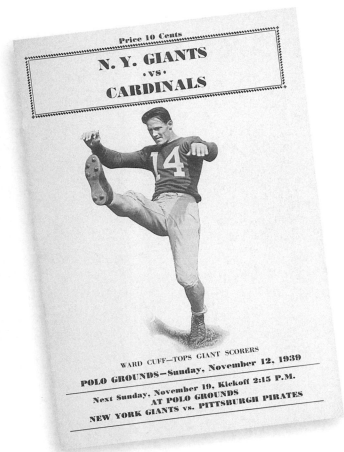

Price 10 Cents

**N. Y. GIANTS**
·vs·
**CARDINALS**

WARD CUFF—TOPS GIANT SCORERS
POLO GROUNDS—Sunday, November 12, 1939
Next Sunday, November 19, Kickoff 2:15 P.M.
AT POLO GROUNDS
NEW YORK GIANTS vs. PITTSBURGH PIRATES

Ward Cuff didn't like to practice. As far back as his college years at Marquette, he would limp into the locker room on days when heavy contact was scheduled, look around, and hope he could convince the trainer to give him an excuse. But there was never a doubt about his athleticism. He threw the javelin. He was the school's heavyweight boxing champion, and he could do an awful lot of things on the football field.

A skilled running back, brilliant on pass defense, a kickoff and extra-point man, Cuff was born to play the game. It did not take the Giants long to develop him into an expert field-goal kicker as well. He led the Giants in scoring six years in a row and played in six championship games.

# 60 Cal Hubbard

One of the strongest and most physical players of his time, Cal Hubbard was one of seventeen charter enshrinees into the Hall of Fame. Out of little Geneva College, he came to the Giants after helping the Packers beat them out of a championship in 1929. In 1927, the Giants' first championship year, he was the dominant player on a defense that allowed just twenty points in thirteen games.

He retired after the 1935 season to become an American League umpire, but when injuries riddled the Giants defense in 1936, Hubbard agreed to a brief comeback. At 270 pounds and in his late thirties, Hubbard single-handedly destroyed Detroit's offensive line in his comeback game. He never played again after that season and a lot of opposing linemen were ecstatic when he left.

**The Giants acquired** Cal Hubbard in 1927 to bolster their defense. He did. New York surrendered only twenty points all season en route to its first NFL championship. In 1929, Green Bay acquired the tackle in a deal that would haunt New York. Hubbard led the 12-0-1 Packers to a 20-6 victory over the 13-1-1 Giants in a game that would decide the NFL champion.

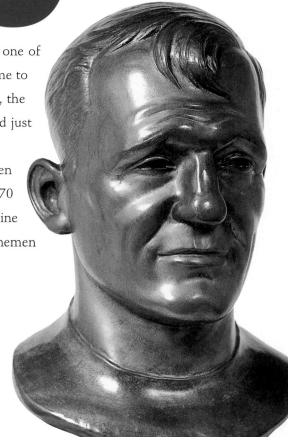

One of the greatest all-around backs in NFL history, Frank Gifford, shown below in his rookie card, accounted for 9,753 yards in his career, including 3,609 rushing yards and a team-record 5,434 receiving yards. Gifford caught 367 passes and ran for 484 points. He made the Pro Bowl as a defensive back in 1953 and as an offensive back the following year—an NFL first. He holds the Giants' record for touchdowns (seventy-eight).

# 16
# Frank Gifford

They never had anyone like him. Perhaps nobody did. If other superstars were the equivalent of featured soloists, Frank Gifford was the whole damned orchestra. When he first reported to the Giants in 1952, head coach Steve Owen thought his running style too "dainty" and converted him to defensive back. He became an All-Pro at the position. The following year, they converted him to offense and he went back to the Pro Bowl as a running back. When Vince Lombardi came down from Army to serve as offensive coordinator, he put in a halfback pass that became a deadly weapon for the Giants. Naturally, Gifford was the guy who threw it.

His numbers were spectacular: seven Pro Bowls . . . 1956 Player of the Year . . . seventy-eight touchdowns . . . 4.3 yards per carry . . . fourteen touchdown passes off the option . . . and on and on. Incredibly, he lost two years of offensive potential when they had him in the defensive backfield and another when a brutal hit by the Eagles' Chuck Bednarik put him out of football for a year.

When he returned, it was to join a team stocked with a wealth of riches at running back. Coach Allie Sherman stunned everyone by converting Gifford to flanker. Gifford's ability to get open and catch the ball made him look as though it had been his natural position all his life. Additionally, he could kick field goals and extra points when called upon and did a brief training-camp stint at quarterback. Small wonder that he was a Hall of Famer. Gifford played in five NFL title games including the 1956 championship won by the Giants. Later, he was a fixture on Monday Night Football telecasts as an analyst. Gifford was inducted into the Hall of Fame in 1977. Wellington Mara calls him the most versatile player the Giants ever had. He should know. He has seen them all.

The place was called Jamison No. 9, tucked deep within the hills of West Virginia, where long hours, short pay days, constant debt to the company store, and the threat of black lung disease was the fate of every boy from this coal-mining town.

But not that of Robert Lee Huff, known to friends and family as Sam. "Nobody in my family had ever graduated high school but I knew I was never, never going down into that mine no matter what it took."

Football was the vehicle that carried him about as far as you could get from that underworld of danger, grime, and despair. He was an All-American tackle at the University of West Virginia, goaded by a coach named Art "Pappy" Lewis, who constantly reminded Huff that if he didn't like the discipline, he could get himself a shovel and go back to where he came from. Consequently, he played with a passion that earned him a national reputation.

The Giants needed no urging to sign him in 1956.

Then came reality.

In camp they decided he was too small to play tackle and too slow to play guard. The coaches did not know what to do with him and he overheard them say as much. Huff decided he was going to make his own move before they cut him. Disheartened, homesick, and depressed, he planned to go AWOL with his roommate, a rookie punter named Don Chandler.

Vince Lombardi, the offensive coordinator, caught Chandler at the airport and brought him back, screaming, "I might cut you, but that's my decision! But I sure as hell won't let you quit on me!" Chandler became a fixture with the team starting with that very championship year.

Huff, meanwhile, had been cornered by line coach Ed Kolman, who told him, "If you leave now you will never forgive yourself. If you leave now you will feel like a quitter for the rest of your life." It was the kind of challenge a young man from Jamison No. 9 could not ignore.

"I'll come back," Huff said, "but [Jim Lee] Howell has to promise to stop yelling at me so much. He's like a marine drill sergeant. I know how to play. All he has to do is take a closer look." Howell agreed. Then, suddenly, the Giants found a place for him. Ray Beck, a converted guard who was supposed to start the season at middle linebacker, went down. Defensive coach Tom Landry had an alternate plan and it focused on the speed, peripheral vision, and physical strength of a rookie who had earlier been thought too small to even make the team.

Sam Huff became the triggerman of a defense that would take the Giants to the world title that very season. Remembered most of all were his brutal individual battles with Green Bay's Jim Taylor, Cleveland's Jim Brown, and Chicago's Rick Casares. They were savage one-on-one physical confrontations. Best remembered was the frigid 1962 title game in New York where the turf took on the consistency of concrete. As Taylor lay at the bottom of the pile, he saw a naked calf and bit it.

"Are you crazy?" Dick Modzelewski, a defensive tackle, shrieked.

"Oh, sorry," Taylor said with genuine sincerity. "I thought you were Huff."

Sam Huff was enshrined in the Pro Football Hall of Fame in 1982.

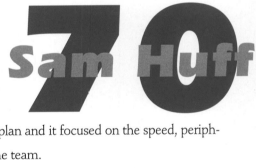

**Sam Huff was** the prototype middle linebacker. Tough and unnerving, Huff won the NFL's Outstanding Lineman award in 1959 and was featured on the cover of TIME in November of that same year. Never before had an NFL player been featured on the cover of a national news magazine. He is best known for his mano-a-mano matches against the great running backs of his era. The documentary "The Violent World of Sam Huff" was one of television's first inside looks at the NFL and helped popularize the league.

Lawrence Taylor, the best football player in Giants history, was a linebacker like no other. He defined the position of outside linebacker, terrorized quarterbacks, inserted sacks into the National Football League's official statistics, popularized the tomahawk tackle that often forced fumbles, dominated opposing coaches' thinking, and continually produced moments magnifying his "L.T." legend.

"In a 1984 game with Tampa Bay," said Phil Simms, his Giants' teammate, "I saw Lawrence trample the tackle, jump over the back who was trying to block him, and pounce on Steve DeBerg for the sack."

As dazzling as Lawrence Taylor, at six-feet-three and 243 pounds, was when healthy, his most theatrical performance occurred on a Sunday night in 1988 in New Orleans when he was wincing with a torn muscle and detached ligament in his right shoulder. Despite having to adjust the protective harness under his jersey after almost every play, he had three sacks, two forced fumbles, and seven tackles. If ever a defensive player won a game, Taylor did that night in the Giants' 13-12 victory.

"It felt," he acknowledged much later, "like somebody had torn my shoulder off my body."

In the locker room after that game, Parcells, knowing the pain L.T. was in, gently hugged him.

"You were great tonight," the coach whispered in his ear. "I just want to say thanks."

The Giants also could thank Lawrence Taylor, more than any single player, for their 1986 and 1990 Super Bowl rings. In 1986, when he had 20.5 sacks, he was voted the NFL's Most Valuable Player, joining tackle Alan Page of the 1976 Minnesota Vikings as the only defensive player so honored. In 1995 he was named to the NFL's 75th Anniversary team. He had ten consecutive All-Pro and Pro Bowl seasons, beginning as a 1981 rookie out of the University of North Carolina.

"I was holding my breath in that draft," recalls George Young, the Giants general manager. "We had the second choice, New Orleans had the first choice. But the Saints took George Rogers, the Heisman Trophy running back from South Carolina."

From the moment Taylor joined the Giants in training camp, he was a starter. His career total of 132.5 sacks doesn't include his 9.5 sacks in 1981 before that category was added to official NFL statistics. Of his ten interceptions, including the postseason, he returned three for touchdowns, notably a ninety-seven-yard dash down the sideline in 1982 in Detroit.

"Regardless of all the individual honors Lawrence received," Parcells said, "he was the consummate team player. That's what separated him. Some guys were more 'me' guys, interested in personal things. With Lawrence, it was always, 'Did we win, and who do we play next?'"

Before a 1987 game in Philadelphia, the Eagles coach, Buddy Ryan, questioned whether L.T. could still catch Randall Cunningham, the Eagles' scrambling quarterback. But with the game at stake in the closing minutes, Cunningham was hurrying down the sideline when L.T., racing across the field, pulled a hamstring muscle but somehow stopped Cunningham short of a first down, preserving a Giants' 20-17 victory. Sprawled on a table in the trainer's room later, Taylor looked up at Parcells.

"Tell Buddy Ryan," he said. "that I can still catch 'em."

In a 1988 late-season game at San Francisco, Taylor suffered what was originally announced as a severely sprained ankle. X rays revealed a broken bone in his ankle. When he was asked if he

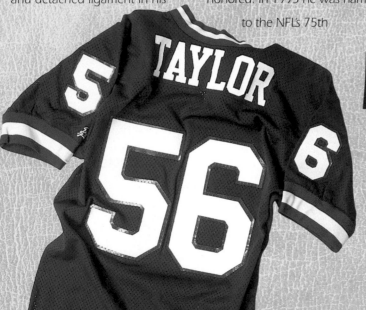

# LAWRENCE TAYLOR

## BY DAVE ANDERSON

now were out for the remainder of the season, he frowned.

"Are you kiddin'?" he asked.

He played the next Sunday. The following year, because of a contract holdout, he didn't join the Giants until the Wednesday before the season started. But in the opener against the Eagles, he had three sacks and a forced fumble. Midway in the 1992 season, which he had announced would be his last, he tore the Achilles tendon in his right heel.

"I'm not going out like this," he said.

He returned in 1993 for one more season. After a 44-3 playoff loss in San Francisco, he hurried onto the field toward referee Bernie Kukar.

"I wanted his flag," Taylor said later with a grin, referring to the official's yellow penalty hanky. "He's thrown it against me enough."

Not really. For all his reputation as a licensed terrorist, he never was accused of a "cheap shot." He never strutted after a sack. He never scuffled with opponents after the whistle. He just hit hard. As hard as any defensive player in NFL history ever did. Archie Manning, then a Saints quarterback, remembers what it was like to be sacked by the young linebacker in the "56" jersey.

"Lawrence hit me so hard, my teeth hurt, " Manning recalled. "On the next play, I called a draw and I hoped it wouldn't work so that I could get off the field."

When the occasion demanded, Taylor hit his Giants teammates hard too. Not physically, but mentally. In a 1986 game in Minnesota, the Giants were hoping to add to a 9-6 lead just before halftime until offensive tackle Brad Benson's illegal-motion penalty forced Raul Allegre to try a sixty-yard field goal. Wide left. Hurrying to the locker room, Parcells was about to scold Benson.

"I'll kill him," Parcells was growling. "I'll kill him."

"You won't have to, Bill," defensive end George Martin said. "Lawrence will kill him before you get there."

Benson somehow survived to help the Giants win Super Bowl XXI.

But in a lifestyle that too often was more reckless than his pass-rushing, Lawrence Taylor was harder on himself than he was on any opponents or teammates. After the 1985 season he spent time in drug rehab for what he acknowledged to be cocaine use. In 1988 he was suspended for the first four games of the season for violating the

NFL's substance-abuse policy. Since he stopped playing football, he has had more drug-related problems.

Those incidents clouded his candidacy for the Pro Football Hall of Fame until Commissioner Paul Tagliabue clarified the criteria before the 1999 meeting of the selection committee.

"The Hall of Fame is about performing on the field," Tagliabue said. "And there, Lawrence Taylor was one of the greatest. I think the public understands that by making a judgment of an athlete, you're not condoning, or accepting, what he did off the field."

The next day, Lawrence Taylor was voted into the Canton, Ohio, shrine.

"When the Giants organization retired my jersey, I said this then and I'll say it now," he said upon learning of his Hall of Fame election. "There has always been and will be a Lawrence Taylor, but without the fans, there would have never been an L.T."

**Although he stood** six-feet-three and weighed 243 pounds, Lawrence Taylor stood head and shoulders above peers and opponents alike. In 1986, he became only the second defensive player ever to be named the Most Valuable Player in the NFL for a season puctuated by 20.5 sacks. The consummate professional, Lawrence Taylor was all business when it came to physical and mental preparation.

# 45 Emlen Tunnell

**Ignored in the** 1948 draft, Emlen Tunnell asked the Giants for a tryout. Two decades later, the Giants' first black player was enshrined in the Pro Football Hall of Fame. In addition to being the Giants' all-time leader in interceptions (seventy-four), Tunnell was superb at returning punts and kickoffs.

It was the kind of legend of which movies are made. Player is ignored by draft. Player wants to play. Player walks off the street and begs for a chance. Player gets in and, in return, team gets a future Hall of Famer.

Only this was real life and Emlen Tunnell, who had played college football at both Iowa and Toledo, was the genuine article. He made history with the Giants even before he played his first game with them. He was the first African American to be signed by the Giants.

In camp before that 1948 season, the story seemed more myth than legend. The thing the Giants staff noticed was that he ran very slow sprints. "What are we gonna do with this guy?" was a common topic at coaching meetings. Then one day somebody asked him to field a punt. He ran it all the way back. When it came to fielding kicks and punts, he did everything wrong. He did not put his hands up for the catch. He waited and then shoved his hands forward, belt-high, almost as though he were Willie Mays making a breadbasket catch.

But it worked.

Somebody else wondered if he could tackle. "He might be too slow to get a jump." Pass receivers in intra-squad games came away with the bruises to answer that question. By the end of camp, he had earned double duty as a punt/kick returner and as a defensive back. The Giants had never had a better one at either spot. Years later he would explain his success as a returner by insisting the position had nothing to do with speed. "It's all about pace," he said. And it surely seemed as though he had an extra gear. He would give a wiggle to the first defender and leave him clawing for his own balance. During the time he bought with that move, he would look for what returners call "the crack"—a seam of daylight wide enough to run through. He would invariably find it and, when he did, he was gone.

He could read a pass receiver's route better than the pass receiver. As a result, his nickname was "offense on defense" and he proved it. Tunnell still holds the Giants' record for interceptions at 74 and punt returns at 257. In 1952 he actually gained more yards (923) on interceptions and kick returns than the NFL rushing leader. Four times, he intercepted three passes in a single game. Over his career he ran back interceptions and kicks for an incredible 4,661 yards. He was inducted into the Hall of Fame in 1967.

Giants fans can only shudder at the thought of what might have happened if the Maras had told Tunnell that day he walked in off the street:

"Hey, this isn't amateur night. Make an appointment."

# Andy Robustelli **81**

If he hadn't been such a good father, Andy Robustelli might never have played a down as premier defensive end for the Giants. But then Robustelli, who took the art of playing defensive end to a new level with the Giants, had a career filled with contradictions. For one thing, he was drafted out of a school that no longer existed by the time he got to New York. The Rams chose him out of tiny Arnold College in Connecticut in 1951. He immediately became a fixture for them, playing on two championship teams.

But in 1956, his wife nine months pregnant, Robustelli asked the Rams for permission to come to camp two weeks late. In an incredible show of damaged logic, the Los Angeles club turned him down. "Fine," Robustelli countered, "then I'll take the whole season off and stay with my wife and my new baby in Connecticut." Neither side backed down.

Then the telephone call came.

"My name is Wellington Mara," the voice on the other end of the line said. "Things being what they are, I was wondering if you would consider playing for the Giants."

Robustelli couldn't get to camp fast enough. It did not take the Giants long to understand what they had. Sam Huff recalls him as "our godfather. He was older and more experienced. He was the leader." He was also a tremendous force on a rush line that was put together with the end-to-end ability to harass the passer. Robustelli's sheer willpower was no small motivator. He played on winning teams thirteen of his fourteen years as a pro.

His numbers took him to seven Pro Bowls and eight title matches. In fourteen years, he missed only one game. Later a player-coach and, for a brief time, director of football operations for the Giants, he became a Hall of Famer in 1971.

**Defensive end Andy Robustelli** *played in eight NFL title games and seven Pro Bowls in his fourteen-year career. Only once did he play on a losing team. A seven-time All-Pro selection, Robustelli was the field leader of the Giants defense.*

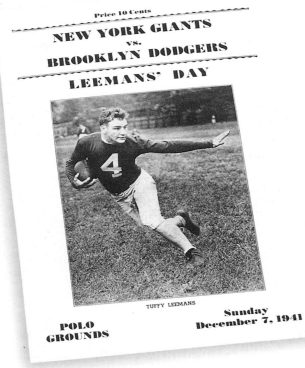

Price 10 Cents

**NEW YORK GIANTS**

vs.

**BROOKLYN DODGERS**

**LEEMANS' DAY**

TUFFY LEEMANS

**POLO GROUNDS**

Sunday
December 7, 1941

**In 1941 Tuffy Leemans** scored a rare double by leading the Giants in both rushing and passing. A second-round pick in the NFL's first draft in 1936, Leemans went from being the Most Valuable Player in the College All-Star Game to the NFL's leading rusher as a rookie. During his career, he accounted for 3,142 rushing yards, 2,324 passing yards, and 442 receiving yards.

He was the product of the strangest scouting system in history. Wellington Mara never saw Tuffy Leemans play a single down but he knew all about him. It was 1935, and with no money to send a scout on the road, Wellington, an undergraduate at Fordham, strained the budget and bought every preseason football magazine printed. He used them to put together his list of players to watch and then went to the out-of-town newsstand in Times Square each Monday and bought the Sunday papers that had covered their Saturday exploits.

In 1935 a hard-running back from a school whose football team didn't draw much attention, George Washington University, caught the eye of Ned Irish from the Giants' public relations department. Wellington added the nation's capital to his Sunday paper list. The back was Alphonse "Tuffy" Leemans. You knew he was tough because any football player with a first name like "Alphonse" damned well better know how to fight. Based solely on Wellington's diligent reading of the Washington newspapers, the Giants selected Leemans in the first draft the NFL ever held in 1936.

"I sent him a telegram," Wellington recalls, "and set up an appointment to meet him at the GW gym. When I arrived he didn't know who I was. I couldn't blame him. I was still at Fordham and just nineteen years old. But we settled on a deal."

Leemans had been around. He was out of Superior, Wisconsin, the son of an iron miner. When his high school coach took a job at the University of Oregon, Leemans went with him and started at halfback. When the coach got fired, Leemans left. He finally settled on George Washington. He was impressed with its high academic standards and the availability of a no-show job—not necessarily in that order.

He made the United Press third team All-America his senior year. In his rookie season with the Giants he led the league in rushing. From 1936 through 1943 he was the team's emotional leader. He ran, he passed, he blocked, and for part of his career, did the play-calling.

For Wellington Mara, he was Exhibit A, proving the case that for a talent scout, the Giants need look no further than the family gene pool.

**For nine seasons** starting in 1927, Red Badgro played offensive and defensive end for the Giants. Although he shared the NFL receiving title in 1934 with sixteen catches, he is best known for a catch he made in 1933—a twenty-nine-yard pass from Harry Newman that resulted in the first touchdown in an NFL Championship game.

# Red Badgro 17

He was the football rebel who came in out of the cold. When Red Grange and a promoter named C. C. Pyle founded the American Football League as an alternative to the NFL in 1926, Morris "Red" Badgro joined their New York Yankees as an end, a position at which he starred as a blocker, receiver, and a tackler. Such was his athleticism that he even played two years of major league baseball with the St. Louis Browns.

When the AFL folded, Badgro was one of several Yankees who joined the Giants. He was a trailblazer in their early history. In 1927, he helped them win the league title. In 1933, when the NFL split into two divisions, he led them to the first championship game in league history and scored the first touchdown ever scored in an NFL title game.

He was inducted into the Hall of Fame in 1981.

# 27 Rodney Hampton

He came to the Giants in 1990 as a first-round draft pick out of Georgia. Rodney Hampton played on one of the best teams in the franchise's history—and some of the worst. He tied the franchise record for most points in a game with twenty-four against New Orleans on September 24, 1995.

Hampton holds the team record for most career rushing attempts (1,284) and most career yards gained (6,897). He had eight games with thirty or more carries and posted five of the nine most productive rushing seasons in the history of the franchise. Hampton was the first Giant to record four consecutive seasons of rushing for more than one thousand yards, and he held the team record of seventeen games in which he rushed for a hundred or more yards. Rodney Hampton played in two Pro Bowls.

**The Giants' all-time** leading rusher, Rodney Hampton was also the first back to lead the Giants in rushing for six straight seasons (1991–96). A first-round pick out of Georgia in 1990, Hampton holds Giants career rushing records for carries (1,824), yards (6,897), and touchdowns (49).

# Dick Modzelewski 77

Part of the 1956 championship team that conquered the heart of New York City and captured the minds of America, Dick Modzelewski was an integral part of a defensive line so strong and talented that at one point it enabled the Giants to win three straight games without scoring a touchdown. He topped five-feet-eleven and weighed 260 pounds. An All-American at the University of Maryland, he had a squat frame that enabled him to "submarine" against taller offensive linemen.

Wellington Mara had gotten him from Pittsburgh in a real steal of a deal. Modzelewski was a great pass rusher, tough and deadly against the run, and on the summer day he arrived at the Giants training camp, he was an All-Pro prophet. He reminded anyone who would listen that the year before, the Browns had traded for his brother Ed and won the title. "This year," he promised, "it's the Giants' turn."

That it was, in no small measure due to his efforts. From 1956 through 1963, he played in four world championship games for New York.

---

**While teammates Rosey** Grier (76) and Sam Huff (70) claimed more headlines, hard-nosed tackle Dick Modzelewski (77) played a pivotal role on defenses that led the Giants to four NFL Championship games. Modzelewski's role was to control the middle of the line of scrimmage.

# Bennie Friedman
## 17

Bennie Friedman is considered the most underrated Giant of all time by Wellington Mara because he never won a title in New York, but Mara believes he may have been one of the best quarterbacks the Giants ever had. In 1928, the Giants were a team in distress. Only one year after their first NFL title, the Giants won just four of eleven. Desperate for someone who could put fire into the team and people into the seats, the Giants once again began their pursuit of Friedman.

An All-American at Michigan and a practitioner of the art of quarterbacking far ahead of his time, Friedman had long been coveted by the Giants. But Friedman was a football nomad of sorts. He played with a team that quickly went broke, the Cleveland Buckeyes. From there he moved to the Detroit Wolverines and after his Giants career he would finish with the Brooklyn Dodgers. Prompted by the disaster of 1928, the Giants were so determined to land him that they made history in the process.

Friedman was under contract to Detroit. When management turned down every offer Tim Mara made for him, the patriarch of the Giants asked, "Well, what's it going to take?"

"His contract is not for sale."

"What about the team?"

"Well, that's different."

Before he put down the phone, Mara had become the owner of the Detroit

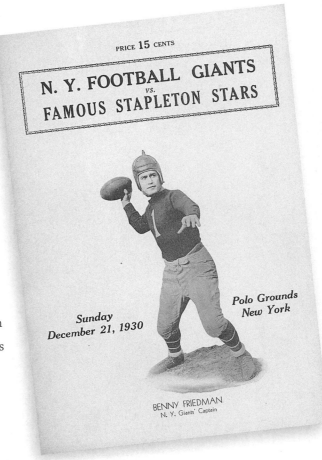

Wolverines. He remained the owner for about two days, during which time he brought Friedman and a handful of other players over and sent the rest home. The Detroit Wolverines were disbanded. Now Tim Mara had to come to terms with Friedman. He did, for what at that time was the incredible season salary of $10,000. Friedman immediately led the Giants to a 13-1-1 record, an eyelash behind the champion Packers. The next year, he again took them to a second-place finish.

"I think," Wellington recalls, "the most amazing thing about him was the way he could throw the kind of football that was in use in his days. Did you ever see that ball?" The football used in the 1930s looked like a pregnant watermelon. It was so round it gave the illusion of being circular. It did not have the twin points at each end that make it move like a missile when thrown.

"It was like trying to throw a wet sock," Wellington explained.

He didn't win a title but Bennie Friedman threw that ball well enough to be remembered by football historians for all time.

---

**The only way** to measure the value of Bennie Friedman is wins and losses, for when Friedman was throwing passes for the Giants from 1929 to 1931, no one kept track of individual statistics. The club's record with Friedman at the helm was 33-11-2 with two runnerup finishes in three seasons.

To celebrate its seventy-fifth anniversary, the National Football League picked its all-time team. Mel Hein was selected as the center—and the center-linebacker on the league's all-time two-way team. Hein's fifteen playing seasons are equalled only by Phil Simms among the Giants. Hein was all-NFL for eight straight years from 1933 to 1940.

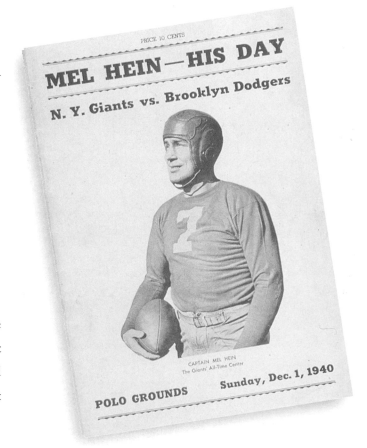

# Mel Hein

Mel Hein was the silent superstar who did his talking on the field. He played a record-setting fifteen years for the Giants and never missed a game—not a single one. Not in high school, not in college, and not with the Giants. He played an incredible 172 consecutive NFL contests. In all those games he took time out only twice and had to leave a game for injury just once.

Who noticed the center in those days of single wing and A formation football? But you had to notice Hein. In the days of two-way players he was spectacular at linebacker defense and a ferocious blocker on offense. In 1938, as the focal point of a line that overpowered Green Bay and brought the Giants the NFL title, he was named the league's Most Valuable Player—an honor no other center ever won.

# Roosevelt Brown, Jr. **79**

Wellington Mara calls him the greatest offensive lineman the Giants ever had. Allie Sherman, one of his coaches, almost waxes poetic over his skills and is quick to add that as a player, Roosevelt Brown gave Sherman an "extra coach" on the field. Upon retirement Brown did, in fact, become an assistant coach on the Giants staff.

"What made him so great," Sherman recalled, "was the fact that there are only two moves a defensive lineman can put on you when you pass-block, and Rosie had a different answer for both ones. For the guy who came at him in a bull rush fueled by sheer brute strength, Rosie would get the first hit and then move into the guy and let him go where he wanted, pushing him even further to that side so that his rush was dead.

"For the shake-and-bake kind of charge, Rosie would let him feint, then cut him low, which was legal back then, and put him on the ground. Nobody could do the things he could. He was so quick that on an end run, in the time it took the quarterback to lay the ball in the runner's belly, he could slide all the way down the line in the direction of the play, get there before the ballcarrier and join in the run block with the two guards at the point of attack."

He came to this team at six-feet-three, 235 pounds with a thirty-two-inch waist. He looked like a walking isosceles triangle. But few players had this Hall of Famer's strength. The Giants even used him on defense in goal-line stand situations.

**Roosevelt Brown went** from being a twenty-seventh-round draft pick in 1953 to being enshrined in the Pro Football Hall of Fame in 1975 as one of the game's greatest offensive tackles. Brown started for thirteen straight seasons and was an eight-time All-NFL pick. He was voted the NFL's Lineman of the Year in 1956.

## Y. A. Tittle

He never won a league championship for them but Tittle's place in the history of the franchise is assured. By the time he got to the Giants, Tittle had spent eleven years in the NFL and two more in the old All-America Conference. He was thirty-five years old. With his bald head and a squint that made him look as though he were forever searching for a very small needle in a very large haystack, there was a great temptation to wonder why the Giants would trade their No. 1 draft choice, a highly ranked lineman out of Clemson named Lou Cordileone, for a well-traveled quarterback whose best years seemed to be behind him.

Allie Sherman was the new coach and before the season began, he told Wellington that he thought this team could surprise everyone if it could get just two things—a reliable backup quarterback for Charlie Conerly, who was forty and whose arm had shown signs of weariness, and a receiver who could outrun somebody.

The receiver was easy—a speedburner named Del Shofner whom the Rams felt they no longer needed. But to find a quarterback, the Giants needed a little touch of fate. They got it when Red Hickey, the coach of the 49ers, looked over his offense and decided to switch to the shotgun attack that, in his version, put more premium on the quarterback's ability to run. Tittle had almost none.

What might have been a disaster for Hickey became a triumph for Sherman. The plan was to start Conerly and alternate him and Tittle as needed. Before it was over, it would become Tittle's team. Charlie retired the following year. Tittle took the Giants to three divisional titles, played in six Pro Bowls, and in his very first year with New York, threw seven touchdown passes in a single game against Washington. He was the NFL's Player of the Year twice for the Giants and once for the 49ers, and was inducted into the Hall of Fame in 1971.

**San Francisco believed** Y. A. Tittle's best days were over when they traded the thirty-five-year-old quarterback to the Giants in 1961. Tittle responded with record-setting seasons that led New York to consecutive Eastern Division titles in 1961 through 1963. Tittle was the NFL Player of the Year in 1957 with the 49ers and 1961 and 1963 with the Giants, when he threw a then NFL-record thirty-six touchdown passes. That remains the Giants' single-season record. Above are Tittle's battle-worn shoulder pads.

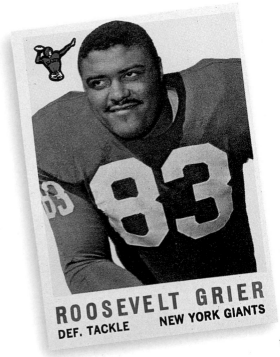

ROOSEVELT GRIER
DEF. TACKLE    NEW YORK GIANTS

# Roosevelt Grier 76

During the defensive hysteria that swept New York City in the Giants' championship year of 1956, Roosevelt Grier was the other half of the tackle tandem that battered opponents all season long. Operating in conjunction with Dick Modzelewski, his counterpart on the other side of the line, Grier had the ability to plug a hole, terrorize a passer, and freeze everything in front of him so linebackers like Sam Huff could have a clear shot at the ballcarrier.

"He was something very special," Huff recalled. "He was so strong and so gifted. The thing is that he played up to the level of any opposition. If, on the other hand, the guy in front of him was ordinary, Rosey never really cut loose all of which he was capable. If he could have done that every game, nobody would have gained a yard over him."

"He used to bring a guitar to training camp," recalled Allie Sherman, who coached Grier for several years. "We trained at Fairfield University back then and because the guys were so exhausted from two-a-day drills, we put him up on the top floor so we could all get some sleep. Then every year there would come a time when we were in a coaches' meeting and we'd hear this very soft music coming from Rosey's guitar instead of the kind of music that kept us all awake.

"That's when we'd look at each other and one of us would say, 'no more two-a-days. Rosey is ready.'" He was an All-Pro and a winner for as long as he was with the team.

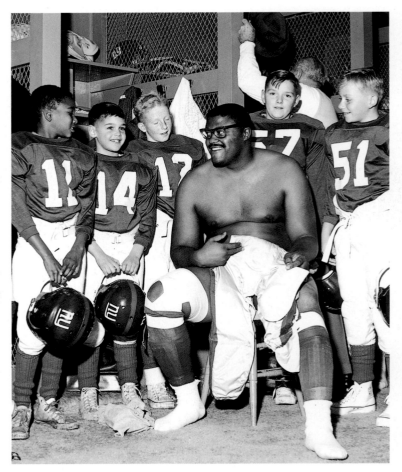

**Off the field,** Rosey Grier delighted in working with children and creating crafts with his hands. On the field, he was a mountain-sized terror. He was superb at both defending the run and rushing the passer. In his second season, Grier earned All-Pro honors while anchoring a defense that carried the Giants to the NFL title.

More than a half-century ago, when football players wore leather helmets and high-top black shoes, the colleges were king and the pros were struggling for recognition. The great chronicler of football then was Grantland Rice, the nationally syndicated sports columnist, and he fanned the stove-hot fires by choosing an all-time, All-America team. One of his halfbacks was Ken Strong.

"If Ken Strong isn't the greatest all-around player in the game's history," Rice asked, "who is? Considering the test of both college and pro football, I'd say the battle of the swift and the strong was among Ken Strong, Jim Thorpe, and Ernie Nevers, with Bronko Nagurski close up."

But which was the best? Rice picked two: Strong and Thorpe.

Thorpe's exploits, especially his Olympic heroics and off-the-field struggles, have been well documented. Strong, because of

a fragmented fourteen-year pro career, never received such recognition. That didn't bother him. This did:

"People used to say to me, 'You're that kicker.' I wanted them to know I was more than a kicker."

He certainly was. At five-feet-eleven and 210 pounds, he was a rugged tailback and fullback. He blocked fiercely. He could pass and catch passes. He could play defense. He could punt and placekick. And at a time when pro football was a grind-it-out, low-scoring game, he scored 479 points as a pro and led the National Football League in scoring three times.

Actually, Elmer Kenneth Strong, Jr. might have been better at baseball than football. He starred in both at West Haven (Connecticut) High School and New York University, where he was an All-America halfback.

Tim Mara, the Giants owner, wanted to sign the local college hero, and he sent LeRoy Andrews, the Giants coach, to offer him $4,000. Andrews figured he could get him for less and offered $3,000. He didn't know that Strong had a better offer from the Staten Island Stapletons, an NFL weak sister, and Strong took that money instead.

He quickly became the star of the Stapletons. When they played the Giants in the Stapletons' bandbox park, Strong was tackled by Ray Flaherty and they slid into the crowd. The whistle sounded, but Flaherty kept a stranglehold on him.

"Let go," Strong said.

"As soon as you stop kicking me," Flaherty said.

"I'm not touching you," Strong said.

Then, out of the corner of his eye, Strong caught the culprit. It seemed that a little old lady, objecting to Flaherty's treatment of her hero, was jabbing him with an umbrella.

When the Stapleton money ran out, Strong went to the Giants. In 1933 and 1934, Strong led the Giants to the NFL's Eastern Division title. In 1934, when he scored seventeen points in the famous Sneakers Game, he was a unanimous All-Pro, making $4,000, good money in those days. In 1935, he got a raise to $6,000.

In 1936, NFL teams, hurt by the depression, reduced salaries. Strong was offered $150 a game. Instead, the New York Yankees of the new American Football League signed him as player-coach for $5,000. An angry NFL, citing his "extreme disloyalty," suspended

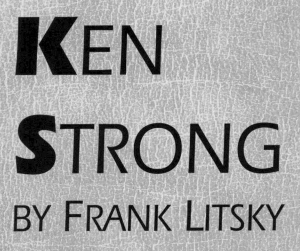

# KEN
# STRONG
## BY FRANK LITSKY

him for five years.

He played for the Yankees in 1936 and 1937. When that league folded, the Giants made a deal with him. If he would coach and play for their new farm team in Jersey City in 1938, they would ask the NFL to let him return to the Giants in 1939. He did and they did, but in his first game of 1939 he broke three vertebrae. For the rest of the season he only kicked, and after the season he retired.

Some retirement. In 1940, he helped coach the Giants and played some for a farm team until a bleeding ulcer hospitalized him for a month. In 1942, he played four games for the semipro Long Island Clippers. With wartime talent scarce, the Giants asked him to play again, and from 1944 to 1947 he did. But he said it would be kicking only, and to make sure he didn't try to do more he wore a wristwatch and no shoulder pads.

He relented only once. Riding a train to Washington for the last game of 1944, his son, Ken III, remarked that he had never seen his father do anything in football except kick. So in the fourth quarter, thirty-eight-year-old Ken Strong asked quarterback Tuffy Leemans to let him carry once. With the Giants leading, 31-0, and the game almost over, Strong got his wish.

He was so excited that he ran into the wrong hole and was smothered. On the last play, he tried again. The Redskins veterans, who knew what was going on, gave him room to run, but an unknowing Redskins rookie smacked him down.

Still, Strong was happy thinking his son had seen this. He was not so happy when he learned that his son had a cold and hadn't gone to the game.

After the 1947 season, Strong retired for good. He worked as a full-time liquor salesman and part-time Giants' kicking coach. In 1962, after Pat Summerall had retired, Strong taught punter Don Chandler to double as a kicker. At 56, Strong tried some kicks himself and made them from thirty-five and forty yards.

In 1967, Strong was elected to the Pro Football Hall of Fame in a distinguished class that included Paul Brown, Bobby Layne, Emlen Tunnell, and Chuck Bednarik.

"I was a little disappointed in other years when I didn't make it," he said, "but as long as it happens before you're dead."

In 1978, he suffered a massive heart attack but survived. In 1979, walking on the West Side of Manhattan, he suffered another heart attack, and a football legend fell dead.

**There wasn't an** aspect of football at which Ken Strong didn't excel. Although best remembered for his placekicking (he was the Giants' all-time scoring leader when he retired in 1947) and punting, Strong, whose shoulder pads are a featured display at the Pro Football Hall of Fame, was also a two-way back.

# Al Blozis

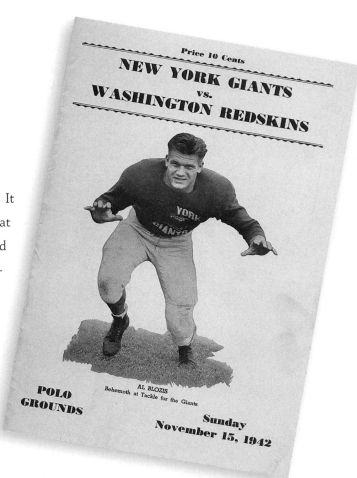

Price 10 Cents

## NEW YORK GIANTS
### vs.
## WASHINGTON REDSKINS

**POLO GROUNDS**

AL BLOZIS
Behemoth at Tackle for the Giants

**Sunday**
**November 15, 1942**

It is not so much what Al Blozis did—which was considerable. It was more a case of what might have been, what could have been, and what should have been. As America approached World War II, no lineman could match his credentials. Blozis was a superstar at Georgetown, an All-American in both football and track. Opposing teams both in college and the pros would try to trap the six-foot-five, 250-pound Blozis at the line of scrimmage. But with his long arms and massive brute strength, more often than not Blozis heaved the trapper into the ballcarrier and everyone went down.

A shot-putter at Georgetown, he set records for heaving the sixteen-pound, twelve-pound, and eight-pound shots. But luck always seemed to elude him. At one Madison Square Garden meet a photographer asked Blozis to heave one for him so he would have a protective photo to fall back on if he couldn't get one during the competition.

Blozis obliged during warm-ups—and threw it a world record distance.

Nobody saw it to confirm the record.

The year before Blozis joined the Giants, United Press picked its three greatest athletes of the year. They were Joe Louis, Ben Hogan, and Al Blozis. Drafting Blozis was a no-brainer. From training camp on he was spectacular. He leveled punt returners in the open field and continued to terrorize ballcarriers and blockers alike. He was a two-year All-Pro. He looked as though he could play and dominate his opponents forever.

But in 1944, as the war intensified, Blozis won a battle he had been waging for two years. Under army regulations he was too tall to serve. He finally got the military to grant him a waiver. At the apex of the Battle of the Bulge, Lt. Al Blozis was killed leading his first patrol into an area dominated by a German machine-gun nest in the Vosges Mountains.

He was so good in the brief time he played, that five years after his death he was named to the NFL team of that decade.

**Al Blozis was** a giant among men in both size and stature. The six-feet-five, 250-pound Blozis, shown hovering over five-foot-nine, 177-pound Andy Tomasic at the 1942 College All-Star Game, was a student leader as well as a two-sport star at Georgetown before joining the Giants. In two short seasons, he became an NFL star. Killed in action during the Battle of the Bulge in 1944, Blozis became only the third Giant to have his number retired and was posthumously named to the NFL's All-'40s team.

# Harry Carson 53

He was the bridge that spanned the years between the franchise's perennial disaster and its emergence as Super Bowl King of the Hill. Drafted out of South Carolina State in the fourth round, Harry Carson found himself being asked to play a position he had never before played in a city in which he didn't particularly want to be.

The Giants joined by Harry Carson in 1976 were a study in inertia. Playing their inaugural season in their spectacular new stadium in the New Jersey meadowlands, the Giants were a franchise all dressed up with no place to go. Short on players, their coaching staff in constant flux, the Giants of Harry Carson's first five years won just twenty-four games and lost a staggering fifty-two.

"It's funny," Carson will tell you, "but without those years I couldn't have really appreciated what the years that followed meant."

Discovering Carson as a down lineman in college and desperately in search of a linebacker who could start, Marty Schottenheimer, the Giants defensive coordinator, saw what nobody else did. He saw a player he could move to a position he needed to fill and who had enough talent to make this strange gamble pay off. Toward that end, Schottenheimer brought him to camp a month early and made him his personal project. By opening day Carson's weight had grown from 230 to 245 and his forty-yard time trial speed had gone from 4.7 to 4.5 seconds.

For more than a decade he was a major force. From the inside linebacker spot his primary responsibility was to stop the run. He played in nine Pro Bowls and finally got to the Super Bowl. But of equal importance were his inspirational qualities both on and off the field.

"George Martin," Carson said of the outstanding defensive end who played in front of him, "was the preacher who inspired the defense, but I was its drill sergeant. I was the guy with the four-letter words. Together we reminded the defense when it needed to be reminded."

**Harry Carson was** a seven-time All-National Football League selection and a nine-time Pro-Bowler at inside linebacker—a position he had never played until he joined the Giants in 1976.

1950s Sweater

1930s Jersey

1940s Jersey

From a fashion angle, the Giants game face has always been simple and straightforward. Due to the winter conditions the Giants can encounter, sweatshirts have long been a bench option. Early uniforms were loose-fitting sweaters. One-piece jerseys were in vogue in the 1960s and 1970s. Short sleeves and putting names on the jerseys became the National Football League style a quarter of a century ago. The Lawrence Taylor jersey shows the Giants' added touch of neck and sleeve stripes. And low-cut cleats are just one of the many shoes—sneakers included—worn by the Giants over seventy-five seasons.

1960s Cleats

1980s Jersey

1990s Jersey

1900s Helmet

1920s Helmet

1930s Helmet

1910s Helmet

**Little in football** has evolved more over the years than the helmet. The Giants' first versions were leather caps with flaps designed to protect the ears and scalp since interior line play involved considerable pulling and tugging. Influenced by the training headgear used by boxers, the football helmet was continually modified in the 1930s and 1940s to offer more protection from blows to the head. It was during this period that the Giants' team colors also adorned the headgear. The plastic helmet and primitive, single-bar mouth guards came into vogue after World War II. The modern Giants helmet features a full face mask with foam-and-air-cushioned padding around the head.

1930s Helmet

1950s Helmet

1960s Helmet

1970s Helmet

1990s Helmet

The Giants of Bill Parcells didn't need to look at the schedule to know it was time for their annual visit to Washington.

The ringing in their ears served as a warning.

Prior to the Washington trip each season, Parcells would circle the Giants practice field with loudspeakers, bombarding his players with crowd noise—jeers, catcalls, and assorted obscenities—taped from previous visits to Washington.

Such was the Giants-Redskins rivalry that the fans' vocal chords were as much a concern as any trick play.

Certainly, the Giants-Redskins rivalry is one of the most storied in the National Football League's history. And it tops one of three categories of great Giants rivalries:

geographical, circumstantial, and personal.

Each is a story unto itself.

The longest ongoing rivalries in the Giants record book are the battles with the Redskins and Philadelphia Eagles—the other two of the three cornerstone franchises of the powerful NFC East.

Since they first played in 1932, when the Redskins were known as the Boston Braves, the Giants and Washington have met twice annually during the regular season, except for the 1967 and 1969 campaigns. Twice they have met three times when the rivalry extended to the playoffs. The road to the Giants' first Super Bowl victory included three victories over the Redskins, including a 17-0 triumph in the 1986 NFC Championship game.

No team loves taking on the Giants more than Washington, which traditionally would goad Giants fans by parading the Redskins marching band up Broadway to the Polo Grounds during visits to New York City. Since Washington has no baseball team, football is the one area

where the city's fans can challenge New Yorkers.

Some of the earliest Giants-Redskins showdowns were dominated by Sammy Baugh— perhaps the most dangerous passer and punter the Giants ever faced.

A threat to run or pass out of

# GREATEST RIVALRIES

## BY MARTY GLICKMAN

**The collisions between** Cleveland Browns running back Jim Brown and New York Giants middle linebacker Sam Huff (70) became the matter for television documentaries, right. If Brown was the greatest runner the Giants ever defensed, Sammy Baugh was the most feared passer. Two decades before Brown, Baugh, shown above in his "slingin'" style, revolutionized the game.

**Don Hutson, above,** was pro football's first great wide receiver and helped Green Bay defeat the Giants in the National Football League's 1939 and 1944 championship games.

the single-wing when he joined the Redskins in 1937, the six-feet-two, 180-pound Baugh could throw a football the way most athletes could throw a baseball, and developed into one of the first great T formation quarterbacks—largely at the Giants' expense. And to this day, he is still No. 1 in the NFL record book for career punting average.

In 1943, Baugh completed sixteen of twenty-one passes to lead the Redskins to a 28-0 victory over the Giants in the Eastern Division Playoff game—after New York had twice upset the Redskins during the regular season.

Although Baugh was the focus of early Redskins-Giants battles, the spotlight in the 1980s moved to the sidelines and the matchups of two coaching legends, Parcells and Washington's Joe Gibbs.

Even more heated and physical during that era were the battles between Parcells' Giants and the Eagles of Buddy Ryan. The two teams just didn't like one another—as if any Eagles and Giants teams ever did. There was

never an abundance of brotherly love between the loyalists of New York Giants football and their highly partisan peers from Philadelphia.

Growing in intensity is the same-town rivalry between the Giants and Jets that is rooted in the old war between the rival National and American football leagues. Jets owner Sonny Werblin and Giants president Wellington Mara are two intensely passionate men who once fought the idea of a merger from two different perspectives.

Ironically, it was the NFL-AFL merger that spawned the "neighbors-on-the-field series," an annual preseason showdown that began in 1969. The Giants-Jets showdown has become the league's most attractive late summer game. In the eight games that have counted in the standings, the teams have split, 4-4. But the most memorable was the Jets' 27-21 final-game victory in 1988 that knocked the Giants out of the playoffs.

It is the playoffs that serve as the backdrop for the Giants'

rivalries with the Green Bay Packers, Chicago Bears, and San Francisco 49ers.

In six meetings in NFL Championship Games, the Giants won two, in 1934 (the famous "sneakers game") and 1956. The Bears took four, in 1933, 1941, 1946, and 1963. Two of the Chicago wins were engineered by another Giants nemesis—quarterback Sid Luckman, who also happened to be the greatest football player ever to be raised in the New York area.

Luckman played high school football at Erasmus Hall in Brooklyn and college football under Lou Little at Columbia. Luckman was the personal choice

of Bears head coach George Halas to introduce the T formation to the NFL in 1939. The following year, Luckman and the Bears shellacked the Redskins 73-0 in the NFL Championship game and the T formation was on its way. Although he played for the "big, bad Bears," Luckman was always a fan favorite in New York.

But New York fans were less kindly toward the Packers, who have four straight wins over the Giants in NFL Championship games (1939, 1944, 1961, and 1962) since the Giants' lone triumph in 1938. Green Bay's victories in the early '60s were designed by Vince Lombardi, the former Giants assistant coach who became a legend in Wisconsin.

ny
125

**Sid Luckman's arrival** in the National Football League in 1939 also marked the beginning of the T formation era. Luckman led the Chicago Bears to two victories over the Giants in NFL championship games: 37-9 in 1941 and 24-14 in 1946 when he threw for one touchdown and ran for another.

If the Packers of Lombardi were the team to beat in the 1960s, the 49ers were the NFL's great team of the 1980s. And the Giants twice defeated the 49ers en route to their Super Bowl triumphs in a pair of games highlighted by the very nature of the physical play. In 1986, the Giants dominated San Francisco 49-3 in an NFC Semifinal game that featured four touchdown passes by Phil Simms and two touchdowns and 159 yards rushing by Joe Morris. Four years later, the Giants prevailed 15-13 in a game so physical that New York defensive end Leonard Marshall drove San Francisco quarterback Joe Montana to the sidelines on one sack.

In terms of great individual clashes, it all began in 1925 when the Galloping Ghost, Red Grange, drew a guess-timated seventy-three thousand people to the Polo Grounds to watch the Giants play the Chicago Bears. That game, a 20-3 Bears victory, set the standard for the seventy-five years of Giants football.

Grange had the first of the great nicknames carried to town by visiting greats. There followed Bronko Nagurski, Crazy Legs Hirsch, Bulldog Turner, Mean Joe Greene, Slinging Sammy Baugh, Buckets Goldenberg, Bullet Bill Omanski, Night Train Lane, and on and on.

But the greatest individual ever to line up against the Giants needed no nickname.

Jimmy Brown was simply Jimmy Brown—and the Cleveland Browns fullback is as much a part of Giants history as Tuffy Leemans.

An "all-everything" athlete as a youth at nearby Manhasset High in Long Island, Brown developed at Syracuse University into the greatest lacrosse player of all time as well as an All-American in football and regular in basketball. The six-feet-three, 235-pound Brown then led the NFL in rushing eight times in nine years.

But Brown approached games against the Giants as though on a quest. And the Giants answered with linebacker Sam Huff leading a gang-tackling defense.

The drama seldom varied. Brown would pound off-tackle into the heart of the Giants defense where, eventually, he'd go down in a Huff-led pile. Brown would then rise slowly, walk back to the Cleveland huddle, usually get the same play, and pound away again—and again and again. The stakes were huge. One slip by the Giants defense and Brown, who also had a sprinter's speed, would break away for a touchdown. And a touchdown sometimes was all that separated the Giants or the Browns from the top of the Eastern Conference standings.

It was football in its simplest, purest form. Strength vs. strength. The will of one team and its star pitted against the will of another team and its star.

It was Jimmy Brown vs. the Giants. But it could have been Sammy Baugh or Don Hutson or Sid Luckman. And it could have been the Eagles, Packers, 49ers, or Redskins.

Picture it—the Redskins marching band parading up Broadway.

That's a rivalry.

**T**his is the franchise that was born in and survived during the Great Depression at a time when nobody on the West Coast had even seen an NFL game. It is a franchise that held together during World War II at a time when money was so tight and the NFL future so bleak that two of the league's eastern teams—the Eagles and the Steelers—actually had to merge into a single two-city team called the Steagles just to survive.

It is a franchise that survived wars with at least three rebel leagues, played its home games in four different stadiums, and flourished through labor wars, fan anger, and some horrendous seasons.

In the end each battle was won because of the leadership—leadership in the locker room, leadership on the field, and leadership in the front office. These are the stories of coaches who best demonstrated that quality, and of ownership that was not afraid to look in the mirror during its darkest hour and make overdue changes that shook the franchise to its very core and eventually brought it to a new plateau.

From an impact status, the continuity began with a man named Steve Owen. Discovered almost by accident as a player, Owen would become such a part of the franchise's leadership that for more than two decades his name became synonymous with the Giants.

He graduated from Phillips University, a tiny college located on the historic Cherokee Strip ninety miles north of Oklahoma City. Back in 1922, that meant it was nowhere. The town was called Enid, and Steve Owen was about the best football player anyone in that little dot on the map of North Central Oklahoma had ever seen.

But to get to Enid you had to want to get there and apparently no scout for the National Football League was overpowered by that desire. So for two years Owen, a massive tackle with serious physical skills, drifted throughout the Midwest, hooking up with a myriad of anonymous semipro teams until he joined one in Kansas City that was affiliated with the embryonic NFL.

# 75 YEARS OF LEADERSHIP

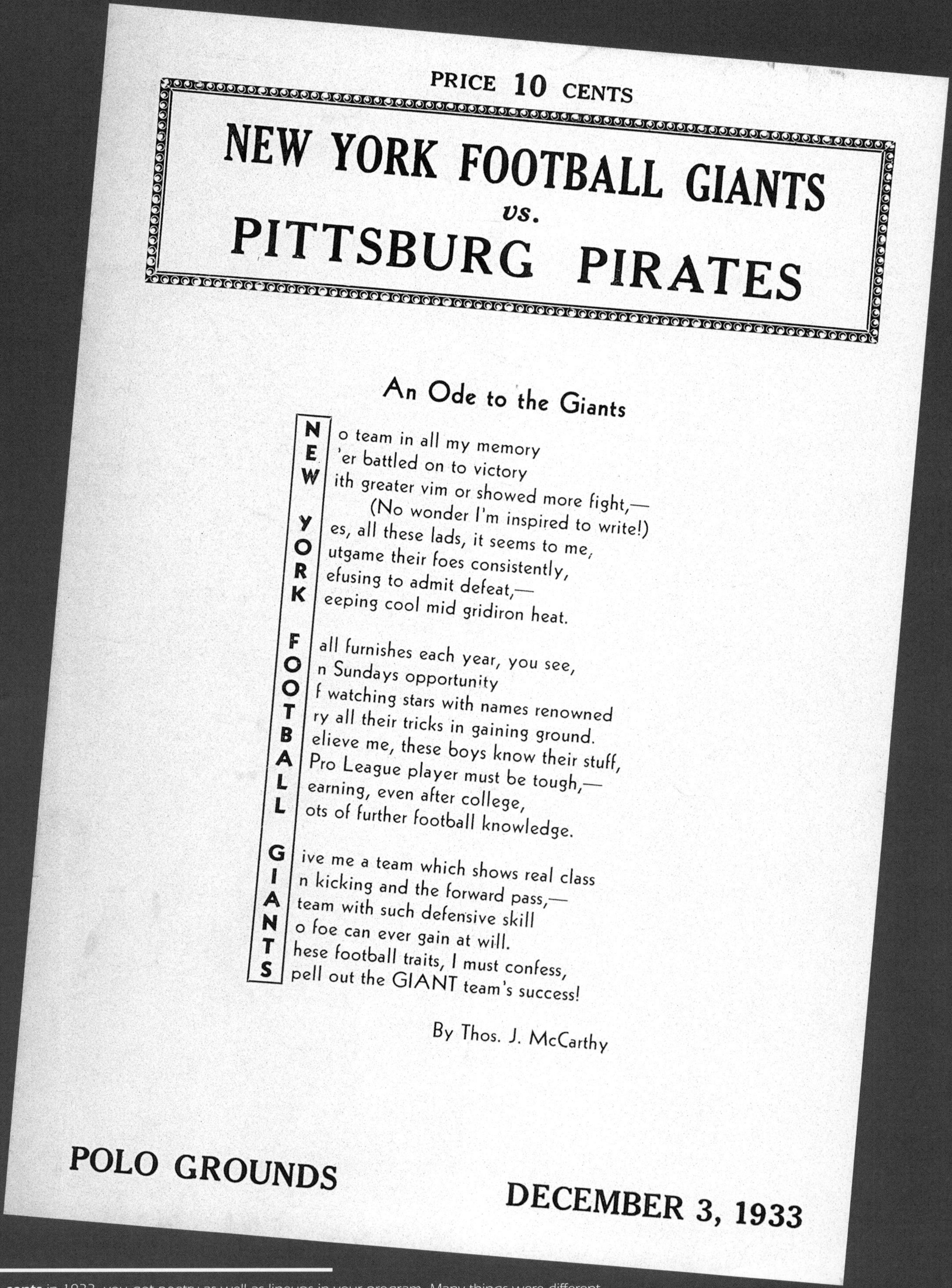

PRICE 10 CENTS

# NEW YORK FOOTBALL GIANTS
*vs.*
# PITTSBURG PIRATES

## An Ode to the Giants

**N**o team in all my memory
**E**'er battled on to victory
**W**ith greater vim or showed more fight,—
(No wonder I'm inspired to write!)
**Y**es, all these lads, it seems to me,
**O**utgame their foes consistently,
**R**efusing to admit defeat,—
**K**eeping cool mid gridiron heat.

**F**all furnishes each year, you see,
**O**n Sundays opportunity
**O**f watching stars with names renowned
**T**ry all their tricks in gaining ground.
**B**elieve me, these boys know their stuff,
**A** Pro League player must be tough,—
**L**earning, even after college,
**L**ots of further football knowledge.

**G**ive me a team which shows real class
**I**n kicking and the forward pass,—
**A** team with such defensive skill
**N**o foe can ever gain at will.
**T**hese football traits, I must confess,
**S**pell out the GIANT team's success!

By Thos. J. McCarthy

POLO GROUNDS

DECEMBER 3, 1933

**For ten cents** in 1933, you got poetry as well as lineups in your program. Many things were different back then, including the helmet and publicity pictures. Left: Giants back Hap Moran showed his best form for the widely used "posed action" newspaper photos of the era.

**Ken Strong (50) kicks** a thirty-eight-yard field goal to give the Giants an early 3-0 lead on the Bears in the 1934

NFL Championship game. At halftime, the Giants changed from the stiff football cleats of the day to sneakers for

better traction on the frozen field at the Polo Grounds. The result was a 30-13 Giants' victory.

It was here at the tail end of their 1925 season that the Giants stumbled across him. The word "stumbled" is used advisedly because of the way he hammered Giants ballcarriers into the ground over and over again. The Giants won 9-3 against a team they figured to beat by at least twenty-one points. Owen impressed them so much they invited him on a post-season barnstorming tour and signed him to a contract for the following year.

They got him for $500.

The Giants couldn't have gotten a better deal with a ski mask and a gun. It was the football steal of the decade.

As a player, he captained the 1927 team that won New York's first world title when he anchored a defense that held the collective opposition to a grand total of twenty points. Owen was a great football player but it was as a coach that he helped write history for the young franchise. Ironically, it was by sheer accident that he got the job. Over the next twenty-three years, he was not just a coach to the Giants. He was THE coach.

He got half the job with just two games left during the 1930 season when, disgusted by consecutive losses to Frankford and Brooklyn, Tim Mara fired LeRoy Andrews, the head coach, but couldn't figure out who should replace him.

Since his quarterback, Bennie Friedman, was receiving the unheard of salary of $10,000 he tapped Friedman. But Friedman was already a part-time coach at Yale and expected to eventually go full-time there. He didn't really want to coach the Giants and he told Mara so. In the end, Friedman agreed to coach the last two games of the 1930 season only if he had help. Mara gave him Owen as his temporary co-coach. They won the last two games.

The following year, Owen agreed to take the job until the Giants could find a full-time man. Owen would remain a player through 1936. He would serve as head coach for twenty-three years.

From 1930 to 1953, teams coached by Steve Owen won 153 games, lost 100, and tied 17. They also won two world titles, eight divisional titles outright, and tied twice more for first in the East, forcing playoffs.

Owen was the coach who gave the Giants stability and status. In his first four years as head coach, he took them to the championship game three times. When the rival All America Conference collapsed and the Cleveland Browns came into the NFL with a spectacular team, it was Owen who emerged as their nemesis and the Giants who emerged as their greatest rivals.

Nobody expected it, but in their first meeting the Giants beat the Browns, who had never before been shut out, 6-0. Then they beat them 17-13. The Browns finally won, 8-3, that year in a divisional playoff. But nobody expected Owen to take on this powerhouse in its first NFL season and put together a string of great defensive games that would continue against the Browns through much of his career.

He did it with coaching genius and players suited to his kind of football gambles. On offense, he had already the invented the A formation, which for a time was very difficult to defend against. Now he came up with something called the umbrella defense, which he designed primarily to take the Browns' strength and turn it against them. It worked for years against a lot of other teams as well.

The Browns were quarterbacked by Otto Graham, whose ability to spot a receiver out of the corner of his eye was uncanny. Against Graham's quick release, a lot of teams felt that defensive pressure was the only way to stop him. Rush him with the

**Steve Owen, above,** was a Giants' legend as a player and coach—and was both from 1930 to 1936. His coaching career spanned twenty-three seasons, from 1930 to 1953. In addition to a pair of world championships, Owen is best known for introducing the A formation, umbrella defense, and the two-platoon system to football. Right: Back in 1933, the loyalty of a season ticket holder was worth a 25-cent discount off a $2.25 ticket.

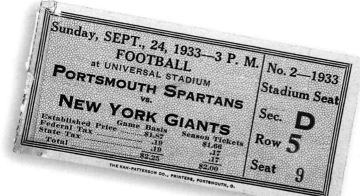

Sunday, SEPT., 24, 1933—3 P. M.
FOOTBALL
at UNIVERSAL STADIUM
PORTSMOUTH SPARTANS
vs.
NEW YORK GIANTS
Game Basis
Established Price .......... $1.87        Season Tickets
Federal Tax .......... .19                $1.66
State Tax .......... .19                    .17
Total .......... $2.25                    $2.00

No. 2—1933
Stadium Seat
Sec. D
Row 5
Seat 9

THE KAH-PATTERSON CO., PRINTERS, PORTSMOUTH, O.

Timothy J. Mara, the Giants' founding father, was as New York as a subway platform at rush hour, late-night jazz along 52nd Street, or the Easter Parade. New York was the city of his birth and the city of his choice. During the Giants' early years it was still very much a city where hard work and dreams often merged into spectacular New York success stories. His rise from the Lower East Side was typical of such civic love affairs.

Consequently, when New York staggered under the weight of the Great Depression that followed the stock market crash of 1929, Tim Mara took it as seriously as an illness in the family. "He always believed," his son Wellington once explained, "that he owed the city all he could give it."

In 1930 bankers were selling apples on street corners and financial geniuses were seriously thinking of taking long walks off very short piers. The signs of despair were everywhere. With that as a backdrop, Jimmy Walker, New York's flamboyant mayor,

came to Mara for help.

"We have so many unemployed that we can't help," the mayor said. "Play a game for our unemployment fund."

The Giants were in the middle of a desperate pennant fight with Green Bay, but Mara still agreed. Bill Abbott, the Giants' publicity man, immediately suggested the greatest attention-getter of all. "Play Notre Dame," he told his boss. Mara, himself, was one of that vociferous group of Notre Dame fans known as "the subway alumni" and thought the idea was terrific. Knute Rockne, the coach of the Irish, did not for obvious reasons. Instead, Rockne offered to put together a team of former Notre Dame stars, including the Four Horsemen. The game was scheduled for December 14, 1930.

As the Giants continued to play their regular season games and with Notre Dame's season finished, Rockne kept his word.

He assembled a group of "yesterday's heroes." They were out of shape and over their heads, and with just four days of practice behind them, they left for New York.

What followed was a tribute to Mara's love for his city and his city's love for Notre Dame. More than 55,000 people showed up at the Polo Grounds—the second largest crowd in the Giants' young history.

Rockne's pregame advice to his former players was an indication of how little regard he had for professional football. "They're big but they're slow," he said. His plan was to hit quickly, gain the lead, play defense, and keep his out-of-shape charges

from getting hurt. These goals, as the day developed, proved not to be in order of importance.

When Rockne got a look at the Giants before the game, he asked Bennie Friedman, the Giants coach, to cut the quarters from fifteen minutes to twelve. Friedman, no sadist he, agreed.

There is a story, perhaps apocryphal, that when Johnny Law, a 170-pound Notre Dame guard, looked at the Giants

running out on the field before the opening kickoff, he asked one of the officials:

"Excuse me, sir, but could you please tell me how much time is left?"

It was even more one-sided than the Giants expected. That

# THE NOTRE DAME GAME

**Few games have** ever bonded a team to a city more than the unofficial one played by the Giants on December 14, 1930. With New York City suffering through the Great Depression, Giants owner Tim Mara promoted an exhibition game against an alumni team from collegiate power Notre Dame—a team that had a huge following in New York City. Although the best seats went for $3, a huge sum considering the times, more than 55,000 turned out to see the Giants win 22-0. But the big winner was the New York City Unemployment Fund, to the tune of $115,153. Tim Mara paid Notre Dame's expenses out of his own pocket.

the final score was 22-0 was a tribute to Mara mercy. Afterward, Mara confided to Friedman that he was somewhat disturbed because while the gross check (the baseball Giants had given Mara the stadium at no cost) was $115,153, Notre Dame wanted what he considered an unreasonable sum of $5,000 for expenses.

"Look, this is a great cause," Friedman said, "but you're entitled to make some money, too. Why not chalk up $15,000 to expenses and give them an even $100,000?"

Mara just smiled. Then he gave the New York City Unemployment Fund a check for $115,153—an enormous sum of money in 1930. He kept nothing for the Giants and paid Notre Dame's $5,000 out of his own pocket.

No pro franchise in any sport has ever done anything quite like that—before or since.

"The Duke," named in honor of Giants president Wellington Mara, was the official ball of the National Football League at the time of Super Bowl I. Because the rival National and American Leagues used different balls, The Duke was used when the NFL champions were on offense. Below: If the field was iced over, the Giants loved switching from football cleats to sneakers. Changing shoes led to NFL Championship game victories in 1934 and 1956. Here a ballboy carries a load of sneakers into Yankee Stadium for a game against Dallas. Giants were larger than life in programs as well as on the field, but they respected the diminutive yet fiery head coach Allie Sherman.

kitchen sink if you had to but knock him down before he could throw. Owen saw that it didn't work and came up with a plan nobody had ever used.

It was Owen's idea to use Graham's ability to quickly unload to the Giants' advantage. He no longer had his defense rush the passer. Instead, much like an offensive lineman whose technique lets a pass rusher go where he wants and then uses the rusher's momentum to push him further in that direction, Owen would permit Graham to throw wherever he wanted to throw. He designed a way that ensured wherever it was, the Giants' defense would get there first. He reached back to when the Redskins had Sammy Baugh and Owen had first utilized a crude version of his umbrella.

Against Graham, he put together a 6-1-4 formation. Sometimes he had the ends drop back in pass coverage, giving the secondary the look of an umbrella top. It was a defensive concept based on coverage rather than pressure. It stamped Owen as a master innovator.

It worked and for a time kept the Giants in games with the Browns when Cleveland was a juggernaut to most opponents.

Unhappily, even an innovator can't stand still. Owen did.

Ultimately, the magic and the gimmicks were gone. His A formation gave way to the T formation out of desperation. The umbrella finally sprung a leak. When the Browns, whom he had handled so effectively in the past, beat him 42-14 at the end of the 1953 season, the Giants let him go.

He was followed by Jim Lee Howell, whose 1956 team won a world title, capping a season that forever will remain as the benchmark year for the Giants and possibly for all of pro football. This was the team that turned the blood, mud, and grunt work of defense into a heroic focal point. Howell's teams also competed for two other NFL championships but his success was built on his ability to delegate power to assistants like Vince Lombardi, Allie Sherman, and Tom Landry.

When Howell, a former Giants player and a favorite of the Maras, decided to retire, Sherman proved to be much of his own man at the helm. Allie Sherman had played his football at, of all places, Brooklyn College, a city-run school where grades impacted far more on the student body than touchdowns. As a pro, he had been a skinny quarterback, more in demand for his brain than his body. There was an NFL stint in Philadelphia under a brilliant coach named Greasy Neale, who became his mentor. In Philly he was relegated to the role of setting up the ball for placekicker Augie Lio, but his relationship with Neale would change the direction of his life.

They spent hours together as teacher and pupil and Sherman's football mind was the best any teacher-coach could ask for. Sherman's odyssey took him to vastly different corners of the football world . . . to Paterson, New Jersey, as a minor league player-coach . . . to New York as Howell's backfield coach . . . to Canada as a head coach . . . and finally back to New York, where he took over the team he had wanted to coach ever since he was a teenager in Brooklyn.

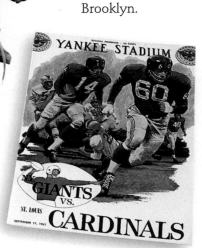

They were the oddest odd couple among all the assistant coaches ever assembled on the same NFL staff. Tom Landry was a soft-spoken man from the Texas Bible Belt. Vince Lombardi was the very essence of the Italian-American Brooklyn neighborhood from which he came.

Landry was a refugee from the All-America Conference, who became the leader of what Giants coach Steve Owen called his "umbrella defense"—a 6-1-4 alignment that for a time dominated the NFL.

Lombardi never played pro football. An overworked football coach at tiny St. Cecilia's High School in New Jersey, he also taught science, math, and history; served as the school's dean of discipline; and coached basketball occasionally—all for $3,500 a year. He was as far removed from pro football as you could get.

His later dossier included a stop as freshman football coach at Fordham, where he had played, and a frustrating career under Col. Earl "Red" Blaik at West Point where he waited to be discovered

by a world that had few if any head coaches of Italian-American ancestry. Frustrated, now nearing forty-five years of age and still looking for that elusive head coaching job, he joined the Giants staff under newly appointed Jim Lee Howell in 1954 as what today would be considered the offensive coordinator.

Landry meanwhile retired as a player and moved into what evolved as the defensive coordinator's job. Both had interesting problems at the outset.

# LOMBARDI & LANDRY

Landry was put in the unique position of coaching a number of players who had played alongside him. He got their attention by changing Owen's old umbrella defense from a 6-1-4 to a 4-3-4. This was the birth of what for years became a traditional

three-linebacker defense.

"He never yelled," Sam Huff, the focal point of the Giants' defense for a number of championship years, explained. "He would just stare at you with that look of disgust when you made a mistake. I remember one time I dropped off in coverage when I wasn't supposed to and intercepted a pass. But it wasn't where I was supposed to be. I gambled and won but as soon as I came off the field he made it very clear to me that he would not tolerate anyone who could

not put the team ahead of himself. He was chilling when he got mad but he was never loud."

Lombardi, on the other hand, had to struggle to keep his emotions under control.

He would chase players on the practice field and whack them

on the helmet when he was angry. When he put a halfback option in for the multi-talented Frank Gifford to exploit, the players originally laughed, telling him it was a college play. "I don't care if it's a nursery school play!" Lombardi shrieked back at them. "You are going to run it."

Run it they did and nobody ever threw that pass with better results than Frank Gifford. "I loved the man," says Gifford. "I had played defense for the Giants and then some offense and I really didn't know what they expected of me. Then he came along and he really taught me what this game was all about and how good I could become."

What was so interesting about both coaches was their intellects. Rarely have two such intellectually curious men coached on the same staff. Landry, who had played both quarterback and fullback at the University of Texas, had earned twin degrees in business administration and mechanical engineering. Lombardi, who had seriously considered studying for the priesthood, had a classical education background at Fordham, heavily larded with studies in philosophy. He was a classmate of Wellington Mara there. "He was the guy in every class who always had the answer to the question that stumped the rest of us," Wellington recalled.

The two assistant coaches also shared an intense work ethic. They were perfect in what they did for the Giants, primarily because Jim Lee Howell knew exactly how to use them. Lombardi and Landry would turn over their notes in midweek to Howell, who would use them to put together the game plan. After the game he would tell reporters things like, "I don't know why we ran that play, you'll have to ask Vince" or "Tom was the guy who made that defensive call on the goal line. Ask him about it."

In 1956, this tandem under Howell brought the Giants their first world title since 1938. Small wonder that Lombardi at Green Bay and Landry at Dallas went on to dominate this league, which could not have surprised Howell. Each time he was asked what was left for him to do as a head coach with this pair of assistants, Howell invariably replied:

"Keep order and check and see that the footballs are pumped up."

**Two future coaching** legends, Vince Lombardi and Tom Landry, were assistants under Jim Lee Howell with the Giants in the 1950s. Lombardi was with the Giants from 1954 to 1958 before becoming head coach of the Green Bay Packers and Landry was with the Giants from 1954 to 1959 before becoming head coach of the Dallas Cowboys. The coaching staff (clockwise from upper left) posed in Yankee-style jackets: Landry, Jim Lee Howell, Ken Kavanaugh, John Dell Isola, and Lombardi.

He was not a popular choice because he was remembered more for being the keeper of Owen's offense and the A formation that had gone down in flames rather than the installer of Howell's successful T formation, which he now took to new heights. Sherman, with a brilliant tactical mind, proved to be rich in innovations but unlucky in matchups.

Sherman would take his teams to three straight divisional titles and then lose three straight world title games: two to Green Bay and one to Chicago.

The first Green Bay match was a disaster on a frozen field fit only for abominable snowmen, penguins, and Green Bay Packers. These were Lombardi's Packers of destiny at their best—Bart Starr, Paul Hornung, Max McGee, and Willie Davis. They battered the Giants, 37-0, and the only quotable comment out of the Giants locker room that dismal afternoon was the sound of Frank Gifford yelling over and over again each time somebody came in, "Shut the damned door NOW!"

In the Green Bay title rematch in 1962, the weather was even more of a factor. The wind in Yankee Stadium and the bounces of the windblown football all went the Packers' way. It was close at 16-7 but the outcome was never really in doubt because the Giants could not move the ball. Their only score came when Jim Collier blocked a punt and recovered in the end zone.

And fate wasn't finished with the Sherman regime. In 1963, with Y. A. Tittle as the quarterback, they went into Chicago's ancient Wrigley Field as a cinch to win. Over a fourteen-game season they had failed to score thirty or more points in only four games and even managed to put up twenty-four in two of those.

But in the second quarter on another frigid day, Tittle's knee collided with a Bears' helmet and Tittle was carried off the field in agonizing pain. He tried to return but couldn't move on the bad knee. Instead, the Giants had to trust everything to a rarely used rookie quarterback named Glynn Griffing.

They also relied on prayer and defense. It wasn't enough. Without the brilliance of Tittle, they lost 14-10. Griffing never played another game for them.

Sherman never did get his world title. After his brilliant three-year start, the Giants inexplicably began to fade at a staggering pace. He was gone by 1968, and the Giants were already locked in the most serious slide in franchise history.

It would lead to a grave internal crisis. Management couldn't conceive of anything more depressing than what it had weathered back in 1946 when, on the morning of the NFL Championship game against the Bears at the Polo Grounds, Tim Mara was summoned to City Hall.

Both quarterback Frank Filchock and halfback Merle Hapes had been approached by a gambler named Alvin Paris and offered money to throw the championship game. Filchock denied any knowledge of it and was permitted to play. Hapes said it was true but they had declined the money. He was barred for not reporting the incident. That day Filchock, finishing with a broken nose, was magnificent in defeat. Afterward, he confessed that he too had been approached. Both players were banned from football.

It was axiomatic to the owners, to the team's front office, and especially to its fans that nothing could test the Mara family more than the events leading up to that traumatic Sunday afternoon.

**Leaping through a** huge hole opened by Roosevelt Brown's (79) pancake block, Giants running back Joe Morrison heads into the Cardinals' secondary. An all-around back, Morrison led the Giants in rushing in 1969 and in receiving in 1965 and 1969. He is the Giants' all-time leader in receptions (395) and second in receiving yards (4,993) and touchdowns (47). Opposite: Quarterback Y. A. Tittle kneels battered and bloodied in the end zone during a 27-24 loss to Pittsburgh in 1964. Tittle's broken helmet was symbolic of the worst season in the Giants' history: 2-10-2. Both Tittle and Frank Gifford retired at season's end. Two short seasons later, the Giants hit rock bottom at 1-12-1.

**The grim faces** on the Giants appear to acknowledge the ending of an era as they prepare to meet Pittsburgh in 1965.

It was the last season for Hall of Fame offensive tackle Roosevelt Brown (79) and late in the Giants careers of defensive

ends Andy Stynchula (72) and Jim Katcavage (75), an unidentified player (84), and middle linebacker Jerry Hillebrand (87).

Pacing is linebacker Tom Scott (82).

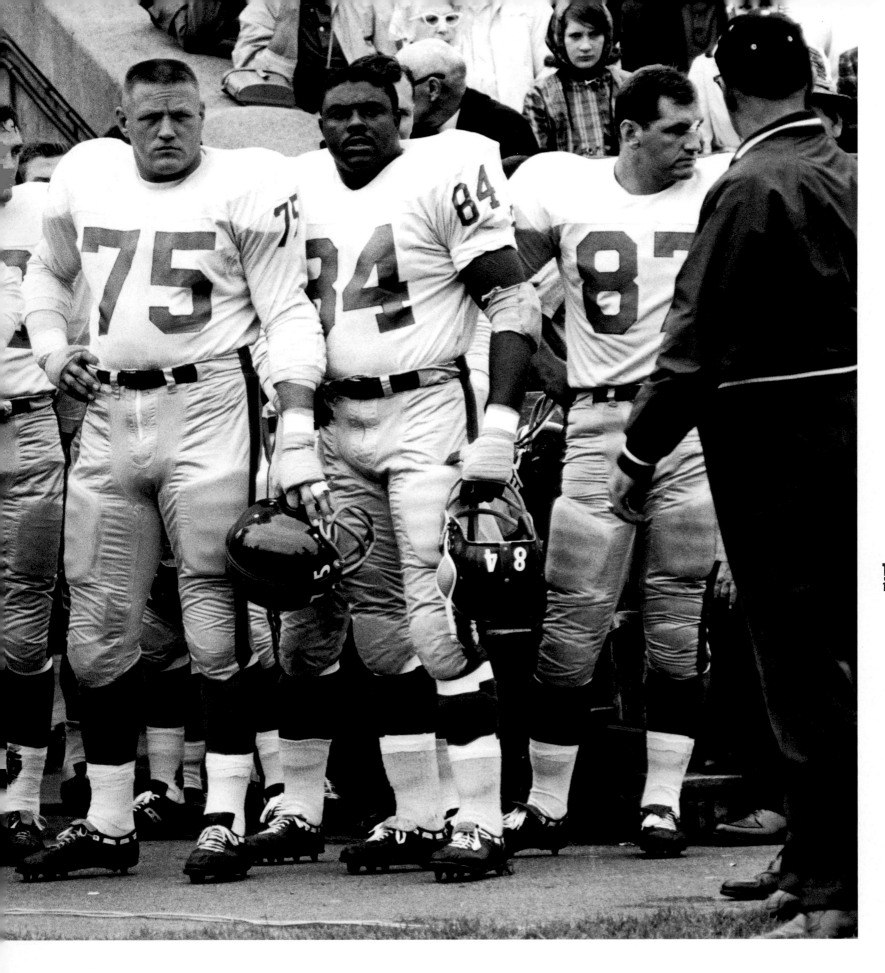

THE GIANTS, A CONTINUING TRADITION

**Aside from an** *occassional great hit, like this one administered by middle linebacker Brian Kelley (55) on a Green Bay running back, the Giants continued to struggle in the 1970s. The decade's one bright light was the announcement of the building of a new home for the Giants in New Jersey. Right: A game-day program commemorates the Meadowlands deal.*

All of them were wrong.

It began with what the front office believed to be a temporary state of affairs. Following Sherman's three near-misses in the early 1960s, the Giants never again topped .500 during Sherman's final five seasons as head coach. Meanwhile, a new force was impacting on the Giants. The New York Jets had won Super Bowl III in 1969, and for the first time ever, the Giants became No. 2 in the two-team megalopolis.

This became apparent when the two teams met in the Yale Bowl for an exhibition game.

It was the first time they had ever played each other. The Jets won it in a laugher. But Wellington Mara wasn't laughing as the game grew more lopsided. When the Giants traveled to Montreal for an exhibition game against the Steelers, Giants fans, who had adopted the refrain "Goodbye, Allie" as a battle cry, sang it in French. Sherman was fired and replaced by longtime Giants' favorite Alex Webster.

The hiring of Big Red, as he was known when he was a popular running back, was as much a public relations move as a change. He had never coached before. What he brought to the moment was passion. Several times he threatened to take recalcitrant players out in the hall and "beat the hell out of them." Sometimes it worked when players were more afraid of him than the opposition.

But Webster had only one winning season in five. Under his successors, Bill Arnsparger and John McVay, the record was a nightmarish 21-51. Economically, the Giants prospered when old nemesis and Jets president Sonny Werblin became a New Jersey state official and built the Meadowlands sports complex. Emerging as the Giants' new savior, Werblin brought his former archenemy Wellington Mara and his team across the Hudson River to their own 76,000-seat stadium.

Artistically, however, the Giants were living a nightmare that reached Friday-the-thirteenth dimensions. Through good

years and bad the one thing the Giants could always count on was the devotion and goodwill of their fans. Steadily and painfully, the team began to lose that in the widening wake of losing seasons that seemed to grow exponentially. Fan disaffection (although the Sunday sellouts continued) was now focused on Wellington Mara. Since his days as a student at Fordham, Mara has been an integral part of the football operation. He scouted players, he learned from coaches, he made technical suggestions—and the franchise was successful. But by the 1970s it was apparent that the game had drastically changed.

In an attempt to acknowledge that fact, Tim and Wellington named one-time Giants hero Andy Robustelli as "director of football operations." Fans, noting Mara's refusal to give Robustelli the title of general manager, felt that Wellington was not backing away enough. Nothing really seemed to improve. Two more coaches failed miserably. The Giants remained a profitable franchise but was lacking the on-field success to match its financial returns.

But even that problem paled with the shocking turn of events that, almost without warning, gripped the family of the patriarch. For the first time in its genuinely close-knit existence, the Mara family was torn apart. Thus began the kind of painful battle that would emerge as the bloody metamorphosis of a franchise reborn.

It would begin with a fumble.

Not just any fumble.

But the one Giants fans today still call "The Fumble."

Wellington Mara owned half of the franchise's stock. The other half was held by his late brother Jack's widow, Helen, and her adult children, Tim and Maura. For voting purposes, Tim controlled the stock owned by his side of the family. Their split with Wellington had its roots in the losing streak that they felt Wellington was to blame for, but there were other factors as well: Maura was passionately tied to the Giants and hurt deeply by the losing; her husband, Dick Concannon, was a lawyer who saw things from a business perspective.

"I didn't blame [Dick] for that," Wellington said. "But what he didn't understand was that while it was a business, it was a business like no other. He would say things like 'Why did you give Spider Lockhart all that money when Dallas gave less to Herb Adderly?' Well, I knew why, but they didn't."

Tim resented what he considered a lack of respect right down to the way he was called Timmy rather than Tim. His discontent was fed by a group of former Giants players and team camp followers whom he hung out with at P. J. Clarke's, an east-side Manhattan bar. The Clarke Axis had great influence over Tim, who was the team's treasurer and not without influence of his own. The fact that the stock was split 50-50 only added to the tension. Wellington and Tim stopped speaking. They could agree on nothing.

And then came "The Fumble."

The 1978 Giants were lurching—to nobody's surprise. The coach, John McVay, was on borrowed time and would finish at 6-10, a feat the team would manage by losing seven of their last eight games. But on November 19, 1978, in front of their usual sellout crowd—miracle of miracles—the Giants were just thirty-one seconds short of winning one. They led the Eagles 17-12 and they had the ball on their own twenty-nine. All that quarterback Joe Pisarcik, whose entire Giants career will be remembered for this one play, had to do was take a knee and the victory would go into the books.

This was one the Giants couldn't screw up . . . could they?

They could.

They did.

Pisarcik did not take a knee. Instead he tried to hand off to

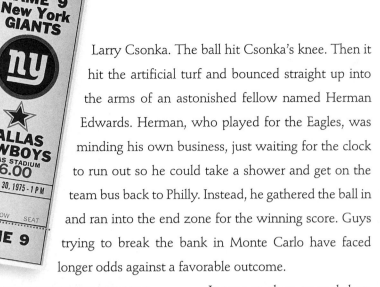

Larry Csonka. The ball hit Csonka's knee. Then it hit the artificial turf and bounced straight up into the arms of an astonished fellow named Herman Edwards. Herman, who played for the Eagles, was minding his own business, just waiting for the clock to run out so he could take a shower and get on the team bus back to Philly. Instead, he gathered the ball in and ran into the end zone for the winning score. Guys trying to break the bank in Monte Carlo have faced longer odds against a favorable outcome.

It was as close to rock bottom as the Mara family could get. But neither Wellington nor Tim was prepared for what followed. The rage that gripped the customers in Giants Stadium was as ugly as it was passionate. Never before had a crowd turned against a home team the way this one did. Within a week, fans—the most disorganized group in America—were actually organizing opposition. Management kept McVay but fired his offensive coordinator Bob Gibson. The fans ignored the human sacrifice.

On December 10, with the Cardinals in town, a small number of hard-core fans gathered around a metal trash barrel just outside the stadium and burned their tickets.

It got nobody's attention.

But during the game a small, single-engine plane buzzed the stadium trailing a banner that read: "Fifteen Years of Lousy Football."

It got everybody's attention.

The crowd came to its feet in concurring tribute. Both Wellington and Tim were traumatized. As angry as their intra-family feud had become, neither could conceive of this kind of

**Five Giants defenders** ganged up to stop Miami running back Jim Kiick in a 23-13 loss to the Dolphins in 1972. Identifiable are end Jack Gregory (81), linebacker Pat Hughes (56), tackle Larry Jacobson (75), safety Richmond Flowers (44) and Dolphin Larry Czonka (39). Above: In 1975, tickets to NFL games were still going for six dollars.

**The efforts to** rebuild the Giants during the mid-1960s included bringing Hall of Fame quarterback Fran Tarkenton to New York in a stunning 1967 trade. In five seasons with the Giants, the famed scrambler astonished and delighted the crowds and departed as the team's No. 3 all-time passer. But the Giants were only 33-37 with him at the controls.

**F**or George Young, the general manager who took the Giants to their two Super Bowls, it was never the money: certainly not when he was a high school teacher-coach in Baltimore . . . not when he was breaking down films for the old Baltimore Colts . . . not when he coached the offensive line there for Don Shula . . . not when he moved into the front office for Shula's Dolphins . . . not even when the strangest of circumstances elevated him to serious power with the Football Giants.

He came to what was a critically wounded franchise on Valentine's Day of 1979. The way he put dignity and victory back into this badly limping franchise you could swear his résumé included a coaching stint at Lourdes. He did it through nineteen years that included three rebuilding jobs, two Super Bowls, Bill Parcells, and Jim Fassel— nineteen years in which he

taught the professional football world a few lessons about patience, dedication, and loyalty.

It isn't often that intellect and football talent merge the way they did in Young. Here was a general manager who could debate the strict construction of

the Constitution with you at lunch one day and then argue the art and science of a man-in-motion attack the next. For the Giants he was the right GM at the right time in the right place.

Fortunately for the Giants, George Young was Baltimore blue

collar. Think of where the train races into the tunnel that leads to the city; just above it you will find Preston Street in the ninth ward where he lived on the second floor of his grandfather's German Bakery.

George Young was the guy who gave the team to Bill Parcells after his first hire, Ray Perkins, quit—and Parcells made history. Young was also the man who rebuilt the team after the near-debacle of Parcells' sudden departure.

It was never the money.

It was the challenge.

On the day he retired, he spoke before enough media to chronicle the original exodus:

"I have done everything in this business except sell tickets. When you love your work, it's . . ."

And then he broke down.

It was a football man's valedictory.

# GEORGE YOUNG

**The Giants had** weathered six straight losing seasons when George Young was named general manager in 1979. Rather than go for quick fixes, Young carefully acquired new coaching talent and rebuilt the club through the draft.

embarrassment and humiliation being heaped upon a franchise that was the most glamorous in the NFL and their own family heirloom. But neither man knew what to do.

By season's end the franchise was paralyzed. McVay was fired. There was no coach. There was no general manager. There was no operation at all. Wellington agreed to hire a general manager for the first time in the team's history, but he and Tim had stopped speaking to each other and couldn't agree on whom it should be.

As the days dragged through January, Wellington announced a press conference at which he alone would hire a coach. All hell broke loose. Commissioner Pete Rozelle stepped in and asked the two Maras to make their own lists of potential general managers for him. Neither would agree to anyone who placed highly on the other's list. Rozelle took matters into his own hands. He called Tim.

"I want you to choose between George Young [a fixture in the Dolphins front office] and Frank Ryan [former Browns quarterback and then athletic director at Yale]." Then he called Wellington, with whom he was very close, and told him to "make sure George Young is somewhere on your list."

On Valentine's Day the deal that saved the franchise was concluded in the early evening in Rozelle's office. George Young would be the new general manager of the Giants with total autonomy and the right to pick his coaching staff. It was 7 P.M. by then and there was nobody left in the NFL offices to write a press release, so Rozelle, who had begun his NFL career as a publicist for the Rams, walked over to the typewriter and began to write.

"Hell of a way to spend Valentine's Day," he looked up and said. "Today's my wedding anniversary."

Young was a brilliant choice. He hired Ray Perkins as his head coach and there was immediate improvement. The record stayed at 6-10 but the change was noticeable. "At least now,"

one New York columnist wrote, "they come out of the huddle with their shirts tucked in."

Perkins remained for five seasons. When he left to return to Alabama, his alma mater, as its new head coach, Young tapped his defensive coordinator to take over.

The guy's name was Bill Parcells.

Two Super Bowl victories later, it was clear the franchise had been saved.

But things would never be quite the same. In 1991, Tim Mara developed terminal cancer and sold his stock to an industrialist-developer named Bob Tisch, who had once been the Postmaster General of the United States. Over the years, he had been involved in unsuccessful (through no fault of his) attempts to purchase the New Jeresy Nets, the Baltimore Colts, and the Dallas Cowboys.

His deal with Tim Mara was delayed not by Tim but rather by the Giants' abilities. All Tisch had to do was wait for the Bears to beat the Giants in the first round of the playoffs.

But the Giants won, so Tisch had to wait for the 49ers to beat the Giants in the NFC title game.

But the Giants won again.

So then he had to wait for the Super Bowl.

"Tim was a man of his word," Tisch says. "It was just that the Giants kept winning and he told me that his sister, Maura, was so passionate about this team that there was no way she would let him sell until they were eliminated."

Of course, they weren't. They won it all.

Just before the game, meeting with Tim and Wellington on separate floors (naturally) of the Tampa Hyatt, Bob Tisch became the owner of the longest-running superstar franchise in the NFL.

---

**Lawrence Taylor grabbed** more headlines, but linebacker Harry Carson (53) was a seven-time All-Pro and a hero of the Giants' Super Bowl XXI victory.

**Physical defense has** always been the forte of Giants championship teams. San Francisco fans will always remember the hit by Giants lineman Jim Burt, below, that knocked quarterback Joe Montana unconscious during New York's 49-3 rout in the 1986 NFC Semifinal game. Opposite: Linebacker Gary Reasons clobbers a Denver running back in a goal-line stop against the Broncos in the 1989 blizzard-swept game at Denver, sending the back's mouthpiece flying.

You could make the case that Bill Parcells, the Giants' double Super Bowl winner, was born to coach this team; history would be very much on your side. Long before the new Giants Stadium rose out of what had once been a neglected tract of land called the New Jersey Meadowlands, Parcells had been a local high school sports star just up the road. Ironically, his coaching career had crisscrossed the face of America from Florida in the South to Colorado in the West. But for him, New Jersey always held an emotional light in the window, calling him home.

None of the men who had coached this team since it moved over from New York had exhibited any real feeling for New Jersey. But because of Parcells' boyhood there was a bond between him and his constituency. So strong was his feeling of return that whenever a nagging roster problem or a faulty game plan arose during the season, he would often leave his office by 9 P.M., make the hour drive to Sea Girt, New Jersey, sit on the empty boardwalk sipping coffee and staring at the waves, and then return to his office by first light with the problem solved.

For the most part, New Jersey is a blue-collar state that refused to surrender to the blight of the Northeastern Rust Belt. The truth is that Parcells "spoke New Jersey." "This [coaching pro football] isn't about fancy. It's about going to the diner on Monday mornings for your 'coffee-and' and knowing that there's only one question they will ask. It ain't about how you looked. All they want to know is 'Did you win?'"

He was a bottom-line coach with a bottom-line fan base. His football odyssey had taken him to places like the grim, gray towers of West Point; to the muggy, sweat-soaked heat of Lubbock, Texas, and Tallahassee, Florida; to the flat-as-a-tabletop land of Wichita; and to the rarefied altitude of Colorado.

But starting at a place called Hastings College in Nebraska, where he and his wife lived in a dentist's basement apartment and made cultural way stops for games in places with names like Kearney and Doan, was all basic training for his stint with the Giants.

During Parcells' first year with the Giants, the minimal talent he had inherited was not up to the

# BILL PARCELLS

task. He finished at 3–12–1 and there was serious thought given to replacing him.

But then something happened that nobody expected. Hell, nobody dared expect it since the Giants had only had four winning seasons over the previous nine years. The Giants won, went to the playoffs, and won a game before being eliminated. By 1985, no longer did Mara Tech's Turnpike Alumni hope to win—they expected it.

Now the roster began to burst with outstanding talent: Phil Simms, the quarterback; Joe Morris, the low-center-of-gravity, record-setting running back; receivers like Mark Bavaro, a tight end for whom the position appeared to have been invented; capable if not speedy receivers; and a defense whose linebackers, Lawrence Taylor, Carl Banks, and Harry Carson, had the blue-collar hearts of a state yearning for a championship team. The offensive line was probably the best of its time.

Parcells won with talent, desire, and psychology. Sometimes, in manipulating his quarterback, he did not speak to Simms for an entire week. "That's the worst," Simms once said. "You do well, you want to hear it. You do poorly, you expect to hear it. But if you don't hear anything, you don't know what to think. It drives you crazy. You play like hell and hope he'll say something."

Parcells could read his football team like a book. He knew who responded to what. Before their second Super Bowl

title—they had already beaten Denver on January 25, 1987—Buffalo was a one-point chiller. During that week, Parcells sensed a lack of intensity in his premier blocker, offensive tackle Jumbo Elliott.

"Come here a minute," Parcells told Lawrence Taylor. "During the last practice in full pads, I want you to start a fight with Elliott. We have to get something going. Do you think you can do that?"

"Yes," Lawrence told him. "I think I can do that." Lawrence

would have had the same response if Parcells had taken him to the zoo and asked:

"Do you think you could bite that lion for me?"

And in that Super Bowl, forced to rely on backup quarterback Jeff Hostetler, who played the entire game in place of the injured Simms, the newly aroused Jumbo was a serious force. He anchored an offensive line that wrapped Hostetler and his runners in a shield of muscular Teflon that enabled the Giants to hold the ball an incredible forty minutes and fifteen seconds.

The state of New Jersey celebrated.

And then Bill Parcells retired.

He was back in football with the Patriots after a year in the broadcast booth. He eventually took them to the Super Bowl.

Then he took over the hated Jets—rivals who share the same stadium. But no Giants fan has ever booed him at a Jets-Giants game.

No state hath greater love for one of its own.

**The coaching style** of Bill Parcells can only be described as "hands on." A dynamic leader, Parcells was also a tireless worker who attended to the smallest detail. The Giants had one winning season in the decade before Bill Parcells became head coach in 1983. By the time his fourth season had concluded, Parcells had turned the Giants into Super Bowl champions. In eight seasons, Parcells compiled a 77-49-1 record and led the Giants to two Super Bowl titles and three NFC East championships.

**Joe Morris (20),** left, bursts through a hole created by his blockers en route to the Giants' single-season rushing record of 1,516 yards in 1986. During the Giants 1985 campaign leading up to their first Super Bowl triumph, Morris rushed for 1,336 yards and a team-record and NFL-leading twenty-one touchdowns. Above: Ernie Accorsi succeeded the retired George Young as the Giants general manager in 1998. Accorsi had assisted Young for four seasons.

So Bob Tisch, a winner in business and now the co-owner of a world championship franchise, had the best of all possible worlds. All he had to do after that was show up with Wellington, share the owners' box and enjoy the victories.

Not exactly.

The headaches began anew for this franchise almost immediately when Bill Parcells announced the following May that he was leaving the locker room in favor of the broadcast booth. This timing of his move sent the franchise into a perilous situation. So much had to be done before the team assembled in training within the next sixty days. Young, who stressed his belief in continuity when he chose Parcells to succeed Perkins, now reached into the same bag. Tommy Coughlin, who would later establish himself as a fine pro coach when he took over the brand-new Jacksonville franchise had taken a head coaching job at Boston College during the 1990 season, but stayed on through the Super Bowl.

Desperate for a stopgap measure that might stretch into a long-term move, Young surprised everyone by tapping Ray Handley, who had been a Parcells assistant for six years but who had little persona in terms of public image. Beat men who regularly covered the club knew only that he was not very communicative with them and that he held some kind of advanced degree from Stanford in the sciences. It was also pretty much common knowledge that his mind was so mathematical that if he had chosen to do so he could have played blackjack in Las Vegas and successfully counted all the cards in the deck as the game progressed.

Beyond that not much was known about him by the

media. Still, there was little obvious cause to worry. The Giants began the season with a surprising rush. Late in the year, Handley had them at 7-5 and a playoff berth seemed within reach. Hostetler surprisingly was Handley's choice to start at quarterback but an injury late in the season returned Simms to the starting lineup.

When they lost three out of four in December and missed the playoffs, nobody seemed over alarmed. After all, the new coach had won his spurs, finished at 8-8, and barely missed making the playoffs. Next year the franchise would be back in stride, fans reasoned.

And then the bottom fell out. The Giants of '92 played about as badly as any Giants team had played since the nightmare years of the family feud. Everything collapsed. Simms was hurt. Hostetler limped off after just nine games. Taylor badly damaged an Achilles tendon and his career was in serious jeopardy. With all of that compounding what already were serious management doubts about Handley, his firing was a forgone conclusion at season's end. Just two years after the dramatic Super Bowl victory over Buffalo, the Giants were in total collapse. They lost six of their last seven games and finished the season at 6-10.

Rebuffed by Coughlin, who didn't want the job, and several other candidates, Young finally turned to a man who publicly proclaimed he did. Dan Reeves, fired as the head man in Denver, seemed like a perfect fit. With a reasonably healthy Simms at quarterback and Rodney Hampton having a fine season at running back, the Giants went 11-5 and were back in the playoffs when they won

**Running back Charles** Way prepares to drive through an Arizona defender.

As the new co-owner of the Giants, Bob Tisch immediately ordered alterations to the owners box. But this wasn't the prima-donna-like move of a corporate mogul: What Tisch wanted and Mara agreed to was to have the partition that had divided the owners box for several years removed. It was as symbolic as it was practical. The old feud was over and now there were owners who could live with each other.

Tisch, co-chairman of the Loews Corporation, had long desired to own a professional team, particularly a football team. His neighbors and friends Giants Head Coach Allie Sherman and NFL Commissioner Pete Rozelle introduced him to the NFL community during the 1960s. Not that this guy needed any introducing; Bob Tisch is a schmoozer and above all a people person.

"Over the years I've learned to work with and get along with a lot of different kinds of people."

His relaxed nature and overarching calm about business matters was just the break the Mara family needed after the period of acrimony that led to Tim's selling his half of the team in 1991. After Tisch bought Tim's share for a reported $75 million, the Mara and Tisch families mingled comfortably at home and road games.

Through almost a decade as the Giants co-owner, Tisch has maintained that he ventured into football purely for the fun of it. In fact, some of his first banter with Wellington was on this subject. During a meeting to discuss the possibility of partnering, Tisch levelled with Wellington, "I'd like to be owner of the Giants. I'd like to get in ten years of fun."

"Bob," Wellington replied, "to get in ten years of fun, you have to be in it for thirty."

Besides attending all games, Tisch exercises his business muscle in advising on the financial, marketing, and stadium-improvement fronts. He watches practice about once a week and would regularly discuss football over lunch with George Young when he was the GM, but in general Tisch lets the Maras handle the day-to-day operations.

Tisch has no plans to sell his half of the team. "Let me put it this way. I see owning the team for the rest of my life. If anything happens to me, then my share would go to my wife and children."

ny
155

# BOB TISCH

**Giants new co-owner**, Preston Robert Tisch, reviews prospects during the 1991 NFL Draft.

Following pages: defensive tackle Chad Bratzke (77), linebacker Jessie Armstead (98), cornerback Phillippi Sparks (22), and strong safety Sam Garnes (20) get physical as the Giants successfully battle Washington's offensive line for control of the line of scrimmage.

**Giants head coach** Jim Fassel is escorted by his son Mike after a Giants' victory .

the wild card over Minnesota. When the 'Niners ripped them 44-3, well, that was the 'Niners and there was every reason to think the ship had righted itself.

Once again, the optimism was premature. Simms and Taylor both retired. Reeves' Giants next went 9-7, 5-11, and 6-10. Moreover, there was sniping between the coach and the front office. He said he wanted more say in things, to which Young replied, "When was he ever turned down when he wanted to sign a player?" Reeves even complained about the team's psychologist. This had become a marriage made in Football Purgatory.

Reeves was fired at the end of the 1996 season. Once again it was rebuilding time. Now the Giants turned to a man who had once been their quarterback coach, Jim Fassel, which made perfect sense since the player billed as their "quarterback of the future," Dave Brown, had failed miserably thus far. It was hoped that Fassell would teach him how to win.

In three seasons, the team showed signs of progress and signs of despair. Brown was eventually cut. Fassel made the playoffs in his second year but, as always happens with rebuilding, familiar faces began to disappear. Rodney Hampton, who held Giants records for most career yards rushing, most career attempts, and most rushing touchdowns in both career and individual games, was released and then retired.

Defensively, encouraging things had begun to happen. Cornerback Jason Sehorn missed the 1998 season due to an injury but had already established himself as one of the league's best. Mike Strahan became the glue that held together a rapidly improving defense down front. But how the rebuilding would go was anybody's guess. Once, you could have said of this team's glorious past that it drafted well, traded brilliantly, and hired the right coaches.

And that would have been enough.

But in the ever-growing, more transient world of free agency, the race does not always go to the smartest and most dedicated. Sometimes it goes to the one who can best look inside a free agent's head and know whether he will play hard after he gets the money, whether he will like the city in which he plays, and whether he will fit in with the chemistry of his teammates, some of whom will be paid far less money.

In short, with all the glorious history and with all the deep roots in this love affair between fans and franchise, the truth is that pro football is no less a gamble now than it was when Mr. Mara first bought his football team.

But sing no sad songs for this franchise.

What ownership in this league has understood that better and risen to the challenge more often than the men who have owned the Giants?

ny
159

**Defensive end Michael** Strahan, the first player selected by the Giants in the 1993 draft, has quickly developed into a two-time All-Pro and one of the National Football League's top pass rushers. Following spread: Tackle Jumbo Elliott (76) and guard William Roberts (66) clear a path for running back Jarrod Bunch (33) in the 1998 game against the Green Bay Packers.

**Outside linebacker Jessie** Armstead (98) has quickly advanced from being an eighth-round draft choice in 1993 to a Pro Bowl selection in 1997 and 1998. Armstead, left, is one of the more feared pass rushers in the National Football League. Below: Cornerback Jason Sehorn (31), shown wrapping up a Cincinnati ballcarrier, was a second-round pick in the 1994 draft who has proved a phenomenal player.

**O**n behalf of my family—especially my father Tim and my brother Jack, who were the backbone of this organization for many years—and Bob Tisch, I want our fans to know how proud the Giants are to have represented you for the past seventy-five years.

It has not always been pretty. We have had our ups and we have had some low points as well. For sixteen weeks of every season we place our product before you to be judged. We know when we are succeeding, and we know when we are missing the mark. All we have to do is listen to our faithful followers. They tell us in no uncertain terms just how we are doing. And we, the Giants, appreciate that feedback. It tells us you care.

We care, too. We care about being the best we can be. And we care about the legacy of decency established in 1925 by my father and maintained and advanced by my brother.

The New York Giants: Seventy-five Years is our story. It is the story about the game we play and the people who are the Giants: the administrators, the coaches and scouts, and the players—especially the players. The players are the heart and soul of our great game. And it is a great game.

As we close out this century and move into the next, we do so with a sense of responsibility. We are responsible to the tradition of this franchise, and we are responsible to you, our fan.

# THE FUTURE

### BY WELLINGTON MARA

# GIANTS RECORDS SECTION

## GIANTS INDIVIDUAL RECORDS

### SERVICE

#### MOST SEASONS, ACTIVE PLAYER
15  Phil Simms (1979-93)
15  Mel Hein (1931-45)
14  George Martin (1975-88)
14  Joe Morrison (1959-72)
14  Charlie Conerly (1948-61)
13  Lawrence Taylor (1981-93)
13  Harry Carson (1976-88)
13  Greg Larson (1961-73)
13  Jim Katcavage (1956-68)
13  Rosie Brown (1953-65)

#### MOST CONSECUTIVE GAMES PLAYED, CAREER
172  Mel Hein (1931-45)
165  Dave Jennings (1974-84)
140  Bart Oates (1985-93)
126  Emlen Tunnell (1948-58)
124  Ray Wietecha (1953-62)

#### MOST SEASONS, HEAD COACH
23  Steve Owen (1931-53)
8  Bill Parcells (1983-90)
8  Allie Sherman (1961-68)
7  Jim Lee Howell (1954-60)

### SCORING

#### MOST SEASONS LEADING LEAGUE
1  Don Chandler (1963)
1  Gene Roberts (1949–tied)
1  Ken Strong (1933–tied)

#### MOST POINTS, CAREER
646  Pete Gogolak (1966-74)
     (268-pat, 126-fg)
484  Frank Gifford (1950-60, 62-64)
     (78-td, 10-pat, 2-fg)
482  Joe Danelo (1976-82)
     (170-pat, 104-fg)
411  Brad Daluiso (1993-98)
     (114-pat, 99-fg)
390  Joe Morrison (1959-72)
     (65-td)

#### MOST POINTS, SEASON
127  Ali Haji-Sheikh (1983) (22-pat, 35-fg)
126  Joe Morris (1985) (21-tds)
107  Pete Gogolak (1970) (32-pat, 25-fg)
106  Don Chandler (1963) (52-pat, 18-fg)

#### MOST POINTS, ROOKIE SEASON
127  Ali Haji-Sheikh (1983) (22-pat, 35-fg)

#### MOST POINTS, GAME
24  Rodney Hampton, vs. New Orleans
    Sept. 24, 1995
24  Earnest Gray, at St. Louis
    Sept. 7, 1980
24  Ron Johnson, at Philadelphia
    Oct. 2, 1972
20  Joe Danelo, at Seattle
    Oct. 18, 1981

#### MOST CONSECUTIVE GAMES SCORING
61  Pete Gogolak (1969-73)

57  Ben Agajanian (1949, 54-57)
46  Pat Summerall (1958-61)

### TOUCHDOWNS

#### MOST SEASONS LEADING LEAGUE
2  Bill Paschal (1943–tied, 1944–tied)
1  Joe Morris (1985)
1  Homer Jones (1967)
1  Gene Roberts (1949)

#### MOST TOUCHDOWNS, CAREER
78  Frank Gifford (1952-60, 62-64)
65  Joe Morrison (1959-72)
56  Alex Webster (1955-64)

#### MOST TOUCHDOWNS, SEASON
21  Joe Morris (1985)
17  Gene Roberts (1949)
14  Rodney Hampton (1992)
14  Ottis Anderson (1989)
14  Joe Morris (1986)
14  Ron Johnson (1972)
14  Homer Jones (1967)
12  Ron Johnson (1970)
12  Del Shofner (1962)
12  Bill Paschal (1943)

#### MOST TOUCHDOWNS, ROOKIE SEASON
12  Bill Paschal (1943)

#### MOST TOUCHDOWNS, GAME
4  Rodney Hampton, vs. New Orleans
   Sept. 24, 1995
4  Earnest Gray, at St. Louis
   Sept. 7, 1980
4  Ron Johnson, at Philadelphia
   Oct. 2, 1972
3  by many players
   Last: Rodney Hampton,
   vs. Kansas City Dec. 19, 1992

#### MOST CONSECUTIVE GAMES SCORING TOUCHDOWNS
10  Frank Gifford (1957-58)
7  Kyle Rote (1959-60)
7  Bill Paschal (1944)
6  Frank Gifford (1953)

### POINTS AFTER TOUCHDOWN

#### MOST SEASONS LEADING LEAGUE
1  Don Chandler (1963)
1  Pat Summerall (1961)
1  Ward Cuff (1938)

#### MOST POINTS AFTER TOUCHDOWN ATTEMPTED, CAREER
278  Pete Gogolak (1966-74)
176  Joe Danelo (1976-82)
159  Ben Agajanian (1949, 54-57)

#### MOST POINTS AFTER TOUCHDOWN ATTEMPTED, SEASON
56  Don Chandler (1963)
48  Don Chandler (1962)
46  Pat Summerall (1961)

#### MOST POINTS AFTER TOUCHDOWN (NO MISSES), GAME
8  Pete Gogolak, vs. Philadelphia
   Nov. 26, 1972
7  by five players

#### MOST POINTS AFTER TOUCHDOWN, CAREER
268  Pete Gogolak (1966-74)
170  Joe Danelo (1976-82)
157  Ben Agajanian (1949, 54-57)

#### MOST POINTS AFTER TOUCHDOWN, SEASON
52  Don Chandler (1963)
47  Don Chandler (1962)
46  Pat Summerall (1961)

#### MOST POINTS AFTER TOUCHDOWN, GAME
8  Pete Gogolak, vs. Philadelphia
   Nov. 26, 1972
7  Raul Allegre, vs. Green Bay
   Dec. 20, 1986
7  Pete Gogolak, vs. St. Louis
   Dec. 7, 1969
7  Don Chandler, vs. Washington
   Oct. 28, 1962
7  Pat Summerall, vs. Washington
   Nov. 5, 1961
7  Ray Poole, at Baltimore
   Nov. 19, 1950
7  Len Younce, at Green Bay
   Nov. 21, 1948

#### MOST CONSECUTIVE POINTS AFTER TOUCHDOWN
133  Pete Gogolak (1967-72)
126  Pat Summerall (1958-61)

#### MOST POINTS AFTER TOUCHDOWN (NO MISSES), SEASON
46  Pat Summerall (1961)
36  Pete Gogolak (1968)
35  Ben Agajanian (1954)

### FIELD GOALS

#### MOST SEASONS LEADING LEAGUE
3  Ward Cuff (1938–tied, 1939, 1943–tied)
1  Ali Haji-Sheikh (1983)
1  Pat Summerall (1959)
1  Ken Strong (1944)

#### MOST FIELD GOALS ATTEMPTED, CAREER
219  Pete Gogolak (1966-74)
176  Joe Danelo (1976-82)
128  Brad Daluiso (1993-98)
112  Pat Summerall (1958-61)

#### MOST FIELD GOALS ATTEMPTED, SEASON
42  Ali Haji-Sheikh (1983)
41  Pete Gogolak (1970)
38  Joe Danelo (1981)
34  Pat Summerall (1961)
32  Brad Daluiso (1997)
32  Raul Allegre (1986)

31  David Treadwell (1993)
31  Pete Gogolak (1972)

#### MOST FIELD GOALS ATTEMPTED, GAME
6  Raul Allegre, at Minnesota
   Nov. 16, 1986
6  Ali Haji-Sheikh, at Washington
   Dec. 17, 1983
6  Joe Danelo, at Seattle
   Oct. 18, 1981
6  Pete Gogolak, at Philadelphia
   Nov. 25, 1973
6  Ben Agajanian, vs. Philadelphia
   Nov. 14, 1954

#### MOST FIELD GOALS, CAREER
126  Pete Gogolak (1966-74)
104  Joe Danelo (1976-82)
99  Brad Daluiso (1993-98)
75  Raul Allegre (1986-90)
59  Pat Summerall (1958-61)

#### MOST FIELD GOALS, SEASON
35  Ali Haji-Sheikh (1983)
25  David Treadwell (1993)
25  Pete Gogolak (1970)
24  Brad Daluiso (1996)
24  Raul Allegre (1986)
24  Joe Danelo (1981)
22  Brad Daluiso (1997)
22  Matt Bahr (1991)
21  Brad Daluiso (1998)
21  Joe Danelo (1978)
21  Pete Gogolak (1972)

#### MOST FIELD GOALS, GAME
6  Joe Danelo, at Seattle
   Oct. 18, 1981
5  Raul Allegre, at Minnesota
   Nov. 16, 1986
5  Eric Schubert, vs. Tampa Bay
   Nov. 3, 1985
5  Ali Haji-Sheikh, at Washington
   Dec. 17, 1983
4  David Treadwell, at Chicago
   Sept. 5, 1993
4  Raul Allegre, at Philadelphia
   Oct. 8, 1989
4  Raul Allegre, vs. Phoenix
   Sept. 24, 1989
4  Raul Allegre, at Washington
   Nov. 29, 1987
4  Raul Allegre, vs. Denver
   Nov. 23, 1986
4  Ali Haji-Sheikh, at Dallas
   Nov. 4, 1984
4  Ali Haji-Sheikh, vs. Seattle
   Dec. 11, 1983
4  Joe Danelo, at Philadelphia
   Jan. 2, 1983
4  Joe Danelo, vs. Washington
   Nov. 14, 1976
4  Pete Gogolak, at Cleveland
   Dec. 4, 1966
4  Pete Gogolak, vs. St. Louis
   Oct. 9, 1966

4    Don Chandler, vs. Philadelphia
     Nov. 18, 1962

**MOST CONSECUTIVE GAMES
KICKING FIELD GOALS**

18   Joe Danelo (1977-79)
15   Raul Allegre (1988-89)
15   Ali Haji-Sheikh (1983)
14   Pat Summerall (1960-61)
12   Matt Bahr (1990-91)
11   Brad Daluiso (1995-96)
9    Pete Gogolak (1972)
7    Ali Haji-Sheikh (1984)
7    Pat Summerall (1959)
7    Pat Summerall (1958-59)

**LONGEST FIELD GOAL (IN YARDS)**

56   Ali Haji-Sheikh, at Detroit
     Nov. 7, 1983
56   Ali Haji-Sheikh, vs. Green Bay
     Sept. 26, 1983
55   Joe Danelo, vs. New Orleans
     Sept. 20, 1981
54   Brad Daluiso, vs. Phoenix
     Nov. 28, 1993
54   Matt Bahr, vs. Houston
     Dec. 21, 1991
54   Joe Danelo, at Seattle
     Oct. 18, 1981
54   Pete Gogolak, vs. Dallas
     Nov. 8, 1970
53   Raul Allegre, at Philadelphia
     Nov. 15, 1987
53   Don Chandler, at Dallas
     Dec. 1, 1963
52   Brad Daluiso, at Detroit
     Oct. 19, 1997
52   Brad Daluiso, vs. Cincinnati
     Dec. 11, 1994
52   Raul Allegre, at Washington
     Sept. 11, 1989
52   Raul Allegre, at Philadelphia
     Nov. 15, 1987
52   Ali Haji-Sheikh, at Green Bay
     Sept. 15, 1985
52   Joe Danelo, at San Francisco
     Nov. 29, 1981
52   Joe Danelo, vs. San Francisco
     Sept. 24, 1978
51   Brad Daluiso, at Arizona
     Dec. 6, 1998
51   Brad Daluiso, at Arizona
     Nov. 30, 1995
51   Brad Daluiso, vs. New Orleans
     Sept. 24, 1995
51   Joe Danelo, at Dallas
     Oct. 5, 1980
51   Joe Danelo, vs. Dallas
     Nov. 6, 1977
50   Paul McFadden, vs. Dallas
     Nov. 6, 1988
50   Joe Danelo, at Philadelphia
     Sept. 22, 1980
50   Joe Danelo, at New Orleans
     Oct. 29, 1978
50   Joe Danelo, vs. Washington
     Nov. 14, 1976
50   Ben Agajanian, at Washington
     Oct. 13, 1957

**HIGHEST FIELD GOAL PERCENTAGE,
CAREER (50 ATTEMPTS)**

77.3  Brad Daluiso 99/128 (1993-98)

75.3  Matt Bahr 55/73 (1990-92)
74.3  Raul Allegre 75/101 (1986-91)
67.5  Ali Haji-Sheikh 54/80 (1983-85)
59.0  Joe Danelo 104/176 (1976-82)
57.1  Pete Gogolak 126/219 (1966-74)
54.8  Ben Agajanian 46/84 (1949, 54-57)

**HIGHEST FIELD GOAL PERCENTAGE,
SEASON (14 ATTEMPTS)**

88.9  Brad Daluiso 24/27 (1996)
83.3  Ali Haji-Sheikh 35/42 (1983)
80.6  David Treadwell 25/31 (1993)
77.8  Brad Daluiso 21/27 (1998)
76.9  Raul Allegre 20/26 (1989)
76.2  Matt Bahr 16/21 (1992)
75.8  Matt Bahr 22/29 (1991)
75.0  Raul Allegre 24/32 (1986)
75.0  Ray Poole 12/16 (1951)
73.9  Matt Bahr 17/23 (1990)
73.7  Paul McFadden 14/19 (1978)
72.4  Joe Danelo 21/29 (1978)
71.4  Brad Daluiso 20/28 (1995)
69.0  Pat Summerall 20/29 (1959)

**HIGHEST FIELD GOAL PERCENTAGE,
GAME (4 ATTEMPTS)**

100   David Treadwell, at Chicago
      Sept. 5, 1993 (4-4)
100   Raul Allegre, at Washington
      Nov. 29, 1987 (4-4)
100   Raul Allegre, vs. Denver
      Nov. 23, 1986 (4-4)
100   Eric Schubert, vs. Tampa Bay
      Nov. 3, 1985 (5-5)
100   Ali Haji-Sheikh, at Dallas
      Nov. 4, 1984 (4-4)
100   Joe Danelo, at Seattle
      Oct. 18, 1981 (6-6)
100   Don Chandler, at Chicago
      Dec. 2, 1962 (4-4)
83.3  Raul Allegre, at Minnesota
      Nov. 16, 1986 (5-6)
83.3  Ali Haji-Sheikh, at Washington
      Dec. 17, 1983 (5-6)
80.0  Ali Haji-Sheikh, vs. Seattle
      Dec. 11, 1983 (4-5)
80.0  Joe Danelo, at Philadelphia
      Jan. 2, 1983 (4-5)
80.0  Joe Danelo, vs. Washington
      Nov. 14, 1976 (4-5)
80.0  Pete Gogolak, at Detroit
      Nov. 17, 1974 (4-5)
80.0  Pete Gogolak, at St. Louis
      Oct. 9, 1966 (4-5)
80.0  Don Chandler, at Cleveland
      Oct. 27, 1963 (4-5)
80.0  Don Chandler, vs. Philadelphia
      Nov. 18, 1962 (4-5)

**MOST FIELD GOALS,
50 OR MORE YARDS, CAREER**

9    Joe Danelo (1976-82)
6    Brad Daluiso (1993-98)
3    Raul Allegre (1986-91)
3    Ali Haji-Sheikh (1983-85)

**MOST FIELD GOALS,
50 OR MORE YARDS, SEASON**

3    Joe Danelo (1981)
2    Brad Daluiso (1995)
2    Raul Allegre (1987)
2    Ali Haji-Sheikh (1983)
2    Joe Danelo (1978 and 1980)

**MOST FIELD GOALS,
50 OR MORE YARDS, GAME**

2    Raul Allegre, at Philadelphia
     Nov. 15, 1987
1    20 times
     Last: Brad Daluiso, at Arizona
     Dec. 6, 1998

**SAFETIES**

**MOST SAFETIES, CAREER**

3    Jim Katcavage (1956-68)
2    Leonard Marshall (1983-92)
1    by many players

**MOST SAFETIES, SEASON**

1    by many players
     Last: Tito Wooten (1996)

**MOST SAFETIES, GAME**

1    by many players
     Last: Tito Wooten, at Detroit
     Oct. 27, 1996

**RUSHING**

**MOST SEASONS LEADING LEAGUE**

2    Bill Pascal (1943-44)
1    Eddie Price (1951)
1    Tuffy Leemans (1936)

**MOST ATTEMPTS, CAREER**

1,824  Rodney Hampton (1990-97)
1,318  Joe Morris (1982-89)
1,196  Alex Webster (1955-64)
1,066  Ron Johnson (1970-75)
919    Tuffy Leemans (1936-43)

**MOST ATTEMPTS, SEASON**

341  Joe Morris (1986)
327  Rodney Hampton (1994)
325  Ottis Anderson (1989)
307  Joe Morris (1988)
306  Rodney Hampton (1995)
298  Ron Johnson (1972)
294  Joe Morris (1985)
292  Rodney Hampton (1993)
271  Eddie Price (1951)

**MOST ATTEMPTS,
GAME**

43   Butch Woolfolk, at Philadelphia
     Nov. 20, 1983
41   Rodney Hampton, vs. Rams
     Sept. 19, 1993
38   Harry Newman, vs. Green Bay
     Nov. 11, 1934
36   Joe Morris, vs. Pittsburgh
     Dec. 21, 1985
36   Ron Johnson, at Philadelphia
     Oct. 2, 1972
34   Rodney Hampton, at Dallas
     Dec. 17, 1995
34   Rodney Hampton, at Washington
     Nov. 27, 1994
34   Rodney Hampton, at Houston
     Nov. 21, 1994
33   Rodney Hampton, vs. New Orleans
     Sept. 24, 1995
33   Rodney Hampton, vs. Indianapolis
     Dec. 12. 1993
32   Rodney Hampton, at Buffalo
     Oct. 3, 1993
32   Joe Morris, vs. Phoenix
     Dec. 4, 1988

32   Eddie Price, at Chicago Cardinals
     Nov. 25, 1951
31   Joe Morris, vs. Kansas City
     Dec. 11, 1988
31   Joe Morris, vs. Washington
     Oct. 27, 1986
30   Rodney Hampton, vs. Detroit
     Oct. 30, 1994
30   Rodney Hampton, vs. Dallas
     Jan. 2, 1994
30   Joe Morris, vs. San Diego
     Sept. 14, 1986
30   Ron Johnson, vs. Philadelphia
     Sept. 23, 1973
30   Eddie Price, at N.Y. Yanks
     Dec. 16, 1951
30   Bill Paschal, vs. Washington
     Dec. 3, 1944

**MOST YARDS GAINED, CAREER**

6,897  Rodney Hampton (1990-97)
5,296  Joe Morris (1982-89)
4,638  Alex Webster (1955-64)
3,836  Ron Johnson (1970-75)
3,609  Frank Gifford (1952-60, 62-64)

**MOST YARDS GAINED, SEASON**

1,516  Joe Morris (1986)
1,336  Joe Morris (1985)
1,182  Rodney Hampton (1995)
1,182  Ron Johnson (1972)
1,141  Rodney Hampton (1992)
1,083  Joe Morris (1988)
1,077  Rodney Hampton (1993)
1,075  Rodney Hampton (1994)
1,063  Gary Brown (1998)
1,059  Rodney Hampton (1991)
1,027  Ron Johnson (1970)
1,023  Ottis Anderson (1989)
971    Eddie Price (1951)
928    Alex Webster (1961)

**MOST YARDS GAINED, GAME**

218  Gene Roberts, vs. Chicago Cardinals
     Nov. 12, 1950
202  Joe Morris, vs. Pittsburgh
     Dec. 21, 1985
188  Bill Paschal, vs. Washington
     Dec. 5, 1943
187  Rodney Hampton, at Dallas
     Dec. 17, 1995
181  Joe Morris, vs. Washington
     Oct. 27, 1986
181  Joe Morris, vs. Dallas
     Nov. 2, 1986
179  Joe Morris, vs. St. Louis
     Dec. 14, 1986
173  Rodney Hampton, vs. Indianapolis
     Dec. 12, 1993
171  Eddie Price, at Philadelphia
     Dec. 9, 1951

**MOST GAMES 100 YARDS OR MORE
RUSHING, CAREER**

19   Joe Morris (1982-89)
17   Rodney Hampton (1990-97)
11   Eddie Price (1950-55)
10   Ron Johnson (1970-75)
7    Rob Carpenter (1981-83)
6    Gary Brown (1998)
5    Bill Paschal (1943-47)
5    Tuffy Leemans (1936-43)
4    Doug Kotar (1974-81)

4 Alex Webster (1955-64)
4 Gene Roberts (1947-50)

**MOST GAMES, 100 YARDS OR MORE RUSHING, SEASON**

8 Joe Morris (1986)
6 Gary Brown (1998)
6 Joe Morris (1985)
5 Rodney Hampton (1993)
4 Rodney Hampton (1994)
4 Rob Carpenter (1981)
4 Ron Johnson (1972)
4 Ron Johnson (1970)
4 Eddie Price (1952)
4 Eddie Price (1951)
3 Rodney Hampton (1991)
3 Joe Morris (1988)
3 Rob Carpenter (1983)
3 Eddie Price (1950)
3 Tuffy Leemans (1936)
2 Rodney Hampton (1995)
2 Rodney Hampton (1992)
2 Billy Taylor (1979)
2 Doug Kotar (1976)
2 Ron Johnson (1973)
2 Gene Roberts (1949)
2 Ward Cuff (1944)
2 Bill Paschal (1944)
2 Bill Paschal (1943)

**LONGEST RUN FROM SCRIMMAGE**

91 Hap Moran, vs. Green Bay
Nov. 23, 1930
80 Eddie Price, at Philadelphia
Dec. 9, 1951
79 Frank Gifford, vs. Washington
Nov. 29, 1959
77 Bill Paschal, vs. Cleveland Rams
Nov. 4, 1945

**HIGHEST AVERAGE GAIN, CAREER (500 ATTEMPTS)**

4.30 Frank Gifford (1952-60, 62-64)
840/3609
4.14 Mel Triplett (1955-60)
553/2289
4.02 Joe Morris (1982-88)
1318/5296
3.88 Alex Webster (1955-64)
1196/4638
3.78 Rodney Hampton (1990-97)
1824/6897
3.75 Doug Kotar (1974-81)
900/3378

**HIGHEST AVERAGE GAIN, SEASON (QUALIFIERS)**

5.58 Eddie Price (1950) 126/703
5.15 Frank Gifford (1956) 159/819
4.95 Alex Webster (1955) 128/634
4.62 Charles Way (1997) 151/698

**HIGHEST AVERAGE GAIN, GAME (10 ATTEMPTS)**

13.30 Frank Reagan, vs. Rams
Dec. 1, 1946 (10-133)
12.23 Tuffy Leemans, vs. Green Bay
Nov. 20, 1938 (13-159)
11.43 Ernie Koy, at Washington
Oct. 1, 1967 (14-160)

**MOST RUSHING TOUCHDOWNS, CAREER**

49 Rodney Hampton (1990-97)

48 Joe Morris (1982-89)
39 Alex Webster (1955-64)
34 Frank Gifford (1952-60, 62-64)
33 Ron Johnson (1970-75)

**MOST RUSHING TOUCHDOWNS, SEASON**

21 Joe Morris (1985)
14 Rodney Hampton (1992)
14 Ottis Anderson (1989)
14 Joe Morris (1986)
11 Ottis Anderson (1990)
10 Rodney Hampton (1995)
10 Rodney Hampton (1991)
10 Bill Paschal (1943)
9 Ron Johnson (1972)
9 Gene Roberts (1949)
9 Bill Paschal (1944)
8 Ottis Anderson (1988)
8 Ron Johnson (1970)
8 Frank Gifford (1958)

**MOST RUSHING TOUCHDOWNS, GAME**

4 Rodney Hampton, vs. New Orleans
Sept. 24, 1995
3 Rodney Hampton, vs. Kansas City
Dec. 19, 1992
3 Ottis Anderson, vs. Phoenix
Dec. 4, 1988
3 Joe Morris, vs. St. Louis
Dec. 14, 1986
3 Joe Morris, vs. Pittsburgh
Dec. 21, 1985
3 Joe Morris, at Houston
Dec. 8, 1985
3 Joe Morris, vs. Cleveland
Dec. 1, 1985
3 Joe Morris, at Washington
Nov. 18, 1985
3 Joe Morris, vs. Washington
Oct. 28, 1984
3 Charlie Evans, vs. San Diego
Nov. 7, 1971
3 Mel Triplett, at Chicago Cardinals
Oct. 7, 1956
3 Gene Roberts, at N.Y. Bulldogs
Sept. 30, 1949
3 Bill Paschal, vs. Pittsburgh Cardinals
Oct. 22, 1944
2 by many players
Last: Charles Way, Tyrone Wheatley,
vs. Cincinnati, Oct. 26, 1997

**MOST CONSECUTIVE GAMES RUSHING FOR TOUCHDOWNS**

7 Bill Paschal (1944)
5 Rodney Hampton (1991)
5 Ottis Anderson (1989)
5 Bill Gaiters (1961)
4 Joe Morris (1985)
4 Ron Johnson (1970)
4 Bill Paschal (1943)
4 Ken Strong (1934)

**PASSING**

**MOST SEASONS LEADING LEAGUE**

2 Ed Danowski (1935,1938)
1 Phil Simms (NFC, 1990)
1 Norm Snead (1972)
1 Y. A. Tittle (1963)
1 Charlie Conerly (1959)
1 Harry Newman (1933)

**MOST PASSES ATTEMPTED, CAREER**

4,647 Phil Simms (1979-93)
2,833 Charlie Conerly (1948-61)
1,898 Fran Tarkenton (1967-71)
1,391 Dave Brown (1992-97)
1,308 Y. A. Tittle (1961-64)

**MOST PASSES ATTEMPTED, SEASON**

533 Phil Simms (1984)
495 Phil Simms (1985)
479 Phil Simms (1988)
468 Phil Simms (1986)
456 Dave Brown (1995)
409 Fran Tarkenton (1969)
405 Phil Simms (1989)
402 Phil Simms (1980)
400 Phil Simms (1993)
398 Dave Brown (1996)
389 Fran Tarkenton (1970)
386 Scott Brunner (1983)
386 Fran Tarkenton (1971)

**MOST PASSES ATTEMPTED, GAME**

62 Phil Simms, at Cincinnati
Oct. 13, 1985
53 Charlie Conerly, at Pittsburgh
Dec. 5, 1948
52 Jeff Rutledge, vs. Seattle
Dec. 11, 1983
51 Scott Brunner, vs. San Diego
Oct. 2, 1983
51 Scott Brunner, at St. Louis
Dec. 26, 1982
50 Dave Brown, at Green Bay
Sept. 17, 1995
50 Phil Simms, at Dallas
Dec. 15, 1985
49 Phil Simms, vs. Rams
Sept. 25, 1988
49 Phil Simms, at Philadelphia
Sept. 22, 1980
48 Phil Simms, at San Francisco
Nov. 27, 1989
48 Phil Simms, at St. Louis
Dec. 13, 1987
47 Jeff Rutledge, at Washington
Dec. 17, 1989
47 Randy Johnson, vs. Philadelphia
Dec. 19, 1971

**MOST PASSES COMPLETED, CAREER**

2,576 Phil Simms (1979-93)
1,418 Charlie Conerly (1948-61)
1,051 Fran Tarkenton (1967-71)
766 Dave Brown (1992-97)
731 Y. A. Tittle (1961-64)

**MOST PASSES COMPLETED, SEASON**

286 Phil Simms (1984)
275 Phil Simms (1985)
263 Phil Simms (1988)
259 Phil Simms (1986)
254 Dave Brown (1995)
247 Phil Simms (1993)
228 Phil Simms (1989)
226 Fran Tarkenton (1971)
221 Y. A. Tittle (1963)
220 Fran Tarkenton (1969)

**MOST PASSES COMPLETED, GAME**

40 Phil Simms, at Cincinnati
Oct. 13, 1985

36 Charlie Conerly, at Pittsburgh
Dec. 5, 1948
31 Scott Brunner, vs. San Diego
Oct. 2, 1983
30 Phil Simms, at St. Louis
Dec. 13, 1987
30 Randy Johnson, vs. Philadelphia
Dec. 19, 1971
29 Phil Simms, vs. Rams
Sept. 25, 1988
29 Scott Brunner, at St. Louis
Dec. 26, 1982
28 Dave Brown, vs. Baltimore
Sept. 14, 1997
28 Jeff Hostetler, at Dallas
Sept. 29, 1991
28 Jeff Rutledge, vs. Seattle
Dec. 11, 1983
28 Phil Simms, vs. New Orleans
Sept. 20, 1981
28 Norm Snead, vs. New England
Sept. 22, 1974
28 Randy Johnson, at St. Louis
Oct. 28, 1973

**MOST CONSECUTIVE PASSES COMPLETED**

13 Phil Simms, at Cincinnati
Oct. 13, 1985
12 Y. A. Tittle, vs. Washington
Oct. 28, 1962

**HIGHEST PASSING EFFICIENCY, CAREER (1000 ATTEMPTS)**

55.89 Y. A. Tittle (1961-64) 731/1308
55.43 Phil Simms (1979-93) 2576/4647
55.37 Fran Tarkenton (1967-71) 1051/1898
55.07 Dave Brown (1992-97) 766/1391
50.05 Charlie Conerly (1948-61) 1418/2833

**HIGHEST PASSING EFFICIENCY, SEASON (QUALIFIERS)**

62.81 Jeff Hostetler (1991) 179/285
61.80 Phil Simms (1993) 247/400
60.31 Norm Snead (1972) 196/325
60.22 Y. A. Tittle (1963) 221/367
59.20 Phil Simms (1990) 184/311
58.55 Fran Tarkenton (1971) 226/386
58.25 Charlie Conerly (1959) 113/194

**HIGHEST PASSING EFFICIENCY, GAME (20 ATTEMPTS)**

82.35 Jeff Hostetler, at Dallas
Sept. 29, 1991 (28/34)
80.95 Phil Simms, at Indianapolis
Nov. 5, 1990 (17/21)
80.95 Phil Simms, vs. St. Louis
Oct. 25, 1987 (17/21)
80.76 Phil Simms, vs. Green Bay
Dec. 19, 1987 (21/26)
80.00 Norm Snead, vs. New England
Sept. 22, 1974 (28/35)
80.00 Fran Tarkenton, vs. San Diego
Nov. 7, 1971 (16/20)
80.00 Y. A. Tittle, vs. Philadelphia
Nov. 10, 1963 (16/20)
77.80 Phil Simms, vs. Rams
Sept. 19, 1993 (21/27)
77.27 Bob Clatterbuck, vs. Pittsburgh
Dec. 5, 1954 (17/22)
76.92 Phil Simms, vs. Detroit
Sept. 17, 1989 (20/26)

76.70 Phil Simms, vs. Philadelphia
Sept. 2, 1984 (23/30)
76.19 Phil Simms, at Dallas
Sept. 16, 1990 (16/21)
76.00 Dave Brown, vs. Detroit
Oct. 30, 1994 (19/25)
75.00 Dave Brown, at Miami
Dec. 8, 1996 (21/28)
75.00 Norm Snead, vs. Green Bay
Oct. 7, 1973 (21/28)
75.00 Y. A. Tittle, vs. Philadelphia
Nov. 12, 1961 (18/24)

## MOST YARDS PASSING, CAREER

33,462 Phil Simms (1979-93)
19,488 Charlie Conerly (1948-61)
13,905 Fran Tarkenton (1967-71)
10,439 Y. A. Tittle (1961-64)

## MOST YARDS PASSING, SEASON

4,044 Phil Simms (1984)
3,829 Phil Simms (1985)
3,487 Phil Simms (1986)
3,359 Phil Simms (1988)
3,224 Y. A. Tittle (1962)
3,145 Y. A. Tittle (1963)
3,088 Fran Tarkenton (1967)

## MOST YARDS PASSING, GAME

513 Phil Simms, at Cincinnati
Oct. 13, 1985
505 Y. A. Tittle, vs. Washington
Oct. 28, 1962
432 Phil Simms, vs. Dallas
Oct. 6, 1985
409 Phil Simms, vs. Philadelphia
Sept. 2, 1984
395 Scott Brunner, vs. San Diego
Oct. 2, 1983
388 Phil Simms, at San Francisco
Dec. 1, 1986
372 Randy Johnson, vs. Philadelphia
Dec. 19, 1971
368 Jeff Hostetler, at Dallas
Sept. 29, 1991
363 Charlie Conerly, at Pittsburgh
Dec. 5, 1948

## MOST GAMES, 300 YARDS OR MORE PASSING, CAREER

21 Phil Simms (1979-93)
9 Y. A. Tittle (1961-64)
4 Scott Brunner (1980-83)
4 Fran Tarkenton (1967-71)
3 Jeff Rutledge (1982-88)
3 Charlie Conerly (1948-61)

## MOST GAMES, 300 YARDS OR MORE PASSING, SEASON

4 Phil Simms (1986)
4 Phil Simms (1984)
4 Y. A. Tittle (1962)
3 Phil Simms (1988)
3 Phil Simms (1985)
3 Jeff Rutledge (1983)
3 Y. A. Tittle (1961)
2 Scott Brunner (1983)
2 Scott Brunner (1982)
2 Phil Simms (1980)
2 Y. A. Tittle (1963)

## LONGEST PASS COMPLETION (IN YARDS)

98 Earl Morrall (to Homer Jones)
at Pittsburgh, Sept. 11, 1966
94 Norm Snead (to Rich Houston)
vs. Dallas, Sept. 24, 1972
89 Earl Morrall (to Homer Jones)
vs. Philadelphia, Oct. 17, 1965
88 Frank Reagan (to George Franck)
vs. Washington, Oct. 12, 1947
87 Kent Graham (to Tiki Barber)
at Arizona, Dec. 6, 1998

## MOST TOUCHDOWN PASSES, CAREER

199 Phil Simms (1979-93)
173 Charlie Conerly (1948-61)
103 Fran Tarkenton (1967-71)
96 Y. A. Tittle (1961-64)

## MOST TOUCHDOWN PASSES, SEASON

36 Y. A. Tittle (1963)
33 Y. A. Tittle (1962)
29 Fran Tarkenton (1967)

## MOST TOUCHDOWN PASSES, GAME

7 Y. A. Tittle, vs. Washington
Oct. 28, 1962
6 Y. A. Tittle, vs. Dallas
Dec. 16, 1962
5 Phil Simms, at St. Louis
Sept. 7, 1980
5 Fran Tarkenton, vs. St. Louis
Oct. 25, 1970

## MOST CONSECUTIVE GAMES TOUCHDOWN PASSES

13 Y. A. Tittle (1963-64)
10 Phil Simms (1988-89)
10 Phil Simms (1986-87)
10 Charlie Conerly (1948-49)
9 Earl Morrall (1965-66)

## FEWEST PASSES HAD INTERCEPTED, CAREER (1000 ATTEMPTS)

49 Dave Brown (1992-97) 1391
68 Y. A. Tittle (1961-64) 1308
72 Fran Tarkenton (1967-71) 1898
157 Phil Simms (1979-93) 4647
167 Charlie Conerly (1948-61) 2833

## FEWEST PASSES HAD INTERCEPTED, SEASON (QUALIFIERS)

3 Gary Wood (1964)
4 Jeff Hostetler (1991)
4 Phil Simms (1990)
4 Charlie Conerly (1959)
4 Ed Danowski (1937)

## FEWEST PASSES HAD INTERCEPTED, GAME (MOST ATTEMPTS)

0 Scott Brunner, vs. St. Louis
Dec. 26, 1982 (51 attempts)
0 Dave Brown, vs. Baltimore
Sept. 14, 1997 (46 attempts)
0 Fran Tarkenton, at Dallas
Oct. 11, 1971 (46 attempts)
0 Fran Tarkenton, vs. Dallas
Dec. 15, 1968 (43 attempts)
0 Dave Brown, at Seattle
Nov. 5, 1995 (41 attempts)
0 Phil Simms, vs. Phoenix
Nov. 28, 1993 (41 attempts)

0 Y.A. Tittle, vs. Washington
Oct. 28, 1962 (39 attempts)

## MOST PASSES HAD INTERCEPTED, CAREER

167 Charlie Conerly (1949-61)
157 Phil Simms (1979-93)
72 Fran Tarkenton (1967-71)
68 Y. A. Tittle (1961-64)

## MOST PASSES HAD INTERCEPTED, SEASON

25 Charlie Conerly (1953)
25 Frank Filchock (1946)
23 Joe Pisarcik (1978)
22 Phil Simms (1986)
22 Scott Brunner (1983)
22 Norm Snead (1973)
22 Y. A. Tittle (1964)
22 Charlie Conerly (1951)

## MOST PASSES HAD INTERCEPTED, GAME

5 Jeff Rutledge, at New Orleans
Nov. 22, 1987
5 Charlie Conerly, vs. Detroit
Dec. 13, 1953
5 Charlie Conerly, vs. Chicago Cardinals
Oct. 14, 1951
5 Frank Filchock, at Washington
Oct. 13, 1946
5 Harry Newman, at Portsmouth
Sept. 24, 1933
4 by many players
Last: Dave Brown, vs. Washington
Sept. 9, 1996

## LOWEST PERCENTAGE PASSES HAD INTERCEPTED, CAREER (1000 ATTEMPTS)

3.38 Phil Simms (1979-93) 157/4647
3.79 Fran Tarkenton (1967-71) 72/1898
3.52 Dave Brown (1992-97) 49/1391
5.20 Y. A. Tittle (1961-64) 68/1308
5.89 Charlie Conerly (1948-61) 167/2833

## LOWEST PERCENTAGE PASSES HAD INTERCEPTED, SEASON (QUALIFIERS)

1.28 Phil Simms (1990) 4/311
1.40 Jeff Hostetler (1991) 4/285
1.67 Dave Brown (1997) 3/180
1.96 Fran Tarkenton (1969) 8/409
2.06 Charlie Conerly (1959) 4/194
2.10 Gary Wood (1964) 3/143

## PASS RECEPTIONS

### MOST SEASONS LEADING LEAGUE

1 Earnest Gray (1983)
1 Bob Tucker (1971)
1 Tod Goodwin (1935)

## MOST PASS RECEPTIONS, CAREER

395 Joe Morrison (1959-72)
367 Frank Gifford (1952-60, 62-64)
334 Chris Calloway (1992-98)
327 Bob Tucker (1970-77)

## MOST PASS RECEPTIONS, SEASON

78 Earnest Gray (1983)
68 Del Shofner (1961)
66 Mark Bavaro (1986)
65 Lionel Manuel (1988)
64 Del Shofner (1963)
62 Chris Calloway (1998)
59 Bob Tucker (1971)

58 Chris Calloway (1997)
58 Mark Jackson (1993)

## MOST PASS RECEPTIONS, GAME

12 Mark Bavaro, at Cincinnati
Oct. 13, 1985
11 Mark Bavaro, at St. Louis
Dec. 13, 1987
11 Gary Shirk, vs. New Orleans
Sept. 20, 1981
11 Billy Taylor, at Tampa Bay
Nov. 2, 1980
11 Doug Kotar, at St. Louis
Oct. 3, 1976
11 Del Shofner, vs. Washington
Oct. 28, 1962
11 Frank Gifford, vs. San Francisco
Dec. 1, 1957
10 George Adams, vs. Rams
Sept. 25, 1988
10 Ron Johnson, vs. New England
Sept. 22, 1974
10 Tucker Frederickson, vs. Washington
Nov. 15, 1970
10 Alex Webster, vs. Dallas
Dec. 16, 1962
9 by many players
Last: Tiki Barber, vs. Atlanta
Oct. 11, 1998

## MOST CONSECUTIVE GAMES, PASS RECEPTIONS

47 Chris Calloway (1996-98)
46 David Meggett (1989-93)
45 Bob Tucker (1970-73)
41 Chris Calloway (1993-95)
32 Homer Jones (1965-67)
26 Homer Jones (1968-69)
25 Earnest Gray (1982-84)
23 Joe Morrison (1964-65)
23 Kyle Rote (1956-58)
21 Mark Bavaro (1986-87)

## MOST YARDS GAINED, CAREER

5,434 Frank Gifford (1952-60, 62-64)
4,993 Joe Morrison (1959-72)
4,845 Homer Jones (1964-69)

## MOST YARDS GAINED, SEASON

1,209 Homer Jones (1967)
1,181 Del Shofner (1963)
1,139 Earnest Gray (1983)
1,133 Del Shofner (1962)

## MOST YARDS GAINED, GAME

269 Del Shofner, vs. Washington
Oct. 28, 1962
212 Gene Roberts, at Green Bay
Nov. 13, 1949
201 Gene Roberts, vs. Chicago Bears
Oct. 23, 1949

## LONGEST PASS RECEPTION (IN YARDS)

98 Homer Jones (from Earl Morrall)
at Pittsburgh, Sept. 11, 1966
94 Rich Houston (from Norm Snead)
vs. Dallas, Sept. 24, 1972
89 Homer Jones (from Earl Morrall)
vs. Philadelphia, Oct. 17, 1965
88 George Franck (from Frank Reagan)
at Washington, Oct. 12, 1947

## HIGHEST AVERAGE GAIN, CAREER (200 MINIMUM)

22.6 Homer Jones (1964-69) 214/4845
18.1 Del Shofner (1961-67) 239/4315
17.2 Aaron Thomas (1962-70) 247/4253

## HIGHEST AVERAGE GAIN, SEASON (QUALIFIERS)

24.7 Homer Jones (1967) 49/1209
23.5 Homer Jones (1968) 45/1057
21.8 Homer Jones (1966) 48/1044

## HIGHEST AVERAGE GAIN, GAME (4 MINIMUM)

50.3 Gene Roberts, vs. Chicago Bears
Oct. 23, 1949 (4-201)
49.0 Homer Jones, at Washington
Oct. 1, 1967 (4/196)
37.5 Frank Liebel, vs. Detroit
Nov. 18, 1945 (4/150)

## MOST TOUCHDOWNS, CAREER

48 Kyle Rote (1951-61)
47 Joe Morrison (1959-71)
43 Frank Gifford (1952-60, 62-64)

## MOST TOUCHDOWNS, SEASON

13 Homer Jones (1967)
12 Del Shofner (1962)
11 Del Shofner (1961)

## MOST TOUCHDOWNS, GAME

4 Earnest Gray, at St. Louis
Sept. 7, 1980
3 Earnest Gray, vs. Green Bay
Nov. 16, 1980
3 Billy Taylor, at St. Louis
Dec. 9, 1979
3 Ron Johnson, at Philadelphia
Oct. 2, 1972
3 Rich Houston, at Green Bay
Sept. 19, 1971
3 Joe Walton, vs. Dallas
Dec. 16, 1962
3 Del Shofner, at Washington
Nov. 25, 1962
3 Del Shofner, at Dallas
Nov. 11, 1962
3 Joe Walton, vs. Washington
Oct. 28, 1962
3 Del Shofner, at Philadelphia
Dec. 10, 1961
3 Del Shofner, vs. Washington
Nov. 5, 1961
3 Bob Schnelker, at Washington
Oct. 10, 1954
3 Gene Roberts, at Green Bay
Nov. 13, 1949
3 Gene Roberts, vs. Chicago Bears
Oct. 23, 1949
3 Frank Liebel, vs. Philadelphia
Dec. 2, 1945

## MOST CONSECUTIVE GAMES, TOUCHDOWN RECEPTION

7 Kyle Rote (1959-60)
5 Chris Calloway (1997-98)
5 Aaron Thomas (1967)
5 Joe Morrison (1966)
5 Homer Jones (1966)
5 Del Shofner (1963)
5 Frank Liebel (1945)
4 by many players
Last: Thomas Lewis (1996)

## INTERCEPTIONS
## MOST SEASONS LEADING LEAGUE

2 Dick Lynch (1961, 1963)

## MOST INTERCEPTIONS BY, CAREER

74 Emlen Tunnell (1948-58)
52 Jimmy Patton (1955-66)
41 Carl Lockhart (1965-75)

## MOST INTERCEPTIONS BY, SEASON

11 Jimmy Patton (1958)
11 Otto Schellbacher (1951)
10 Willie Williams (1968)
10 Emlen Tunnell (1949)
10 Frank Reagan (1947)
9 by five players
Last: Dick Lynch (1963)

## MOST INTERCEPTIONS BY, GAME

3 Terry Kinard, vs. Dallas
Sept. 20, 1987
3 Carl Lockhart, at Cleveland
Dec. 4, 1966
3 Dick Lynch, at Philadelphia
Sept. 29, 1963
3 Jimmy Patton, at Chicago
Dec. 2, 1962
3 Dick Lynch, vs. Philadelphia
Nov. 12, 1961
3 Dick Lynch, at St. Louis
Oct. 8, 1961
3 Emlen Tunnell, at Chicago Cardinals
Nov. 24, 1957
3 Tom Landry, vs. Philadelphia
Nov. 14, 1954
3 Emlen Tunnell, at Pittsburgh
Nov. 7, 1954
3 Otto Schellbacher, vs. Cleveland
Oct. 22, 1950
3 Emlen Tunnell, at Washington
Oct. 9, 1949
3 Frank Reagan, vs. Boston Yankees
Nov. 28, 1948
3 Emlen Tunnell, at Green Bay
Nov. 21, 1948
3 Art Faircloth, at Boston Yankees
Sept. 23, 1948
3 Frank Reagan, vs. Green Bay
Nov. 23, 1947
3 Frank Reagan, at Detroit
Nov. 2, 1947
3 Howard Livingston, at Brooklyn Tigers
Oct. 15, 1944
3 Ward Cuff, at Philadelphia
Sept. 13, 1941

## MOST CONSECUTIVE GAMES, INTERCEPTIONS BY

6 Willie Williams (1968)
5 Carl Lockhart (1969-70)
5 Emlen Tunnell (1954-55)
4 by many players
Last: Phillippi Sparks (1995)

## MOST YARDS GAINED, CAREER

1,240 Emlen Tunnell (1948-58)
712 Jimmy Patton (1955-66)
574 Terry Kinard (1983-89)
568 Dick Lynch (1959-66)
475 Carl Lockhart (1965-75)

## MOST YARDS GAINED, SEASON

251 Dick Lynch (1963)
251 Emlen Tunnell (1949)

203 Frank Reagan (1947)
195 Erich Barnes (1961)

## MOST YARDS GAINED, GAME

109 Ward Cuff, at Philadelphia
Sept. 13, 1941
104 George Cheverko, at Washington
Oct. 3, 1948
102 Erich Barnes, at Dallas
Oct. 15, 1961

## LONGEST GAIN (IN YARDS)

102 Erich Barnes, at Dallas
Oct. 15, 1961 (TD)
101 Henry Carr, at Rams
Nov. 13, 1966 (TD)
97 Lawrence Taylor, at Detroit
Nov. 25, 1982 (TD)
96 Ward Cuff, vs. Washington
Dec. 4, 1938 (TD)
95 Sam Garnes, vs. Philadelphia
Aug. 31, 1997 (TD)
89 Bruce Maher, at Dallas
Nov. 10, 1968

## MOST TOUCHDOWNS, CAREER

4 Dick Lynch (1959-66)
4 Emlen Tunnell (1948-58)
3 George Martin (1975-86)
3 Carl Lockhart (1965-72)
3 Jerry Hillebrand (1963-66)
3 Erich Barnes (1961-64)
3 Tom Landry (1950-55)
2 Percy Ellsworth (1996-98)
2 Jessie Armstead (1993-98)
2 Jason Sehorn (1994-98)
2 Lawrence Taylor (1981-93)
2 Pepper Johnson (1986-92)
2 Terry Kinard (1983-89)
2 Terry Jackson (1978-82)
2 Jimmy Patton ( 1955-66)
2 Tom Scott (1959-64)
2 Otto Schnellbacher (1950-51)
2 Bill Petrilas (1944-45)

## MOST TOUCHDOWNS, SEASON

3 Dick Lynch (1963)
2 Percy Ellsworth (1998)
2 Carl Lockhart (1968)
2 Erich Barnes (1961)
2 Tom Landry (1961)
2 Otto Schnellbacher (1951)
2 Emlen Tunnell (1949)
2 Bill Petrilas (1944)

## MOST TOUCHDOWNS, GAME

1 by many players
Last: Percy Ellsworth, vs. Kansas City
Dec. 20, 1998

## MOST CONSECUTIVE GAMES, TOUCHDOWNS

2 Carl Lockhart,
at Philadelphia, Sept. 22—
vs. Washington, Sept. 29, 1968
2 Dick Lynch,
vs. Cleveland, Oct. 13—
vs. Dallas, Oct. 20, 1963
2 Tom Landry,
at Cleveland, Oct. 28—
vs. N.Y. Yanks, Nov. 4, 1951

## PUNTING
## MOST SEASONS LEADING LEAGUE

2 Sean Landeta (NFC, 1986, 1990)
1 Dave Jennings (1979, 1980)
1 Don Chandler (1957)

## MOST PUNTS, CAREER

931 Dave Jennings (1974-84)
526 Sean Landeta (1985-93)
525 Don Chandler (1956-64)

## MOST PUNTS, SEASON

111 Brad Maynard (1997)
104 Dave Jennings (1979)
102 Mike Horan (1996)
101 Brad Maynard (1998)
100 Dave Jennings (1977)
97 Dave Jennings (1981)
95 Dave Jennings (1978)
94 Dave Jennings (1980)

## MOST PUNTS, GAME

14 Carl Kinschef, at Detroit
Nov. 7, 1943
13 Brad Maynard, at Washington
Nov. 23, 1997
11 Brad Maynard, at Washington
Nov. 1, 1998
11 Dave Jennings, at Atlanta
Oct. 25, 1981
11 Dave Jennings, at Washington
Sept. 13, 1981
11 Don Chandler, at St. Louis
Oct. 8, 1961
11 Charlie Conerly, vs. Cleveland
Nov. 18, 1951
11 Tom Landry, vs. Philadelphia
Nov. 26, 1950

## MOST YARDS, CAREER

38,792 Dave Jennings (1974-84)
23,019 Don Chandler (1956-64)
22,804 Sean Landeta (1985-93)

## MOST YARDS, SEASON

4,566 Brad Maynard (1998)
4,531 Brad Maynard (1997)
4,445 Dave Jennings (1979)
4,289 Mike Horan (1996)
4,211 Dave Jennings (1980)
4,198 Dave Jennings (1981)
3,995 Dave Jennings (1978)
3,993 Dave Jennings (1977)

## MOST YARDS, GAME

583 Carl Kinscherf, at Detroit
Nov. 7, 1943 (14 punts)
537 Brad Maynard, at Washington
Nov. 23, 1997 (13 punts)
511 Dave Jennings, at Washington
Sept. 13, 1981 (11 punts)
497 Brad Maynard, at Washington
Nov. 1, 1998 (11 punts)
485 Don Chandler, at St. Louis
Oct. 8, 1961 (11 punts)
470 Len Barnum, vs. Green Bay
Nov. 17, 1940 (10 punts)

## LONGEST PUNT

74 Len Younce, vs. Chicago Bears
Nov. 14, 1943
74 Don Chandler, at Dallas
Oct. 11, 1964

73   Dave Jennings, vs. Houston
     Dec. 5, 1982
72   Dave Jennings, vs. Dallas
     Nov. 4, 1979
72   Len Younce, at Brooklyn Tigers
     Oct. 15, 1944
72   Carl Kinscherf, at Pittsburgh
     Oct. 9, 1943
71   Sean Landeta, vs. Green Bay
     Nov. 8, 1992
71   Sean Landeta, vs. Philadelphia
     Dec. 3, 1989

### HIGHEST AVERAGE, CAREER (150 PUNTS)
43.8 Don Chandler (1956-64)
     525 punts
43.4 Sean Landeta (1985-93)
     526 punts
42.1 Mike Horan (1993-96)
     303 punts
41.8 Tom Blanchard (1971-73)
     171 punts
41.7 Dave Jennings (1974-84)
     931 punts

### HIGHEST AVERAGE SEASON (35 PUNTS)
46.6 Don Chandler (1959) 55 punts
45.6 Don Chandler (1964) 73 punts

### HIGHEST AVERAGE, GAME (4 PUNTS)
55.3 Dave Jennings, vs. Houston
     Dec. 5, 1982 (4 punts)
54.1 Don Chandler, at Cleveland
     Oct. 11, 1959 (8 punts)
54.0 Dave Jennings, at Dallas
     Oct. 5, 1980 (5 punts)
53.1 Dave Jennings, at Dallas
     Nov. 30, 1975 (7 punts)
52.4 Sean Landeta, at Denver
     Nov. 15, 1992 (5 punts)
52.1 Dave Jennings, vs. Kansas City
     Sept. 17, 1978 (7 punts)
52.1 Don Chandler, vs. Pittsburgh
     Nov. 15, 1959 (7 punts)

## PUNT RETURNS

### MOST PUNT RETURNS, CAREER
257  Emlen Tunnell (1948-58)
213  Phil McConkey (1984-88)
202  David Meggett (1989-94)
106  Leon Bright (1981-83)
100  Amani Toomer (1996-98)
63   Carl Lockhart (1965-75)

### MOST PUNT RETURNS, SEASON
53   Phil McConkey (1985)
52   Leon Bright (1981)
47   Amani Toomer (1997)
46   David Meggett (1989)
46   Phil McConkey (1984)
43   David Meggett (1990)
42   Phil McConkey (1987)
40   Phil McConkey (1988)
38   Emlen Tunnell (1953)
37   Leon Bright (1982)

### MOST PUNT RETURNS, GAME
9    Phil McConkey, vs. Philadelphia
     Dec. 6, 1987
9    Pete Shaw, at Philadelphia
     Nov. 20, 1983
9    Leon Bright, vs. Philadelphia
     Dec. 11, 1982

8    Phil McConkey, at Dallas
     Nov. 4, 1984
8    Leon Bright, at Washington
     Sept. 13, 1981
8    Emlen Tunnell, vs. N.Y. Yanks
     Dec. 3, 1950
7    Phil McConkey, at St. Louis
     Oct. 5, 1986
7    Phil McConkey, vs. Philadelphia
     Sept. 8, 1985
7    Rondy Colbert, vs. New Orleans
     Dec. 14, 1975
6    Amani Toomer, at St. Louis
     Sept. 21, 1997
6    David Meggett, vs. Cleveland
     Sept. 22, 1991
6    Pete Athas, at St. Louis
     Dec. 15, 1974
6    Emlen Tunnell, at Philadelphia
     Oct. 4, 1952

### MOST FAIR CATCHES, SEASON
25   Phil McConkey (1988)
22   Amani Toomer (1998)
20   David Meggett (1993)
19   Amani Toomer (1997)
18   Phil McConkey (1985)
16   Bobby Duhon (1971)
15   Phil McConkey (1984)
14   David Meggett (1994)
14   David Meggett (1989)
14   Phil McConkey (1987)
14   Pete Athas (1973)
14   Bob Grim (1972)
14   Carl Lockhart (1969)

### MOST FAIR CATCHES, CAREER
84   Phil McConkey (1984-88)
80   David Meggett (1989-94)
59   Carl Lockhart (1965-75)
51   Amani Toomer (1996-98)
40   Bobby Duhon (1968-72)

### FEWEST FAIR CATCHES, SEASON
0    Leon Bright (1983) 17 returns
0    Leon Bright (1982) 37 returns
0    Leon Bright (1981) 52 returns

### MOST FAIR CATCHES, GAME
5    Amani Toomer, at Dallas
     Sept. 8, 1996
5    Phil McConkey, vs. Philadelphia
     Nov. 20, 1988
4    Arthur Marshall, vs. New Orleans
     Dec. 15, 1996
4    David Meggett, vs. Pittsburgh
     Oct. 23, 1994
4    David Meggett, at Pittsburgh
     Oct. 14, 1991
4    Phil McConkey, at Philadelphia
     Sept. 29, 1985
4    Phil McConkey, at Rams
     Sept. 30, 1984
4    Phil McConkey, at Washington
     Sept. 16, 1984
4    Carl Lockhart, vs. Minnesota
     Oct. 31, 1971
4    Eddie Dove, at Cleveland
     Oct. 27, 1963
3    by many players
     Last: Amani Toomer, at Philadelphia
     Dec. 27, 1998

### MOST PUNT RETURNS YARDS, CAREER
2,230 David Meggett (1989-94)
2,206 Emlen Tunnell (1948-58)
1,708 Phil McConkey (1984-88)
1,005 Amani Toomer (1996-98)
852  Leon Bright (1981-83)
512  Bob Hammond (1976-79)
449  Pete Athas (1971-74)

### MOST PUNT RETURN YARDS, SEASON
582  David Meggett (1989)
489  Emlen Tunnell (1951)
467  David Meggett (1990)
455  Amani Toomer (1997)
442  Phil McConkey (1985)

### MOST PUNT RETURN YARDS, GAME
147  Emlen Tunnell, vs. Chicago Cardinals
     Oct. 14, 1951
143  Leon Bright, vs. Philadelphia
     Dec. 11, 1982
114  David Meggett, vs. Raiders
     Dec. 24, 1989
113  Amani Toomer, vs. Buffalo
     Sept. 1, 1996
112  Phil McConkey, vs. Philadelphia
     Dec. 6, 1987
107  David Meggett, at New Orleans
     Dec. 20, 1993
106  Emlen Tunnell, vs. Washington
     Dec. 7, 1952
103  Phil McConkey, vs. Philadelphia
     Sept. 8, 1985
103  Rondy Colbert, vs. New Orleans
     Dec. 14, 1975
101  Leon Bright, vs. Rams
     Dec. 6, 1981

### LONGEST PUNT RETURN
87T  Amani Toomer, vs. Buffalo
     Sept. 1 1996
83   Eddie Dove, at Philadelphia
     Sept. 29, 1963
81   Bosh Pritchard, at Chicago Cardinals
     Nov. 25, 1951
81   Emlen Tunell, vs. Chicago Cardinals
     Oct. 14, 1951
76T  David Meggett, vs. Raiders
     Dec. 24, 1989
75T  David Meggett, at New Orleans
     Dec. 20, 1993
74   Emlen Tunnell, at N.Y. Yanks
     Dec. 16, 1951

### HIGHEST AVERAGE RETURN, CAREER (30 RETURNS)
11.0 David Meggett (1989-94) 202 returns
10.1 Amani Toomer (1996-98) 100 returns
8.8  Pete Athas (1971-74) 51 returns
8.6  Emlen Tunnell (1948-58) 257 returns
8.5  Bob Hammond (1976-79) 60 returns
8.2  Alvin Garrett (1980-81) 35 returns
8.0  Leon Bright (1981-83) 106 returns
8.0  Phil McConkey (1984-88) 213 returns

### HIGHEST AVERAGE RETURN, SEASON (QUALIFIERS)
16.6 Amani Toomer (1996) 18 returns
15.5 Merle Hapes (1942) 11 returns
14.9 George Franck (1941) 13 returns
14.4 Emlen Tunnell (1951) 34 returns

### HIGHEST AVERAGE RETURN, GAME (3 RETURNS)
36.8 Emlen Tunnell, vs. Chicago Cardinals
     Oct. 14, 1951 (4 returns)
35.3 Emlen Tunnell vs. Washington
     Dec. 7, 1952 (3 returns)
32.7 David Meggett vs. Seattle
     Nov. 19, 1989 (3 returns)
31.0 Emlen Tunnell vs. Washington
     Oct. 7, 1951 (3 returns)

### MOST TOUCHDOWNS, CAREER
6    David Meggett (1989-94)
5    Emlen Tunnell (1948-58)
3    Amani Toomer (1996-98)
1    by many players

### MOST TOUCHDOWNS, SEASON
3    Emlen Tunnell (1951)
2    Amani Toomer (1996)
2    David Meggett (1994)
1    by many players
     Last: Amani Toomer (1997)

### MOST TOUCHDOWNS, GAME
1    Amani Toomer, at Detroit
     Oct. 19, 1997
1    Amani Toomer, vs. Philadelphia
     Oct. 13, 1996
1    Amani Toomer, vs. Buffalo
     Sept. 1, 1996
1    David Meggett, vs. Detroit
     Oct. 30, 1994
1    David Meggett, vs. Philadelphia
     Sept. 4, 1994
1    David Meggett, at New Orleans
     Dec. 20, 1993
1    David Meggett, at Tampa Bay
     Nov. 24, 1991
1    David Meggett, vs. Philadelphia
     Sept. 9, 1990
1    David Meggett, vs. Raiders
     Dec. 24, 1989
1    Bob Hammond, at Dallas
     Sept. 25, 1977
1    Rondy Colbert, vs. New Orleans
     Dec. 14, 1975
1    Bobby Duhon, vs. Philadelphia
     Oct. 11, 1970
1    Emlen Tunnell, vs. Philadelphia
     Nov. 20, 1955
1    Jimmy Patton, vs. Washington
     Oct. 30, 1955
1    Herb Johnson, vs. Cleveland
     Nov. 28, 1954
1    Emlen Tunnell, at N.Y. Yanks
     Dec. 16, 1951
1    Bosh Pritchard, at Chicago Cardinals
     Nov. 25, 1951
1    Emlen Tunnell, vs. Philadelphia
     Oct. 21, 1951
1    Emlen Tunnell, vs. Chicago Cardinals
     Oct. 14, 1951
1    Emlen Tunnell, vs. N.Y. Bulldogs
     Nov. 6, 1949
1    Vic Carroll, at Boston Yankees
     Oct. 8, 1944

## KICKOFF RETURNS

### MOST SEASONS LEADING LEAGUE
1    David Meggett (NFC, 1990)
1    Joe Scott (1948)
1    Clarence Childs (1964)

**171**

**MOST KICKOFF RETURNS, CAREER**

146  David Meggett (1989-94)
126  Clarence Childs (1964-67)
67   Phil McConkey (1984-88)
65   Rocky Thompson (1971-73)
54   Joe Scott (1948-53)

**MOST KICKOFF RETURNS, SEASON**

43   David Patten (1998)
41   Herschel Walker (1995)
36   Rocky Thompson (1971)
35   Ronnie Blye (1968)
34   Clarence Jones (1964, 1966)

**MOST KICKOFF RETURNS, GAME**

7    Tiki Barber, vs. Green Bay
     Nov. 15, 1998
7    Alvin Garrett, at San Diego
     Oct. 19, 1980
7    Gene Filipski, at Washington
     Nov. 18, 1956
6    Herschel Walker, at Seattle
     Nov. 11, 1995
6    Clarence Childs, at Cleveland
     Dec. 4, 1966
5    by many players
     Last time: David Patten, vs. Atlanta
     Oct. 11, 1998

**MOST KICKOFF RETURN YARDS, CAREER**

3,163  Clarence Childs (1964-67)
2,989  David Meggett (1989-94)
1,768  Rocky Thompson (1971-73)
1,467  Joe Scott (1948-53)
1,284  Phil McConkey (1984-88)
1,237  Thomas Lewis (1994-97)
1,215  Emlen Tunnell (1948-58)

**MOST KICKOFF RETURN YARDS, SEASON**

987  Clarence Childs (1964)
947  Rocky Thompson (1971)
928  David Patten (1998)
881  Herschel Walker (1995)
855  Clarence Childs (1966)

**MOST KICKOFF RETURN YARDS, GAME**

207  Joe Scott, vs. Rams
     Nov. 14, 1948
198  Rocky Thompson, at Detroit
     Sept. 17, 1972
170  Clarence Childs, at Cleveland
     Dec. 4, 1966
158  Clarence Childs, vs. Cleveland
     Oct. 24, 1965

**LONGEST KICKOFF RETURN**

100  Clarence Childs, vs. Minnesota
     Dec. 6, 1964
100  Emlen Tunnell, vs. N.Y. Yanks
     Nov. 4, 1951
99   Joe Scott, vs. Rams
     Nov. 14, 1948
98   Jimmy Patton vs. Washington
     Oct. 30, 1955

**HIGHEST AVERAGE RETURN, CAREER (40 RETURNS)**

27.2  Rocky Thompson (1971-73) 65 returns
27.2  Joe Scott (1948-53) 54 returns
26.4  Emlen Tunnell (1948-58) 46 returns
25.1  Clarence Childs (1964-67) 126 returns

**HIGHEST AVERAGE RETURN, SEASON (QUALIFIERS)**

31.6  John Salscheider (1949) 15 returns
30.2  John Counts (1962) 26 returns
29.0  Clarence Childs (1964) 34 returns

**HIGHEST AVERAGE RETURN, GAME (3 RETURNS)**

51.8  Joe Scott, vs. Rams
      Nov. 14, 1948 (4 returns)
50.3  Ronnie Blye, at Pittsburgh
      Sept. 15, 1968 (3 returns)
49.5  Rocky Thompson, at Detroit
      Sept. 17, 1972 (4 returns)
44.3  Emlen Tunnell, at Chicago Cardinals
      Nov. 1, 1953 (3 returns)

**MOST TOUCHDOWNS, CAREER**

2    Rocky Thompson (1971-73)
2    Clarence Childs (1964-67)
1    by many players
     Last: David Patten (1997-98)

**MOST TOUCHDOWNS, SEASON**

1    by many players, see next item

**MOST TOUCHDOWNS, GAME**

1    David Patten, at Washington
     Nov. 1, 1998 (90 yards)
1    Thomas Lewis, vs. Washington
     Dec. 10, 1995 (91 yards)
1    David Meggett, vs. Philadelphia
     Nov. 22, 1992 (92 yards)
1    Rocky Thompson, at Detroit
     Sept. 17, 1972 (92 yards)
1    Rocky Thompson, at St. Louis
     Oct. 3, 1971 (93 yards)
1    Clarence Childs, at Cleveland
     Dec. 4, 1966 (90 yards)
1    Clarence Childs, vs. Minnesota
     Dec. 6, 1964 (100 yards)
1    John Counts, at Washington
     Nov. 25, 1962 (90 yards)
1    Jimmy Patton, vs. Washington
     Oct. 30, 1955 (98 yards)
1    Emlen Tunnell, vs. N.Y. Yanks
     Nov. 4, 1951 (100 yards)
1    Jack Salschieder, at Chicago
     Oct. 30, 1949 (95 yards)
1    Joe Scott, vs. Rams
     Nov. 14, 1948 (99 yards)
1    Harry Neuman, at Boston
     Oct. 7, 1934 (93 yards)

**FUMBLES**

**MOST FUMBLES, CAREER**

93   Phil Simms (1979-93)
54   Charlie Conerly (1948-61)
48   Frank Gifford (1952-60, 62-64)
34   Alex Webster (1955-64)

**MOST FUMBLES, GAME**

5    Charlie Conerly, vs. San Francisco
     Dec. 1, 1957
4    Y. A. Tittle, at Philadelphia
     Sept. 13, 1964
3    by many players

**MOST FUMBLES, SEASON**

16   Phil Simms (1985)
11   Dave Brown (1994)
11   Y. A. Tittle (1964)

11   Bobby Gaiters (1961)
11   Charlie Conerly (1957)

**OWN RECOVERIES**

**MOST RECOVERED, CAREER**

30   Phil Simms (1979-93)
26   Charlie Conerly (1948-61)
16   Frank Gifford (1952-60, 62-64)
15   Joe Morrison (1959-72)

**MOST RECOVERED, SEASON**

6    Jeff Hostetler (1991)

5    Phil Simms (1993)
5    Phil Simms (1985)
5    Joe Wells (1961)
5    Frank Gifford (1958)
5    Charlie Conerly (1948, 57)
5    Emlen Tunnell (1952)
5    Gene Roberts (1950)
4    by many players

**MOST RECOVERED, GAME**

3    Jeff Hostetler, vs. Phoenix
     Oct. 21, 1990
2    by many players
     Last: Ottis Anderson, at San Francisco
     Dec. 3, 1990

**TOTAL RECOVERIES**

**MOST RECOVERED, CAREER**

30   Phil Simms (1979-93)
26   Charlie Conerly (1948-61)
19   Jim Katcavage (1956-68)
17   Harry Carson (1976-88)
16   Frank Gifford (1952-60, 62-64)
15   George Martin (1975-88)
15   Joe Morrison (1959-72)

**MOST RECOVERED, SEASON**

6    Jeff Hostetler (1991)
6    Emlen Tunnell (1952)
5    by many players

**MOST RECOVERED, GAME**

3    Jeff Hostetler, vs. Phoenix
     Oct. 21, 1990

**YARDS RETURNING FUMBLES**

**LONGEST FUMBLE RETURN**

87   Keith Hamilton, at Kansas City
     Sept. 10, 1995
81   Andy Headen, vs. Dallas
     Sept. 9, 1984 (td)
72   Wendell Harris, at Pittsburgh
     Sept. 11, 1966 (td)
71   Roy Hilton, vs. Dallas
     Oct. 27, 1974 (td)
67   Horace Sherrod, vs. Washington
     Dec. 7, 1952
65   Lindon Crow, vs. St. Louis
     Oct. 30, 1960 (td)

**MOST TOUCHDOWNS, CAREER (TOTAL)**

2    Tito Wooten (1995, 96, 1-opp)
2    George Martin (1981, 2-opp)
2    Sam Huff (1959, 63, 2-opp)
2    Tom Landry (1950, 51 2-opp)
2    Al De Rogatis (1949, 50, 2-opp)

**MOST TOUCHDOWNS, SEASON (TOTAL)**

2    George Martin, at Washington,
     Sept. 13, 1981 (8 yards) and
     at St. Louis, Dec. 13, 1981 (20 yards)

**MOST TOUCHDOWNS, GAME (TOTAL)**

1    by many players
     Last: Tito Wooten, vs. Dallas
     Nov. 24, 1996 (54 yards)

**QUARTERBACK SACKS**

**(ONLY SINCE 1982)**

**MOST SACKS, CAREER**

132.5  Lawrence Taylor (1981-93)
79.5   Leonard Marshall (1983-92)
47.0   Michael Strahan (1993-98)
46.0   George Martin (1982-88)

**MOST SACKS, SEASON**

20.5  Lawrence Taylor (1986)
15.5  Lawrence Taylor (1988)
15.5  Leonard Marshall (1985)
15.0  Michael Strahan (1998)
15.0  Lawrence Taylor (1989)
14.0  Michael Strahan (1997)
13.5  Lawrence Taylor (1985)

**MOST SACKS, GAME**

4.5  Pepper Johnson, at Tampa Bay
     Nov. 24, 1991
4.0  Lawrence Taylor, vs. Philadelphia
     Oct. 12, 1986
4.0  Lawrence Taylor, vs. Tampa Bay
     Sept. 23, 1984
3.0  Michael Strahan, vs. Arizona
     Nov. 16, 1997
3.0  Michael Strahan, at Green Bay
     Sept. 17, 1995
3.0  Keith Hamilton, vs. Tampa Bay
     Sept. 12, 1993
3.0  Lawrence Taylor, vs. Philadelphia
     Sept. 9, 1990
3.0  Lawrence Taylor, at Phoenix
     Nov. 5, 1989
3.0  Lawrence Taylor, at New Orleanns
     Nov. 27, 1988
3.0  Lawrence Taylor, vs. Detroit
     Oct. 16, 1988
3.0  Lawrence Taylor, at Washington
     Dec. 7, 1986
3.0  Lawrence Taylor, at Philadelphia
     Nov. 9, 1986
3.0  Lawrence Taylor, vs. Washington
     Oct. 27, 1986
3.0  Leonard Marshall, at St. Louis
     Nov. 24, 1985
3.0  George Martin, at St. Louis
     Nov. 24, 1985
3.0  Leonard Marshall, at Philadelphia
     Sept. 29, 1985
3.0  Leonard Marshall, vs. Philadelphia
     Sept. 8, 1985
3.0  Lawrence Taylor, vs. Dallas
     Sept. 9, 1984
3.0  Lawrence Taylor, at Washington
     Dec. 17, 1983
3.0  George Martin, vs. Houston
     Dec. 5, 1982
3.0  Lawrence Taylor, vs. Philadelphia
     Dec. 11, 1982

## TOP TEN RUSHERS
### (Based on Rushing Yardage)

| Player | Years | Attempts | Yards | Avg | Lg | TDs |
|---|---|---|---|---|---|---|
| 1. Rodney Hampton | 1990-97 | 1,824 | 6,897 | 3.8 | 63t | 49 |
| 2. Joe Morris | 1982-89 | 1,318 | 5,296 | 4.0 | 65t | 48 |
| 3. Alex Webster | 1955-64 | 1,196 | 4.638 | 3.9 | 71 | 39 |
| 4. Ron Johnson | 1970-75 | 1,066 | 3,836 | 3.6 | 68 | 33 |
| 5. Frank Gifford | 1952-60, 62-64 | 840 | 3,609 | 4.3 | 79 | 34 |
| 6. Doug Kotar | 1974-81 | 900 | 3,378 | 3.8 | 53 | 20 |
| 7. Eddie Price | 1950-55 | 846 | 3,292 | 3.9 | 74 | 23 |
| 8. Tuffy Leemans | 1936-43 | 919 | 3,142 | 3.4 | NA | 20 |
| 9. Rob Carpenter | 1981-85 | 737 | 2,572 | 3.5 | 46 | 17 |
| 10. Joe Morrison | 1959-72 | 677 | 2,472 | 3.7 | 70 | 18 |

## TOP TEN PASSERS
### (Based on Passing Yardage)

| Player | Years | Att. | Comp. | Yards | Pct. | TDs | Ints |
|---|---|---|---|---|---|---|---|
| 1. Phil Simms | 1979-93 | 4,647 | 2,576 | 33,462 | 55.4 | 199 | 157 |
| 2. Charlie Conerly | 1948-61 | 2,833 | 1,418 | 19,488 | 50.0 | 173 | 167 |
| 3. Fran Tarkenton | 1967-71 | 1,898 | 1,051 | 13,905 | 55.4 | 103 | 72 |
| 4. Y.A. Tittle | 1961-64 | 1,308 | 731 | 10,439 | 55.9 | 96 | 68 |
| 5. Dave Brown | 1992-97 | 1,391 | 766 | 8,806 | 55.1 | 40 | 49 |
| 6. Scott Brunner | 1980-83 | 986 | 482 | 6,121 | 48.9 | 28 | 48 |
| 7. Craig Morton | 1974-76 | 884 | 461 | 5,734 | 52.1 | 29 | 49 |
| 8. Jeff Hostetler | 1984-92 | 632 | 365 | 4,409 | 57.8 | 20 | 12 |
| 9. Norm Snead | 1972-74,76 | 602 | 349 | 4,029 | 57.9 | 24 | 38 |
| 10. Joe Pisarcik | 1977-79 | 650 | 289 | 3,979 | 44.5 | 18 | 43 |

## TOP TEN RECEIVERS
### (Based on Number of Receptions)

| Player | Years | No. | Yards | Avg | Lg | TD |
|---|---|---|---|---|---|---|
| 1. Joe Morrison | 1959-72 | 395 | 4,993 | 12.6 | 70 | 47 |
| 2. Frank Gifford | 1952-60, 62-64 | 367 | 5,434 | 14.8 | 77 | 43 |
| 3. Chris Calloway | 1992-98 | 334 | 4,710 | 14.1 | 68T | 27 |
| 4. Bob Tucker | 1970-77 | 327 | 4,376 | 13.4 | 63 | 22 |
| 5. Kyle Rote | 1951-61 | 300 | 4,795 | 15.9 | 75 | 48 |
| 6. Mark Bavaro | 1985-90 | 266 | 3,722 | 13.9 | 61 | 28 |
| 7. Aaron Thomas | 1962-70 | 247 | 4,253 | 17.2 | 71 | 35 |
| 8. Earnest Gray | 1979-84 | 243 | 3,768 | 15.5 | 62 | 27 |
| 9. Alex Webster | 1955-64 | 240 | 2,679 | 11.2 | 59 | 17 |
| 10. Del Shofner | 1961-67 | 239 | 4,315 | 18.1 | 70 | 35 |

## TOP TEN SCORERS
### (Based on Total Points)

| Player | Years | Touchdowns | | | | Kicking | | Total |
|---|---|---|---|---|---|---|---|---|
| | | Tot | Rush | Rec | Ret | FGs | PATs | Points |
| 1. Pete Gogolak | 1966-74 | 0 | 0 | 0 | 0 | 126 | 268 | 646 |
| 2. Frank Gifford | 1952-60, 62-64 | 78 | 34 | 43 | 1 | 2 | 10 | 484 |
| 3. Joe Danelo | 1976-82 | 0 | 0 | 0 | 0 | 104 | 170 | 482 |
| 4. Brad Daluiso | 1993-98 | 0 | 0 | 0 | 0 | 99 | 114 | 411 |
| 5. Joe Morrison | 1959-72 | 65 | 18 | 47 | 0 | 0 | 0 | 390 |
| 6. Raul Allegre | 1986-91 | 0 | 0 | 0 | 0 | 77 | 109 | 340 |
| 7. Alex Webster | 1955-64 | 56 | 39 | 17 | 0 | 0 | 0 | 336 |
| 8. Ken Strong | 1933-35, 39-47 | 13 | 12 | 1 | 0 | 35 | 141 | 324 |
| 9. Pat Summerall | 1958-61 | 0 | 0 | 0 | 0 | 59 | 136 | 313 |
| 10. Kyle Rote | 1951-61 | 52 | 4 | 48 | 0 | 0 | 0 | 312 |

## TOP TEN INTERCEPTORS
### (Based on Number of Interceptions)

| Player | Years | No | Ret. Yds | Avg | TD |
|---|---|---|---|---|---|
| 1. Emlen Tunnell | 1949-58 | 74 | 1,240 | 16.7 | 4 |
| 2. Jim Patton | 1955-66 | 52 | 712 | 13.7 | 2 |
| 3. Carl Lockhart | 1965-75 | 41 | 475 | 11.6 | 3 |
| 4. Dick Lynch | 1959-66 | 35 | 568 | 16.2 | 4 |
| 5. Willie Williams | 1965, 67-73 | 35 | 462 | 13.2 | 0 |
| 6. Tom Landry | 1950-55 | 31 | 360 | 11.6 | 3 |
| 7. Terry Kinard | 1983-89 | 27 | 574 | 21.3 | 2 |
| 8. Terry Jackson | 1978-83 | 24 | 282 | 11.8 | 2 |
| 9.Phillippi Sparks | 1992-98 | 21 | 135 | 6.4 | 0 |
| 10. Frank Reagan | 1941, 46-48 | 20 | 376 | 18.8 | 0 |
| 11. Howard Livingston | 1944-47 | 20 | 375 | 18.8 | 1 |

## TOP TEN PUNT RETURNERS
### (Based on Return Yardage)

| Player | Years | No | FC | Yds. | Avg. | Long | TD |
|---|---|---|---|---|---|---|---|
| 1. David Meggett | 1989-94 | 202 | 80 | 2,230 | 11.0 | 76t | 6 |
| 2. Emlen Tunnell | 1948-58 | 257 | NA | 2,206 | 8.6 | 74 | 5 |
| 3. Phil McConkey | 1984-88 | 213 | 84 | 1,708 | 8.0 | 37 | 0 |
| 4. Amani Toomer | 1996-98 | 100 | 51 | 1,005 | 10.1 | 87T | 3 |
| 5. Leon Bright | 1981-83 | 106 | 0 | 852 | 8.0 | 55 | 0 |
| 6. Bob Hammond | 1976-79 | 60 | 14 | 512 | 8.5 | 68t | 1 |
| 7. Pete Athas | 1971-74 | 51 | 22 | 449 | 8.8 | 48 | 0 |
| 8. Carl Lockhart | 1965-75 | 63 | 59 | 328 | 5.2 | 28 | 0 |
| 9. Jimmy Robinson | 1976-79 | 56 | 21 | 328 | 5.6 | 50 | 0 |
| 10. Randy Colbert | 1974-76 | 40 | 1 | 310 | 7.8 | 65t | 1 |

## TOP TEN KICKOFF RETURNERS
### (Based on Return Yardage)

| Player | Years | No | Yds. | Avg | Long | TD |
|---|---|---|---|---|---|---|
| 1. Clarence Childs | 1964-67 | 126 | 3,163 | 25.1 | 100 | 2 |
| 2. David Meggett | 1989-94 | 146 | 2,989 | 20.5 | 92t | 1 |
| 3. Rocky Thompson | 1971-73 | 65 | 1,768 | 27.2 | 93 | 2 |
| 4. Joe Scott | 1948-53 | 54 | 1,467 | 27.2 | NA | 1 |
| 5. Phil McConkey | 1984-88 | 67 | 1,284 | 19.2 | 43 | 0 |
| 6. Thomas Lewis | 1994-97 | 53 | 1,237 | 23.3 | 91T | 1 |
| 7. Emlen Tunnell | 1948-58 | 46 | 1,215 | 26.4 | 100t | 1 |
| 8. David Patten | 1997-98 | 51 | 1,051 | 20.6 | 90T | 1 |
| 9. Bob Hammond | 1976-79 | 47 | 983 | 20.9 | 39 | 0 |
| 10. Doug Kotar | 1974-81 | 42 | 920 | 22.0 | 64 | 0 |

## TOP TEN SACK LEADERS

| | Player | Years | Sacks |
|---|---|---|---|
| 1. | Lawrence Taylor | 1981-93 | 142.0 |
| 2. | Jim Katcavage | 1956-68 | 96.5 |
| 3. | George Martin | 1975-88 | 96.0 |
| 4. | Leonard Marshall | 1983-92 | 79.5 |
| 5. | Andy Robustelli | 1956-64 | 79.0 |
| 6. | Jack Gregory | 1972-78 | 65.0 |
| 7. | Michael Strahan | 1993-98 | 47.0 |
| 8. | Keith Hamilton | 1992-98 | 41.5 |
| 9. | John Mendenhall | 1972-79 | 39.5 |
| 10. | Carl Banks | 1984-92 | 36.0 |

GIANTS SEASON LEADERS

## SCORING

| | | TD | PAT | FG | PTS |
|---|---|---|---|---|---|
| 1925 | Jack McBride | 2 | 7 | 2 | 25 |
| 1926 | Jack McBride | 5 | 15 | 1 | 48 |
| 1927 | Jack McBride | 6 | 15 | 2 | 57 |
| 1928 | Henry Haines | 5 | 0 | 0 | 30 |
| 1929 | Len Sedbrook | 11 | 0 | 0 | 66 |
| 1930 | Bennie Friedman | 7 | 12 | 1 | 57 |
| 1931 | Hap Moran | 4 | 8 | 1 | 35 |
| 1932 | Ray Flaherty | 5 | 0 | 0 | 30 |
| 1933 | Ken Strong | 6 | 13 | 5 | 64 |
| 1934 | Ken Strong | 6 | 8 | 4 | 56 |
| 1935 | Dale Burnett | 6 | 0 | 0 | 36 |
| 1936 | Tillie Manton | 1 | 15 | 0 | 21 |
| 1937 | Ward Cuff | 4 | 0 | 2 | 30 |
| 1938 | Ward Cuff | 2 | 18 | 5 | 45 |
| 1939 | Ward Cuff | 2 | 6 | 7 | 39 |
| 1940 | Ward Cuff | 2 | 9 | 5 | 36 |
| 1941 | Ward Cuff | 2 | 19 | 5 | 46 |
| 1942 | Ward Cuff | 2 | 18 | 3 | 39 |
| 1943 | Bill Paschal | 12 | 0 | 0 | 72 |
| 1944 | Bill Paschal | 9 | 0 | 0 | 54 |
| 1945 | Frank Liebel | 10 | 0 | 0 | 60 |
| 1946 | Ken Strong | 0 | 32 | 4 | 44 |
| 1947 | Ken Strong | 0 | 24 | 2 | 30 |
| 1948 | Bill Swiacki | 10 | 0 | 0 | 60 |
| 1949 | Gene Roberts | 17 | 0 | 0 | 102 |
| 1950 | Ray Poole | 0 | 30 | 5 | 45 |
| 1951 | Ray Poole | 0 | 30 | 12 | 66 |
| 1952 | Ray Poole | 0 | 26 | 10 | 56 |
| 1953 | Frank Gifford | 7 | 2 | 1 | 47 |
| 1954 | Ben Agajanian | 0 | 35 | 13 | 74 |
| 1955 | Ben Agajanian | 0 | 32 | 10 | 62 |
| 1956 | Frank Gifford | 9 | 8 | 1 | 65 |
| 1957 | Ben Agajanian | 0 | 32 | 10 | 62 |
| 1958 | Pat Summerall | 0 | 28 | 12 | 64 |
| 1959 | Pat Summerall | 0 | 30 | 20 | 90 |
| 1960 | Pat Summerall | 0 | 32 | 13 | 71 |
| 1961 | Pat Summerall | 0 | 46 | 14 | 88 |
| 1962 | Don Chandler | 0 | *47 | 19 | 104 |
| 1963 | Don Chandler | 0 | 52 | 18 | 106 |
| 1964 | Don Chandler | 0 | 27 | 9 | 54 |
| 1965 | Tucker Frederickson | 6 | 0 | 0 | 36 |
| | Homer Jones | 6 | 0 | 0 | 36 |
| 1966 | Pete Gogolak | 0 | 29 | 16 | 77 |
| 1967 | Homer Jones | 14 | 0 | 0 | 84 |
| 1968 | Pete Gogolak | 0 | 36 | 14 | 78 |
| 1969 | Pete Gogolak | 0 | 33 | 11 | 66 |
| | Joe Morrison | 11 | 0 | 0 | 66 |
| 1970 | Pete Gogolak | 0 | 32 | 25 | 107 |
| 1971 | Pete Gogolak | 0 | 30 | 6 | 48 |
| 1972 | Pete Gogolak | 0 | 34 | 21 | 97 |
| 1973 | Pete Gogolak | 0 | 25 | 17 | 76 |
| 1974 | Pete Gogolak | 0 | 21 | 10 | 51 |
| 1975 | George Hunt | 0 | 24 | 6 | 42 |
| 1976 | Joe Danelo | 0 | 20 | 8 | 44 |
| 1977 | Joe Danelo | 0 | 19 | 14 | 61 |
| 1978 | Joe Danelo | 0 | 27 | 21 | 90 |
| 1979 | Billy Taylor | 11 | 0 | 0 | 66 |
| 1980 | Joe Danelo | 0 | 27 | 16 | 75 |
| 1981 | Joe Danelo | 0 | 31 | 24 | 103 |
| 1982 | Joe Danelo | 0 | 18 | 12 | 54 |
| 1983 | Ali Haji-Sheikh | 0 | 22 | *35 | *127 |
| 1984 | Ali Haji-Sheikh | 0 | 32 | 17 | 83 |
| 1985 | Joe Morris | 21 | 0 | 0 | 126 |
| 1986 | Raul Allegre | 0 | *33 | 24 | 105 |
| 1987 | Raul Allegre | 0 | 25 | 17 | 76 |
| 1988 | Paul McFadden | 0 | 25 | 14 | 67 |
| 1989 | Ottis Anderson | 14 | 0 | 0 | 84 |
| 1990 | Matt Bahr | 0 | 29 | 17 | 80 |
| 1991 | Matt Bahr | 0 | 24 | 22 | 90 |
| 1992 | Rodney Hampton | 14 | 0 | 0 | 84 |
| 1993 | David Treadwell | 0 | 28 | 25 | 103 |
| 1994 | David Treadwell | 0 | 22 | 11 | 55 |
| 1995 | Brad Daluiso | 0 | 28 | 20 | 88 |
| 1996 | Brad Daluiso | 0 | 22 | 24 | 94 |
| 1997 | Brad Daluiso | 0 | 27 | 22 | 93 |
| 1998 | Brad Daluiso | 0 | 32 | 21 | 95 |

* All-Time Single Season Club Record

## RUSHING

| | | YDS | ATT | TD |
|---|---|---|---|---|
| 1932 | John McBride | 302 | 84 | 1 |
| 1933 | Harry Newman | 437 | 130 | 3 |
| 1934 | Harry Newman | 483 | 141 | 3 |
| 1935 | Elvin Richards | 449 | 153 | 4 |
| 1936 | Tuffy Leemans | 830 | 206 | 2 |
| 1937 | Hank Soar | 442 | 120 | 2 |
| 1938 | Tuffy Leemans | 463 | 121 | 4 |
| 1939 | Tuffy Leemans | 429 | 128 | 3 |
| 1940 | Tuffy Leemans | 474 | 132 | 1 |
| 1941 | Tuffy Leemans | 332 | 100 | 4 |
| 1942 | Merle Hapes | 363 | 95 | 3 |
| 1943 | Bill Paschal | 572 | 147 | 10 |
| 1944 | Bill Paschal | 737 | 196 | 9 |
| 1945 | Bill Paschal | 247 | 59 | 2 |
| 1946 | Frank Filchock | 371 | 98 | 2 |
| 1947 | Gene Roberts | 296 | 86 | 1 |
| 1948 | Gene Roberts | 491 | 145 | 0 |
| 1949 | Gene Roberts | 634 | 152 | 9 |
| 1950 | Eddie Price | 703 | 126 | 4 |
| 1951 | Eddie Price | 971 | 271 | 7 |
| 1952 | Eddie Price | 748 | 183 | 5 |
| 1953 | Sonny Grandelius | 278 | 108 | 1 |
| 1954 | Eddie Price | 555 | 135 | 2 |
| 1955 | Alex Webster | 634 | 128 | 5 |
| 1956 | Frank Gifford | 819 | 159 | 5 |
| 1957 | Frank Gifford | 528 | 136 | 5 |
| 1958 | Frank Gifford | 468 | 115 | 8 |
| 1959 | Frank Gifford | 540 | 106 | 3 |
| 1960 | Mel Triplett | 573 | 124 | 4 |
| 1961 | Alex Webster | 928 | 196 | 2 |
| 1962 | Alex Webster | 743 | 207 | 5 |
| 1963 | Phil King | 613 | 161 | 3 |
| 1964 | Ernie Wheelwright | 402 | 100 | 0 |
| 1965 | Tucker Frederickson | 659 | 195 | 5 |
| 1966 | Chuck Mercein | 327 | 94 | 0 |
| 1967 | Ernie Koy | 704 | 146 | 4 |
| 1968 | Tucker Frederickson | 486 | 142 | 1 |
| 1969 | Joe Morrison | 387 | 107 | 4 |
| 1970 | Ron Johnson | 1,027 | 263 | 8 |
| 1971 | Bobby Duhon | 344 | 93 | 1 |
| 1972 | Ron Johnson | 1,182 | 298 | 9 |
| 1973 | Ron Johnson | 902 | 260 | 6 |
| 1974 | Joe Dawkins | 561 | 156 | 2 |
| 1975 | Joe Dawkins | 438 | 129 | 2 |
| 1976 | Doug Kotar | 731 | 185 | 3 |
| 1977 | Bob Hammond | 577 | 154 | 3 |
| 1978 | Doug Kotar | 625 | 149 | 1 |
| 1979 | Billy Taylor | 700 | 198 | 7 |
| 1980 | Billy Taylor | 580 | 147 | 4 |
| 1981 | Rob Carpenter | 748 | 190 | 5 |
| 1982 | Butch Woolfolk | 439 | 112 | 2 |
| 1983 | Butch Woolfolk | 857 | 246 | 2 |
| 1984 | Rob Carpenter | 795 | 250 | 7 |
| 1985 | Joe Morris | 1,336 | 294 | *2 |
| 1986 | Joe Morris | *1,516 | *341 | 14 |
| 1987 | Joe Morris | 658 | 193 | 3 |
| 1988 | Joe Morris | 1,083 | 307 | 5 |
| 1989 | Ottis Anderson | 1,023 | 325 | 14 |
| 1990 | Ottis Anderson | 784 | 225 | 11 |
| 1991 | Rodney Hampton | 1,059 | 256 | 10 |
| 1992 | Rodney Hampton | 1,141 | 247 | 14 |
| 1993 | Rodney Hampton | 1,077 | 292 | 5 |
| 1994 | Rodney Hampton | 1,075 | 327 | 6 |
| 1995 | Rodney Hampton | 1,182 | 306 | 10 |
| 1996 | Rodney Hampton | 827 | 254 | 1 |
| 1997 | Charles Way | 698 | 151 | 4 |
| 1998 | Gary Brown | 247 | 1,063 | 5 |

*All-Time Single Season Club Record

## PASSING

| | | ATT. | COMP. | YDS. | TD | INT. |
|---|---|---|---|---|---|---|
| 1932 | John McBride | 74 | 36 | 363 | 6 | 9 |
| 1933 | Harry Newman | 136 | 53 | 973 | 11 | 17 |
| 1934 | Harry Newman | 93 | 35 | 391 | 1 | 12 |
| 1935 | Ed Danowski | 113 | 57 | 794 | 10 | 9 |
| 1936 | Ed Danowski | 104 | 47 | 515 | 5 | 10 |
| 1937 | Ed Danowski | 134 | 66 | 814 | 8 | 5 |
| 1938 | Ed Danowski | 129 | 70 | 848 | 7 | 8 |
| 1939 | Ed Danowski | 101 | 42 | 437 | 3 | 6 |
| 1940 | Ed Miller | 73 | 35 | 505 | 4 | 7 |
| 1941 | Tuffy Leemans | 66 | 31 | 475 | 4 | 5 |
| 1942 | Tuffy Leemans | 69 | 35 | 555 | 7 | 4 |
| 1943 | Tuffy Leemans | 87 | 37 | 360 | 5 | 5 |
| 1944 | Arnie Herber | 86 | 36 | 651 | 6 | 8 |
| 1945 | Arnie Herber | 80 | 35 | 641 | 9 | 8 |
| 1946 | Frank Filchock | 169 | 87 | 1,262 | 12 | *25 |
| 1947 | Paul Governali | 197 | 85 | 1,461 | 14 | 16 |
| 1948 | Charlie Conerly | 299 | 162 | 2,175 | 22 | 13 |
| 1949 | Charlie Conerly | 305 | 152 | 2,138 | 17 | 20 |
| 1950 | Charlie Conerly | 132 | 56 | 1,000 | 8 | 7 |
| 1951 | Charlie Conerly | 189 | 93 | 1,277 | 10 | 22 |
| 1952 | Charlie Conerly | 169 | 82 | 1,090 | 13 | 10 |
| 1953 | Charlie Conerly | 303 | 143 | 1,711 | 13 | *25 |
| 1954 | Charlie Conerly | 210 | 103 | 1,439 | 17 | 11 |
| 1955 | Charlie Conerly | 202 | 98 | 1,310 | 13 | 13 |
| 1956 | Charlie Conerly | 174 | 90 | 1,143 | 10 | 7 |
| 1957 | Charlie Conerly | 232 | 128 | 1,712 | 11 | 11 |
| 1958 | Charlie Conerly | 184 | 88 | 1,199 | 10 | 9 |
| 1959 | Charlie Conerly | 194 | 113 | 1,706 | 14 | 4 |
| 1960 | George Shaw | 155 | 76 | 1,263 | 11 | 13 |
| 1961 | Y. A. Tittle | 285 | 163 | 2,272 | 17 | 12 |
| 1962 | Y. A. Tittle | 375 | 200 | 3,224 | 33 | 20 |
| 1963 | Y. A. Tittle | 367 | 221 | 3,145 | *36 | 14 |
| 1964 | Y. A. Tittle | 281 | 147 | 1,798 | 10 | 22 |
| 1965 | Earl Morrall | 302 | 155 | 2,446 | 22 | 12 |
| 1966 | Gary Wood | 170 | 81 | 1,142 | 6 | 13 |
| 1967 | Fran Tarkenton | 377 | 204 | 3,088 | 29 | 19 |
| 1968 | Fran Tarkenton | 337 | 182 | 2,555 | 21 | 12 |
| 1969 | Fran Tarkenton | 409 | 220 | 2,918 | 23 | 8 |
| 1970 | Fran Tarkenton | 389 | 219 | 2,777 | 19 | 12 |
| 1971 | Fran Tarkenton | 386 | 226 | 2,567 | 11 | 21 |
| 1972 | Norm Snead | 325 | 196 | 2,307 | 17 | 12 |
| 1973 | Norm Snead | 235 | 131 | 1,483 | 7 | 8 |
| 1974 | Craig Morton | 237 | 122 | 1,510 | 9 | 13 |
| 1975 | Craig Morton | 363 | 186 | 2,359 | 11 | 16 |
| 1976 | Craig Morton | 284 | 153 | 1,865 | 9 | 20 |
| 1977 | Joe Pisarcik | 241 | 103 | 1,346 | 4 | 14 |
| 1978 | Joe Pisarcik | 301 | 143 | 2,096 | 12 | 23 |
| 1979 | Phil Simms | 265 | 134 | 1,743 | 13 | 14 |
| 1980 | Phil Simms | 402 | 193 | 2,321 | 15 | 19 |
| 1981 | Phil Simms | 316 | 172 | 2,031 | 11 | 9 |
| 1982 | Scott Brunner | 298 | 161 | 2,017 | 10 | 9 |
| 1983 | Scott Brunner | 386 | 190 | 2,516 | 9 | 22 |
| 1984 | Phil Simms | *533 | *286 | *4,044 | 22 | 18 |
| 1985 | Phil Simms | 495 | 275 | 3,829 | 22 | 20 |
| 1986 | Phil Simms | 468 | 259 | 3,487 | 21 | 22 |
| 1987 | Phil Simms | 282 | 163 | 2,230 | 17 | 9 |
| 1988 | Phil Simms | 479 | 263 | 3'359 | 21 | 11 |
| 1989 | Phil Simms | 405 | 228 | 3,061 | 14 | 14 |
| 1990 | Phil Simms | 311 | 184 | 2,284 | 15 | 4 |
| 1991 | Jeff Hostetler | 285 | 179 | 2,032 | 5 | 4 |
| 1992 | Jeff Hostetler | 192 | 103 | 1,225 | 8 | 3 |
| 1993 | Phil Simms | 400 | 247 | 3,038 | 15 | 9 |
| 1994 | Dave Brown | 350 | 201 | 2,536 | 12 | 16 |
| 1995 | Dave Brown | 456 | 254 | 2,814 | 11 | 10 |
| 1996 | Dave Brown | 398 | 214 | 2,412 | 12 | 20 |
| 1997 | Danny Kanell | 294 | 156 | 1,740 | 11 | 9 |
| 1998 | Danny Kanell | 299 | 160 | 1,603 | 11 | 10 |

*All-Time Single Season Club Record

## RECEIVING

| | | NO | YDS | TD |
|---|---|---|---|---|
| 1932 | Ray Flaherty | 21 | 350 | 5 |
| 1933 | Dale Burnett | 12 | 212 | 3 |
| 1934 | Morris Badgro | 16 | 206 | 1 |
| 1935 | Tod Goodwin | 26 | 432 | 4 |
| 1936 | Dale Burnett | 16 | 246 | 3 |
| 1937 | Tuffy Leemans | 11 | 157 | 1 |
| 1938 | Hank Soar | 13 | 164 | 2 |
| | Dale Burnett | 13 | 145 | 1 |
| 1939 | Hank Soar | 12 | 134 | 0 |
| 1940 | Leland Shaffer | 15 | 121 | 2 |
| 1941 | Ward Cuff | 19 | 317 | 2 |
| 1942 | Ward Cuff | 16 | 267 | 2 |
| 1943 | Bill Walls | 14 | 231 | 2 |
| 1944 | O'Neal Adams | 14 | 342 | 1 |
| 1945 | Frank Liebel | 22 | 593 | 10 |
| 1946 | Ray Poole | 24 | 307 | 3 |
| 1947 | Ray Poole | 23 | 395 | 4 |
| 1948 | Bill Swiacki | 39 | 550 | 10 |
| 1949 | Bill Swiacki | 47 | 652 | 4 |
| 1950 | Bill Swiacki | 20 | 280 | 3 |
| 1951 | Joe Scott | 23 | 356 | 2 |
| 1952 | Bill Stribling | 26 | 399 | 5 |
| 1953 | Kyle Rote | 26 | 440 | 5 |
| | Eddie Price | 26 | 233 | 1 |
| 1954 | Bob Schnelker | 30 | 550 | 8 |
| 1955 | Frank Gifford | 33 | 437 | 4 |
| 1956 | Frank Gifford | 51 | 603 | 4 |
| 1957 | Frank Gifford | 41 | 588 | 4 |
| 1958 | Frank Gifford | 29 | 330 | 2 |
| 1959 | Frank Gifford | 42 | 768 | 4 |
| 1960 | Kyle Rote | 42 | 750 | 2 |
| 1961 | Del Shofner | 68 | 1,125 | 11 |
| 1962 | Del Shofner | 53 | 1,133 | 12 |
| 1963 | Del Shofner | 64 | 1,181 | 9 |
| 1964 | Aaron Thomas | 43 | 624 | 6 |
| 1965 | Joe Morrison | 41 | 574 | 4 |
| 1966 | Homer Jones | 48 | 1,044 | 8 |
| 1967 | Aaron Thomas | 51 | 877 | 9 |
| 1968 | Homer Jones | 45 | 1,057 | 7 |
| 1969 | Joe Morrison | 44 | 647 | 7 |
| 1970 | Clifton McNeil | 50 | 764 | 4 |
| 1971 | Bob Tucker | 59 | 791 | 4 |
| 1972 | Bob Tucker | 55 | 764 | 4 |
| 1973 | Bob Tucker | 50 | 681 | 5 |
| 1974 | Joe Dawkins | 46 | 332 | 3 |
| 1975 | Walker Gillette | 43 | 600 | 2 |
| 1976 | Bob Tucker | 42 | 498 | 1 |
| 1977 | Jim Robinson | 22 | 422 | 1 |
| 1978 | Jim Robinson | 32 | 620 | 2 |
| | Johnny Perkins | 32 | 514 | 3 |
| 1979 | Gary Shirk | 31 | 471 | 2 |
| 1980 | Earnest Gray | 52 | 777 | 10 |
| 1981 | Johnny Perkins | 51 | 858 | 6 |
| 1982 | Tom Mullady | 27 | 287 | 0 |
| 1983 | Earnest Gray | *78 | 1,139 | 5 |
| 1984 | Zeke Mowatt | 48 | 698 | 7 |
| | Bob Johnson | 48 | 795 | 6 |
| 1985 | Lionel Manuel | 49 | 859 | 6 |
| 1986 | Mark Bavaro | 66 | 1,001 | 4 |
| 1987 | Mark Bavaro | 55 | 867 | 8 |
| 1988 | Lionel Manuel | 65 | 1,029 | 4 |
| 1989 | Odessa Turner | 38 | 467 | 4 |
| 1990 | David Meggett | 39 | 410 | 1 |
| 1991 | Mark Ingram | 51 | 824 | 3 |

| | | | | |
|---|---|---|---|---|
| 1992 | Ed McCaffrey | 49 | 610 | 5 |
| 1993 | Mark Jackson | 58 | 708 | 4 |
| 1994 | Mike Sherrard | 53 | 825 | 6 |
| 1995 | Chris Calloway | 56 | 796 | 3 |
| 1996 | Chris Calloway | 53 | 739 | 4 |
| | Thomas Lewis | 53 | 694 | 4 |
| 1997 | Chris Calloway | 58 | 849 | 8 |
| 1998 | Chris Callloway | 62 | 812 | 6 |

* All-Time Single Season Club Record

## INTERCEPTIONS

| | | NO | YDS |
|---|---|---|---|
| 1940 | Doug Oldershaw | 4 | 48 |
| | Leland Shaffer | 4 | 14 |
| 1941 | Ward Cuff | 4 | 152 |
| | George Franck | 4 | 94 |
| 1942 | Merle Hapes | 3 | 49 |
| | Hank Soar | 3 | 31 |
| 1943 | Dave Brown | 6 | 64 |
| 1944 | Howard Livingston | 9 | 172 |
| | Pete Athas | 4 | 11 |
| 1945 | Howard Livingston | 3 | 65 |
| 1946 | Frank Liebel | 5 | 117 |
| 1947 | Frank Reagan | 10 | 203 |
| 1948 | Frank Reagan | 9 | 145 |
| 1949 | Emlen Tunnel | 10 | 251 |
| 1950 | Otto Schnellbacher | 8 | 99 |
| 1951 | Otto Schnellbacher | *11 | 194 |
| 1952 | Tom Landry | 8 | 99 |

| | | | |
|---|---|---|---|
| 1953 | Emlen Tunnell | 6 | 117 |
| 1954 | Emlen Tunnell | 8 | 108 |
| | Tom Landry | 8 | 71 |
| 1955 | Emlen Tunnell | 7 | 76 |
| 1956 | Emlen Tunnell | 6 | 87 |
| 1957 | Emlen Tunnell | 6 | 87 |
| 1958 | Jim Patton | *11 | 183 |
| 1959 | Dick Nolan | 5 | 57 |
| | Lindon Crow | 5 | 54 |
| | Jim Patton | 5 | 13 |
| 1960 | Jim Patton | 6 | 100 |
| 1961 | Dick Lynch | 9 | 60 |
| 1962 | Jim Patton | 7 | 125 |
| 1963 | Dick Lynch | 9 | *251 |
| 1964 | Dick Lynch | 4 | 68 |
| 1965 | Carl Lockhart | 4 | 117 |
| | Dick Lynch | 4 | 38 |
| 1966 | Carl Lockhart | 6 | 20 |
| 1967 | Carl Lockhart | 5 | 38 |
| 1968 | Willie Williams | 10 | 103 |
| 1969 | Bruce Maher | 5 | 112 |
| 1970 | Willie Williams | 6 | 114 |
| 1971 | Willie Williams | 5 | 58 |
| 1972 | Carl Lockhart | 4 | 56 |
| | Willie Williams | 4 | 42 |
| | Richmond Flowers | 4 | 30 |
| | Pete Athas | 4 | 11 |
| 1973 | Pete Athas | 5 | 52 |

| | | | |
|---|---|---|---|
| 1974 | Chuck Crist | 3 | 20 |
| 1975 | Bobby Brooks | 4 | 38 |
| 1976 | Rick Volk | 2 | 14 |
| | Brad Van Pelt | 2 | 13 |
| | Jim Steinke | 2 | 0 |
| 1977 | Bill Bryant | 3 | 54 |
| 1978 | Terry Jackson | 7 | 115 |
| 1979 | Brian Kelley | 3 | 41 |
| | Harry Carson | 3 | 28 |
| | Terry Jackson | 3 | 10 |
| 1980 | Mike Dennis | 5 | 68 |
| 1981 | Beasley Reece | 4 | 84 |
| 1982 | Terry Jackson | 4 | 75 |
| 1983 | Terry Jackson | 6 | 20 |
| 1984 | Mark Haynes | 7 | 90 |
| 1985 | Elvis Patterson | 6 | 88 |
| 1986 | Terry Kinard | 4 | 52 |
| | Perry Williams | 4 | 31 |
| 1987 | Terry Kinard | 5 | 163 |
| 1988 | Sheldon White | 4 | 70 |
| 1989 | Terry Kinard | 5 | 135 |
| 1990 | Everson Walls | 6 | 80 |
| 1991 | Mark Collins | 4 | 77 |
| | Everson Walls | 4 | 7 |
| 1992 | Greg Jackson | 4 | 71 |
| 1993 | Mark Collins | 4 | 77 |
| | Greg Jackson | 4 | 32 |
| 1994 | John Booty | 3 | 95 |

| | | | |
|---|---|---|---|
| | Phillippi Sparks | 3 | 4 |
| 1995 | Vencie Glenn | 5 | 91 |
| | Phillippi Sparks | 5 | 11 |
| 1996 | Jason Sehorn | 5 | 61 |
| 1997 | Jason Sehorn | 6 | 74 |
| 1998 | Percy Ellsworth | 5 | 92 |

*All-Time Single Season Club Record

## SACKS

| | | Sacks |
|---|---|---|
| 1982 | Lawrence Taylor | 7.5 |
| 1983 | George Martin | 9.0 |
| | Lawrence Taylor | 9.0 |
| 1984 | Lawrence Taylor | 11.5 |
| 1985 | Leonard Marshall | 15.5 |
| 1986 | Lawrence Taylor | *20.5 |
| 1987 | Lawrence Taylor | 12.0 |
| 1988 | Lawrence Taylor | 15.5 |
| 1989 | Lawrence Taylor | 15.0 |
| 1990 | Lawrence Taylor | 10.5 |
| 1991 | Leonard Marshall | 11.0 |
| 1992 | Lawrence Taylor | 5.0 |
| 1993 | Keith Hamilton | 11.5 |
| 1994 | Keith Hamilton | 6.5 |
| 1995 | Michael Strahan | 7.5 |
| 1996 | Chad Bratzke | 5.0 |
| | Michael Strahan | 5.0 |
| 1997 | Michael Strahan | 14.0 |
| 1998 | Michael Strahan | 15.0 |

*All-Time Single Season Club Record

# GIANTS IN THE PRO BOWL

| | | |
|---|---|---|
| 1951 | B | John Cannady (1) |
| | QB | Charlie Connerly (1) |
| | T | Al De Rogatis (1) |
| | RB | Gene Roberts (1) |
| | LB | Emlen Tunnell (1) |
| | DB | Otto Schnellbacher (1) |
| | T | Arnie Weinmeister (1) |
| 1952 | G | Jon Baker (1) |
| | QB | Charlie Conerly (2) |
| | T | Dewitt Coulter (1) |
| | T | Al De Rogatis (2) |
| | RB | Eddie Price (1) |
| | DB | Otto Schnelbacher (2) |
| | DB | Emlen Tunnell (2) |
| | T | Arnie Weinmeister (2) |
| 1953 | G | Jon Baker (2) |
| | B | John Cannady (2) |
| | T | Dewitt Coulter (2) |
| | B-E | Frank Gifford (1) |
| | RB | Eddie Price (2) |
| | DB | Emlen Tunnell (3) |
| | T | Arnie Weinmeister (3) |
| 1954 | G | Bill Austin (1) |
| | B-E | Frank Gifford (2) |
| | E | Kyle Rote (1) |
| | LB | Bill Svoboda (1) |

| | | |
|---|---|---|
| | DB | Emlen Tunnell (4) |
| 1955 | B-E | Frank Gifford (3) |
| | DB | Tom Landry (1) |
| | E | Kyle Rote (2) |
| | G-T | Jack Stroud (1) |
| | DB | Emlen Tunnell (5) |
| | C | Ray Wietecha (1) |
| 1956 | T | Rosie Brown (1) |
| | B-E | Frank Gifford (4) |
| | DE | Andy Robustelli (1) |
| | E | Kyle Rote (3) |
| | DB | Emlen Tunnell (6) |
| 1957 | T | Rosie Brown (2) |
| | QB | Charlie Conerly (3) |
| | B-E | Frank Gifford (5) |
| | DT | Rosey Grier (1) |
| | E | Kyle Rote (4) |
| | DE | Andy Robustelli (2) |
| | G-T | Jack Stroud (2) |
| | DB | Emlen Tunnell (7) |
| 1958 | T | Rosie Brown (3) |
| | B-E | Frank Gifford (6) |
| | LB | Sam Huff (1) |
| | E | Bob Schnelker (1) |
| | RB | Alex Webster (1) |
| | C | Ray Wietecha (2) |

| | | |
|---|---|---|
| 1959 | T | Rosie Brown (4) |
| | DB | Lindon Crow (1) |
| | B-E | Frank Gifford (7) |
| | LB | Sam Huff (2) |
| | DB | Jim Patton (1) |
| | DE | Andy Robustelli (3) |
| | E | Bob Schnelker (2) |
| 1960 | T | Rosie Brown (5) |
| | DT | Rosey Grier (2) |
| | LB | Sam Huff (3) |
| | DB | Jim Patton (2) |
| | DE | Andy Robustelli (4) |
| | G-T | Jack Stroud (3) |
| | C | Ray Wietecha (3) |
| 1961 | DB | Erich Barnes (1) |
| | T | Rosie Brown (6) |
| | LB | Sam Huff (4) |
| | DE | Jim Katcavage (1) |
| | DB | Jim Patton (3) |
| | DE | Andy Robustelli (5) |
| | E | Del Shofner (1) |
| | QB | Y. A. Tittle (1) |
| | RB | Alex Webster (2) |
| 1962 | DB | Erich Barnes (2) |
| | T | Rosie Brown (7) |
| | G | Darrell Dess (1) |

| | | |
|---|---|---|
| | DE | Jim Katcavage (2) |
| | E | Del Shofner (2) |
| | QB | Y. A. Tittle (2) |
| | DB | Jim Patton (4) |
| | C | Ray Wietecha (4) |
| 1963 | DB | Erich Barnes (3) |
| | G | Darrell Dess (2) |
| | B-E | Frank Gifford (8) |
| | DE | Jim Katcavage (3) |
| | DT | John Lovetere (1) |
| | DB | Dick Lynch (1) |
| | E | Del Shofner (3) |
| | QB | Y.A. Tittle (3) |
| 1964 | DB | Erich Barnes (4) |
| | T | Rosie Brown (8) |
| | E | Aaron Thomas (1) |
| 1965 | T | Rosie Brown (9) |
| | RB | Tucker Frederickson (1) |
| 1966 | DB | Carl Lockhart (1) |
| 1967 | E | Homer Jones (1) |
| | RB | Ernie Koy (1) |
| | QB | Fran Tarkenton (1) |
| 1968 | E | Homer Jones (2) |
| | C | Greg Larson (1) |
| | DB | Carl Lockhart (2) |
| | QB | Fran Tarkenton (2) |

# GIANTS IN THE PRO BOWL (con't)

| | | | | | | | | |
|---|---|---|---|---|---|---|---|---|
| 1969 | QB | Fran Tarkenton (3) | 1981 | LB | Harry Carson (3) | | LB | Lawrence Taylor (5) |
| | DB | Willie Williams (1) | | LB | Lawrence Taylor (1) | 1986 | TE | Mark Bavaro (1) |
| 1970 | RB | Ron Johnson (1) | 1982 | LB | Harry Carson (4) | | T | Brad Benson (1) |
| | QB | Fran Tarkenton (4) | | P | Dave Jennings (4) | | DT | Jim Burt (1) |
| 1972 | DE | Jack Gregory (1) | | LB | Lawrence Taylor (2) | | LB | Harry Carson (8) |
| | RB | Ron Johnson (2) | | DB | Mark Haynes (1) | | P | Sean Landeta (1) |
| | QB | Norm Snead (1) | 1983 | LB | Harry Carson (5) | | DE | Leonard Marshall (2) |
| 1976 | LB | Brad Van Pelt (1) | | PK | Ali Haji-Shiekh (1) | | RB | Joe Morris (2) |
| 1977 | LB | Brad Van Pelt (2) | | DB | Mark Haynes (2) | | LB | Lawrence Taylor (6) |
| 1978 | LB | Harry Carson (1) | | LB | Lawrence Taylor (3) | 1987 | LB | Carl Banks (1) |
| | P | Dave Jennings (1) | 1984 | LB | Harry Carson (6) | | TE | Mark Bavaro (2) |
| | LB | Brad Van Pelt (3) | | DB | Mark Haynes (3) | | LB | Harry Carson (9) |
| 1979 | LB | Harry Carson (2) | | LB | Lawrence Taylor (4) | | LB | Lawrence Taylor (7) |
| | P | Dave Jennings (2) | 1985 | LB | Harry Carson (7) | 1988 | DB | Terry Kinard (1) |
| | LB | Brad Van Pelt (4) | | DE | Leonard Marshall (1) | | LB | Lawrence Taylor (8) |
| 1980 | P | Dave Jennings (3) | | RB | Joe Morris (1) | 1989 | RB | David Meggett (1) |
| | LB | Brad Van Pelt (5) | | QB | Phil Simms (1) | | LB | Lawrence Taylor (9) |

| | | |
|---|---|---|
| 1990 | DT | Erik Howard (1) |
| | LB | Pepper Johnson (1) |
| | P | Sean Landeta (2) |
| | C | Bart Oates (1) |
| | T | William Roberts (1) |
| | LB | Lawrence Taylor (10) |
| | DB | Reyna Thompson (1) |
| 1991 | C | Bart Oates (2) |
| 1992 | RB | Rodney Hampton (1) |
| 1993 | RB | Rodney Hampton (2) |
| | T | John Elliott (1) |
| | C | Bart Oates (3) |
| | QB | Phil Simms (2) |
| 1997 | LB | Jessie Armstead (1) |
| | DE | Michael Strahan (1) |
| 1998 | LB | Jessie Armstead (2) |
| | DE | Michael Strahan (2) |

# GIANTS ALL-NFL SELECTIONS, 1925-1998

176

1925 Art Carney (G)
Jack McBride (B)
1927 Cal Hubbard (T);
Steve Owen (T)
1928 Ray Flaherty (E)
1929 Ray Flaherty (E)
Bennie Friedman (QB)
Tony Plansky (B)
Joe Westoupal (C)
1930 Bennie Friedman (QB)
1931 Morris (Red) Badgro (E)
Denver Gibson (G)
1932 Ray Flaherty (E)
1933 Morris (Red) Badgro (E)
Mel Hein (C)
Harry Newman (QB)
1934 Denver Gibson (G)
Mel Hein (C)
Bill Morgan (T)
Ken Strong (HB)
Morris (Red Badgro (E)
1935 Mel Hein (C)
Bill Morgan (T)
Ed Danowski (HB)
1936 Mel Hein (C)
Tuffy Leemans (HB)
1937 Mel Hein (C)
1938 Mel Hein (C)
Ed Danowski (HB)
Ed Widseth (T)
1939 Tuffy Leemans (HB)
Jim Poole (E)
John Dell Isola (G)
Mel Hein (C)
1940 Mel Hein (C)
1942 Bill Edwards (G)
1946 Jim White(T)
Frank Filchock (HB)
1947 Len Younce (G)

1950 Arnie Weinmeister (DT)
1951 Arnie Weinmeister (DT)
Dewitt Coulter (T)
Eddie Price (HB)
Al DeRogatis (DT)
Jon Baker (G)
Otto Schnelbacher (DB)
Emlen Tunnell (DB)
1952 Eddie Price (HB)
Arnie Weinmeister (DT)
Emlen Tunnell (DB)
1953 Arnie Weinmeister (DT)
1954 Tom Landry (DB)
1955 Emlen Tunnell (DB)
Bill Austin (G)
Frank Gifford (HB)
1956 Emlen Tunnell (DB)
Frank Gifford HB)
Roosevelt Brown (T)
Andy Robustelli (DE)
Roosevelt Grier (DT)
1957 Frank Gifford (HB)
Roosevelt Brown (T)
Andy Robustelli (DE)
1958 Roosevelt Brown (T)
Andy Robustelli (DE)
Ray Wietecha (C)
Sam Huff (LB)
Jim Patton (DB)
1959 Frank Gifford (HB)
Roosevelt Brown (T)
Andy Robustelli (DE)
Sam Huff (LB)
Jim Patton (DB)
1960 Roosevelt Brown (T)
Andy Robustelli (DE)
Jim Patton (DB)
1961 Roosevelt Brown (T)
Jim Patton (DB)

Del Shofner (E)
Y.A. Tittle (QB)
Jim Katcavage (DE)
Erich Barnes (DB)
1962 Roosevelt Brown (T)
Jim Patton (DB)
Del Shofner (E)
Y.A. Tittle (QB)
Jim Katcavage (DE)
1963 Roosevelt Brown (T)
Del Shofner (E)
Y.A. Tittle (QB)
Jim Katcavage (DE)
Dick Lynch (DB)
1964 Erich Barnes (DB)
1967 Homer Jones (WR)
1970 Ron Johnson (RB)
1972 Bob Tucker (TE)
Jack Gregory (DE)
1974 John Mendenhall (DT)
1976 Brad Van Pelt (LB), All-NFC
1977 Brad Van Pelt (LB), All-NFC
1978 Brad Van Pelt (LB), All-NFC
Harry Carson (LB); All-NFL
Dave Jennings (P), All-NFL
1979 Harry Carson (LB), All-NFL; All-NFC
Dave Jennings (P), All-NFL, All-NFC;
Brad Van Pelt (LB), All-NFC
1980 Dave Jennings (P), All-NFL, All-NFC
Brad Van Pelt (LB), All-NFC
1981 Lawrence Taylor (LB), All-NFL
Harry Carson (LB), All-NFL
Mark Haynes (CB), All-NFL
Dave Jennings (P), All-NFL, (2nd Team)
1982 Lawrence Taylor (LB), All-NFL
Dave Jennings (P), All-NFL
Mark Haynes (CB), All-NFL
Harry Carson (LB), All-NFL, (2nd Team)
1983 Lawrence Taylor (LB)

Ali Haji Sheikh (PK)
Mark Haynes (CB), (2nd Team)
1984 Lawrence Taylor (LB)
Mark Haynes (CB)
Harry Carson (LB), (2nd Team)
1985 Lawrence Taylor (LB)
Leonard Marshall (DE);
Joe Morris (RB)
Harry Carson (LB)
1986 Lawrence Taylor (LB)
Phil Simms (QB)
Joe Morris (RB)
Mark Bavaro (TE)
Sean Landeta (P)
Jim Burt (DT)
Harry Carson (LB)
Leonard Marshall (DE)
Brad Benson (T)
1987 Mark Bavaro (TE)
Carl Banks (LB)
Lawrence Taylor (LB)
1988 Lawrence Taylor (LB)
1989 Lawrence Taylor (LB)
Sean Landeta (P)
David Meggett (RB)
Mark Collins (CB)
1990 Lawrence Taylor (LB)
Pepper Johnson (LB)
Sean Landeta (P)
David Megget (PR)
Reyna Thompson (CB-ST)
1993 Michael Brooks (LB), All-NFL (2nd Team), All-NFC
Mark Collins (CB), All-NFL (2nd Team)
William Roberts (G), All-NFC
1994 David Meggett (PR)
1997 Jessie Armstead (LB)
Michael Strahan (DE)
1998 Michael Strahan (DE)

# GIANTS RUSHING HONOR ROLL

## 100 OR MORE YARDS IN A GAME, CHRONOLOGICALLY

| | | | | | | |
|---|---|---|---|---|---|---|
| 108 | Harry Newman at. Boston | 10/8/33 | 148 | Billy Taylor vs. Tampa Bay | 10/7/79 |
| 107 | Kink Richards vs. Bkn., | 10/22/33 | 126 | Billy Taylor vs. Washington | 11/25/79 |
| 114 | Harry Newman vs. Green Bay | 11/11/34 | 103 | Billy Taylor at Seattle | 12/7/80 |
| 105 | Ed Danowski vs. Boston | 11/25/34 | 103 | Rob Carpenter vs. St. Louis | 10/11/81 |
| 102 | Tuffy Leemans at. Pittsburgh | 9/27/36 | 116 | Rob Carpenter at Seattle | 10/18/81 |
| 117 | Tuffy Leemans vs. Chicago Cardinals | 10/18/36 | 111 | Rob Carpenter at Philadelphia | 11/22/81 |
| 117 | Tuffy Leemans vs. Philadelphia | 10/25/36 | 117 | Rob Carpenter at St. Louis | 12/13/81 |
| 118 | Hank Soar at Philadelphia | 10/3/37 | 161** | Rob Carpenter at Philadelphia | 12/27/81 |
| 159 | Tuffy Leemans vs. Green Bay | 11/20/38 | 113 | Rob Carpenter vs. L.A. Rams | 9/4/83 |
| 101 | Tuffy Leemans vs. Cleveland | 11/10/40 | 111 | Rob Carpenter at. Atlanta | 9/11/83 |
| 101 | Bill Paschal at. Bkn., | 10/17/43 | 116 | Rob Carpenter vs. Green Bay | 9/26/83 |
| 188 | Bill Paschal vs. Washington | 12/5/43 | 159 | Butch Woolfolk at Philadelphia | 11/20/83 |
| 139 | Bill Paschall vs. Philadelphia | 10/29/44 | 107 | Joe Morris at. St. Louis | 12/9/84 |
| 113 | Bill Paschal vs. Boston | 11/5/44 | 104 | Joe Morris at New Orleans | 10/27/85 |
| 103 | Ward Cuff vs. Green Bay | 11/19/44 | 132 | Joe Morris vs. Tampa Bay | 11/3/85 |
| 100 | Ward Cuff vs. Washington | 12/3/44 | 118 | Joe Morris at Washington | 11/18/85 |
| 143 | Bill Paschal vs. Cleveland | 11/4/45 | 131 | Joe Morris vs. Cleveland | 12/1/85 |
| 108 | Frank Filchock at Pittsburgh | 10/6/46 | 129 | Joe Morris at Houston | 12/8/85 |
| 107 | George Franck vs. Boston | 11/10/46 | 202 | Joe Morris vs. Pittsburgh | 12/21/85 |
| 133 | Frank Reagan vs. Los Angeles | 12/1/46 | 141** | Joe Morris vs. San Francisco | 12/29/85 |
| 125 | "Choo Choo" Roberts vs. Chicago Cardinals | 10/17/48 | 113 | George Adams at St. Louis | 11/24/85 |
| 108 | "Choo Choo" Roberts at.NY Bulldogs | 9/30/49 | 110 | Joe Morris at L.A. Raiders | 9/21/86 |
| 108 | "Choo Choo" Roberts at Chicago Cardinals | 10/30/49 | 116 | Joe Morris at Seattle | 10/19/86 |
| 121 | Joe Scott vs. Cleveland | 10/22/50 | 181 | Joe Morris vs. Washington | 10/27/86 |
| 218* | "Choo Choo" Roberts vs. Chicago Cardinals | 11/12/50 | 181 | Joe Morris vs. Dallas | 11/2/86 |
| 145 | Ed Price at Baltimore | 11/19/50 | 111 | Joe Morris at Philadelphia | 11/9/86 |
| 101 | Randall Clay vs. Philadelphia | 11/26/50 | 106 | Joe Morris vs. Denver, | 11/23/86 |
| 156 | Ed Price vs. N.Y. Yanks. | 12/3/50 | 179 | Joe Morris vs. St. Louis | 12/14/86 |
| 103 | Ed Price at Philadelphia | 12/10/50 | 115 | Joe Morris vs. Green Bay | 12/20/86 |
| 107 | Ed Price vs. Chicago Cardinals | 10/14/51 | 159** | Joe Morris vs. San Francisco | 1/4/87 |
| 101 | Ed Price vs. Philadelphia | 10/21/51 | 132 | Joe Morris vs. Jets | 12/27/87 |
| 171 | Ed Price at Philadelphia | 12/9/51 | 107 | Joe Morris at Dallas | 9/18/88 |
| 138 | Ed Price at N.Y. Yanks | 12/16/51 | 122 | Joe Morris vs. Phoenix | 12/4/88 |
| 130 | Ed Price at Dallas | 9/28/52 | 140 | Joe Morris vs. Kansas City | 12/11/88 |
| 119 | Ed Price at Philadelphia | 10/4/52 | 101 | Ottis Anderson vs. Washington | 10/15/89 |
| 116 | Ed Price at Chicago Cardinals | 11/2/52 | 120** | Ottis Anderson vs. L.A. Rams | 1/7/90 |
| 106 | Ed Price vs. San Francisco | 11/9/52 | 105 | Rodney Hampton vs. Buffalo | 12/15/90 |
| 139 | Alex Webster at Chicago Cardinals | 10/2/55 | 102** | Ottis Anderson vs. Buffalo | 1/27/91 |
| 108 | Frank Gifford vs. Washington | 12/2/56 | 104 | Rodney Hampton vs. Cleveland | 9/22/91 |
| 132 | Alex Webster at Philadelphia | 12/15/56 | 137 | Rodney Hampton vs. Phoenix | 10/6/91 |
| 115 | Bob Epps at Washington | 10/13/57 | 140 | Rodney Hampton vs. Houston | 12/21/91 |
| 126 | Frank Gifford vs. Cardinals | 11/10/57 | 167 | Rodney Hampton vs. Phoenix | 10/11/92 |
| 116 | Mel Triplett vs. Cleveland | 11/29/59 | 138 | Rodney Hampton at Washington | 11/1/92 |
| 137 | Mel Triplett at Cleveland | 11/6/60 | 134 | Rodney Hampton vs. Tampa Bay | 9/12/93 |
| 129 | Bob Gaiters at Dallas | 10/15/61 | 134 | Rodney Hampton vs. Rams | 9/19/93 |
| 100 | Alex Webster vs. Philadelphia | 11/12/61 | 104 | Lewis Tillman at Washington | 10/10/93 |
| 107 | Alex Webster vs. Philadelphia | 11/18/62 | 169 | Lewis Tillman vs. Philadelphia | 10/17/93 |
| 120 | Joe Morrison at Philadelphia | 9/29/63 | 101 | Rodney Hampton at Philadelphia | 11/21/93 |
| 101 | Phil King vs. San Francisco | 11/17/63 | 173 | Rodney Hampton vs. Indiana | 12/12/93 |
| 160 | Ernie Koy at Washington | 10/1/67 | 114 | Rodney Hampton vs. Dallas | 1/2/94 |
| 142 | Ron Johnson vs. Philadelphia | 10/11/70 | 161** | Rodney Hampton vs. Minnesota | 1/9/94 |
| 140 | Ron Johnson vs. Dallas | 11/8/70 | 112 | Rodney Hampton at Rams | 10/16/94 |
| 106 | Ron Johnson vs. Washington | 11/15/70 | 138 | Rodney Hampton vs. Detroit | 10/30/94 |
| 100 | Ron Johnson vs. Buffalo | 12/6/70 | 122 | Rodney Hampton at Houston | 11/21/94 |
| 124 | Ron Johnson at Philadelphia | 10/2/72 | 106 | Rodney Hampton at Washinton | 11/27/94 |
| 134 | Ron Johnson at St. Louis | 11/19/72 | 149 | Rodney Hampton vs. New Orleans | 9/24/95 |
| 123 | Ron Johnson vs. Philadelphia | 11/26/72 | 187 | Rodney Hampton at Dallas | 12/17/95 |
| 119 | Ron Johnson at Cinncinatti | 12/3/72 | 103 | Tyrone Wheatley at Arizona | 10/12/97 |
| 105 | Vin Clements at Dallas | 12/17/72 | 114 | Charles Way vs. Arizona | 11/16/97 |
| 112 | Ron Johnson vs. Philadelphia | 9/23/73 | 114 | Tiki Barber at Philadelphia | 12/7/97 |
| 101 | Ron Johnson at Philadelphia | 11/25/73 | 108 | Gary Brown vs. Arizona | 10/18/98 |
| 119 | Doug Kotar vs. Atlanta | 10/6/74 | 119 | Gary Brown at Dallas | 11/8/98 |
| 108 | Doug Kotar at Rams | 9/26/76 | 124 | Gary Brown at Arizona | 12/6/98 |
| 103 | Doug Kotar vs. St. Louis | 12/12/76 | 112 | Gary Brown vs. Denver | 12/13/98 |
| 100 | Larry Csonka vs. Chicago | 12/18/77 | 103 | Gary Brown vs. Kansas City | 12/20/98 |
| 118 | Doug Kotar vs. St. Louis | 12/10/78 | 112 | Gary Brown at Philadelphia | 12/27/98 |

\* Team Record   \*\* In playoff game

# GIANTS PASSING HONOR ROLL

### 300 or More Yards in a Game, Chronologically

| | | | | | | |
|---|---|---|---|---|---|---|
| 341 | Paul Governali vs. Philadelphia | 11/9/47 | | 326 | Scott Brunner at St. Louis | 12/26/82 |
| 363 | Charlie Conerly at Pittsburgh | 12/5/48 | | 395 | Scott Brunner vs. San Diego | 10/2/83 |
| 357 | Charlie Conerly at Green Bay | 11/13/49 | | 325 | Jeft Rutledge vs. Dallas | 10/30/83 |
| 321 | Charlie Conerly at Rams | 9/26/59 | | 346 | Scott Brunner at Raiders | 11/27/83 |
| 315 | Y. A. Tittle at Washington | 10/1/61 | | 349 | Jeff Rutledge vs. Seattle | 12/11/83 |
| 307 | Y. A. Tittle vs. Philadelphia | 11/12/61 | | 324 | Jeff Rutledge at Washinton | 12/17/83 |
| 314 | Y. A. Tittle vs. Pittsburgh | 11/19/61 | | 409 | Phil Simms vs. Philadelphia | 9/2/84 |
| 332 | Y. A. Tlttle at Pittsburgh | 9/30/62 | | 347 | Phil Simms at Washington | 9/16/84 |
| 505 | Y. A. Tittle vs. Washington | 10/28/62 | | 339 | Phil Simms vs. Washington | 10/28/84 |
| 315 | Y. A. Tittle at Dallas | 11/11/62 | | 343 | Phil Simms vs. Kansas City | 11/25/84 |
| 341 | Y. A. Tittle vs. Dallas | 12/16/62 | | 432 | Phil Simms vs. Dallas | 10/6/85 |
| 324 | Y. A. Tittle at Washington | 10/6/63 | | 513* | Phil Simms at Cinncinatti | 10/13/85 |
| 308 | Y. A. Tittle vs. Pittsburgh | 12/15/63 | | 329 | Phil Simms at Dallas | 12/15/85 |
| 348 | Fran Tarkenton vs. New Orleans | 10/8/67 | | 300 | Phil Simms at Dallas | 9/8/86 |
| 325 | Fran Tarkenton vs. St Louis | 12/8/68 | | 300 | Phil Simms vs. San Diego | 9/14/86 |
| 320 | Fran Tarkenton vs. Washington | 11/15/70 | | 310 | Phil Simms at Minnesota | 11/16/86 |
| 302 | Fran Tarkenton at Pittsburgh | 11/21/71 | | 388 | Phil Simms at San Francisco | 12/1/86 |
| 372 | Randy Johnson vs. Philadelphia | 12/19/71 | | 359 | Phil Simms at St. Louis | 12/13/87 |
| 348 | Randy Johnson at St. Louis | 10/28/73 | | 309 | Phil Simms vs. L.A. Rams | 9/25/88 |
| 300 | Phil Simms vs. San Francisco | 10/14/79 | | 324 | Phil Simms at Philadelphia | 10/10/88 |
| 351 | Phil Simms vs. Dallas | 11/9/80 | | 320 | Phil Simms vs. Detroit | 10/16/88 |
| 322 | Phil Simms vs. Green Bay | 11/16/80 | | 326 | Phil Simms at San Franciso | 11/27/89 |
| 324 | Phil Simms vs. New Orleans | 9/20/81 | | 368 | Jeff Hostetler at Dallas | 9/29/91 |
| 310 | Scott Brunner vs. Atlanta | 9/12/82 | | 337 | Phil Simms vs. Phoenix | 11/28/93 |

\* Team Record

# NEW YORK GIANTS IN THE PRO FOOTBALL HALL OF FAME

| Player | Giants Service | Year Enshrined | Player | Giants Service | Year Enshrined |
|---|---|---|---|---|---|
| Lawrence Taylor | Linebacker | 1999 | Emlen Tunnell | Defensive Back | 1967 |
| Wellington Mara | President, Co-Chief Executive Officer | 1997 | Steve Owen | Coach | 1966 |
| Tom Landry | Coach | 1990 | Cal Hubbard | Tackle | 1963 |
| Arnold Weinmeister | Defensive Tackle | 1984 | Tim Mara | Founder | 1963 |
| Sam Huff | Linebacker | 1982 | **OTHER HALL OF FAME MEMBERS WITH GIANTS EXPERIENCE** | | |
| Morris (Red) Badgro | End | 1981 | Larry Csonka | Fullback | 1987 |
| Alphonse (Tuffy) Leemans | Halfback, Fullback | 1978 | Don Maynard | Wide Receiver | 1987 |
| Frank Gifford | Halfback, Flanker | 1977 | Fran Tarkenton | Quarterback | 1986 |
| Roosevelt Brown | Tackle | 1975 | Ray Flaherty | End, Coach | 1976 |
| Vince Lombardi | Coach | 1971 | Hugh McElhenny | Halfback | 1970 |
| Andy Robustelli | Defensive End | 1971 | Joe Guyon | Hlalfback | 1966 |
| Y. A. Tittle | Quarterback | 1971 | Arnie Herber | Quarterback | 1966 |
| Ken Strong | Halfback | 1967 | Wilber (Pete) Henry | Tackle | 1963 |

# RETIRED GIANTS NUMBERS

| No | Player | Giants Service | Year Retired | No | Player | Giants Service | Year Retired |
|---|---|---|---|---|---|---|---|
| 1 | Ray Flaherty | End-Assistant Coach (1928-35) | 1935 | 32 | Al Blozis | Tackle (1942-44) | 1945 |
| 4 | Tuffy Leemans | Back (1936-1943) | 1940 | 40 | Joe Morrison | End-Halfback (1959-72) | 1972 |
| 7 | Mel Hein | Center-Linebacker (1931-45) | 1963 | 41 | Charlie Conerly | Quarterback (1948-61) | 1962 |
| 11 | Phil Simms | Quarterback (1979-1993) | 1995 | 50 | Ken Strong | Fullback-Kicker (1933-35, 39-47) | 1947 |
| 14 | Y.A. Tittle | Quarterback (1961-64) | 1965 | 56 | Lawrence Taylor | Linebacker (1981-93) | 1994 |

| PLAYER | POS. | SCHOOL | YEARS |
|---|---|---|---|
| **A** | | | |
| Abrams, Bobby | (LB) | Michigan | 1990-92 |
| Adamchik, Ed | (C) | Pittsburgh | 1965 |
| Adams, George | (RB) | Kentucky | 1985-89 |
| Adams, O'Neal | (E) | Arkansas | 1941-45 |
| Adams, Verlin | (T) | Morris Harvey | 1942-45 |
| Agajanian, Ben | (K) | New Mexico | 1949, 54-57 |
| Agnew, Ray | (DT) | N.Carolina St. | 1995-97 |
| Albright, Bill | (G) | Wisconsin | 1951-54 |
| Alexakos, Steve | (G) | San Jose St. | 1971 |
| Alexander, Joe | (G) | Texas A&M | 1928 |
| Alexander, John | (T) | Rutgers | 1926 |
| Alexander, Kevin | (WR) | Utah St. | 1996-97 |
| Allegre, Raul | (K) | Texas | 1986-91 |
| Allen, Derek | (G) | Illinois | 1995 |
| Alford, Brian | (WR) | Purdue | 1998 |
| Allison, Jim | (E) | Texas A&M | 1928 |
| Almodobar, Beau | (WR) | Norwich | 1987 |
| Amberg, John | (B) | Kansas | 1951-52 |
| Anderson, Bob | (B) | Army | 1963 |
| Anderson, Bruce | (DE) | Williamette | 1967-69 |
| Anderson, Cliff | (E) | Indiana | 1953 |
| Anderson, Ottis | (RB) | Miami | 1986-92 |
| Anderson, Roger | (DT) | Virginia Union | 1965-68 |
| Anderson, Winston | (E) | Colgate | 1936 |
| Apuna, Ben | (LB) | Arizona St. | 1980 |
| Ard, Billy | (G) | Wake Forest | 1981-88 |
| Archer, Troy | (DT) | Colorado | 1976-78 |
| Artman, Corwan | (T) | Stanford | 1931 |
| Armstead, Jessie | (LB) | Miami (Fla) | 1993-98 |
| Ashburn, Cliff | (G) | Nebraska | 1929 |
| Athas, Pete | (DB) | Tennessee | 1971-74 |
| Atkinson, Jess | (K) | Maryland | 1985 |
| Atwood, John | (B) | Wisconsin | 1948 |
| Austin, Bill | (G) | Oregon St. | 49-50, 53-57 |
| Avedisian, Charles | (G) | Providence | 1942-44 |
| Averno, Sisto | (G) | Muhlenberg | 1951 |
| Avery, Ken | (LB) | S. Mississippi | 1967-68 |
| Avinger, Clarence | (B) | Alabama | 1953 |
| **B** | | | |
| Badgro, Morris | (E) | USC | 1927-35 |
| Bahr, Matt | (PK) | Penn St. | 1990-1992 |
| Bailey, Carlton | (LB) | N. Carolina | 1993-94 |
| Bain, Bill | (T) | USC | 1978 |
| Baker, Ed | (QB) | Lafayette | 1970-71 |
| Baker, John | (DE) | Norfolk St. | 1970 |
| Baker, Jon | (G) | California | 1949-52 |
| Baker, Stephen | (WR) | Fresno St. | 1987-92 |
| Baldinger, Rich | (OT) | Wake Forest | 1982-83 |
| Ballman, Gary | (TE) | Michigan St. | 1973 |
| Banks, Carl | (LB) | Michigan St. | 1984-92 |
| Banks, Willie | (G) | Alcorn A&M | 1970 |
| Barasich, Carl | (DT) | Princeton | 1981 |
| Barber, Ernie | (C) | San Francisco | 1945 |
| Barber, Tiki | (RB) | Virginia | 1997-98 |
| Barbour, Wes | (QB) | Wake Forest | 1945 |
| Barker, Hubert | (B) | Arkansas | 1942-45 |
| Barnard, Charles | (E) | Edmond St. | 1938 |
| Barnes, Erich | (DB) | Purdue | 1961-64 |
| Barnum, Len | (QB) | W. Va Wesleyan | 1938-40 |
| Barrett, Emmet | (C) | Portland | 1942-44 |
| Barry, Al | (G) | USC | 1958-59 |
| Bavaro, Mark | (TE) | Notre Dame | 1985-90 |
| Barzilauskas, F | (G) | Yale | 1951 |
| Bauer, John | (G) | Illinois | 1954 |
| Beamon, Willie | (CB) | Nthrn. Iowa | 1993-96 |
| Beck, Ray | (G) | Georgia Tech | 1952, 55-57 |
| Beckman, Brad | (TE) | Neb. Omaha | 1988 |
| Bednar, Al | (G) | Lafayette | 1925-26 |
| Beeble, Keith | (B) | Occidental | 1944 |
| Beecham, Earl | (RB) | Bucknell | 1987 |
| Belcher, Kevin | (G) | Texas El-Paso | 1983-85 |
| Beil, Lawrence | (T) | Portland | 1948 |
| Bell, Gordon | (RB) | Michigan | 1976-77 |
| Bell, Kay | (T) | Wash. St. | 1942 |
| Bellinger, Bob | (T) | Gonzaga | 1934-35 |
| Benkert, Harry | (B) | Rutgers | 1925 |
| Benners, Fred | (QB) | SMU | 1952 |
| Benson, Brad | (G) | Penn St. | 1977-87 |
| Bennett, Lewis | (WR) | Flonda A&M | 1987 |
| Benyola, George | (PK) | Louisiana Tech | 1987 |
| Berry, Wayne | (B) | Wash. St. | 1954 |
| Berthusen, Bill | (DE) | Iowa St. | 1987 |
| Besana, Fred | (QB) | California | 1978 |
| Best, Art | (RB) | Kent St. | 1980 |
| Biggs, Riley | (C) | Baylor | 1926-27 |
| Biscaha, Joe | (E) | Richmond | 1959 |
| Bishop, Greg | (G) | Pacific | 1993-98 |
| Black, Mike | (T) | CSU Sacramento | 1987 |
| Blackwell, Kory | (CB) | Massachusetts | 1998 |
| Blanchard, Tom | (P-QB) | Oregon | 1971-73 |
| Blazine, Anthony | (T) | Georgetown | 1942-44 |
| Bloodgood, Elbert | (B) | Nebraska | 1928 |
| Blount, Tony | (S) | Virginia | 1980 |
| Blozis, Al | (T) | Georgetown | 1942-44 |
| Blumenstock, Jim | (B) | Fordham | 1947 |
| Bly, Ron | (B) | Notre Dame | 1968 |
| Boggan, Rex | (T) | Mississippi | 1955 |
| Bookman, John | (DB) | Miami | 1962-67 |
| Bohovich, Reed | (T) | Lehigh | 1962-63 |
| Bolin, Bookie | (G) | Mississippi | 1962-97 |
| Boll, Don | (T) | Nebraska | 1960 |
| Bomar, Lynn | (E) | Vanderbilt | 1925-26 |
| Bonness, Rik | (LB) | Nebraska | 1980 |
| Booty, John | (S) | TCU | 1994 |
| Borcky, Dennis | (DT) | Memphis St. | 1987 |
| Borden, Les | (E) | Fordham | 1935 |
| Boston, McKinley | (DE) | Minnesota | 1968-69 |
| Bowdoin, Jim | (G) | Alabama | 1932 |
| Bowman, Steve | (B) | Alabama | 1966 |
| Boyle, Bill | (T) | No College | 1934 |
| Brackett, M.L. | (G) | Auburn | 1958 |
| Brahm, Larry | (G) | Temple | 1943 |
| Brandes, John | (TE) | Cameron | 1992 |
| Bratzke, Chad | (DE) | E. Kentucky | 1994-98 |
| Brennan, Matt | (B) | Lafayette | 1925 |
| Brenner, Al | (DB) | Michigan St. | 1969-70 |
| Bright, Leon | (RB) | Flonda St. | 1981-83 |
| Broadstone, Manon | (T) | Nebraska | 1931 |
| Brooks, Bobby | (DB) | Bishop Coll. | 1974-76 |
| Brooks, Michael | (LB) | LSU | 1993-95 |
| Brossard, Fred | (C) | N.W. Louisiana | 1955 |
| Brovarney, Casimir | (T) | Detroit | 1941 |
| Brown, Barry | (LB) | Florida | 1968 |
| Brown, Boyd | (TE) | Alcorn St. | 1977 |
| Brown, Dave | (B) | Alabama | 1943, 46-47 |
| Brown, Dave | (QB) | Duke | 1992-97 |
| Brown, Derek | (TE) | Notre Dame | 1992-94 |
| Brown, Donald | (CB) | Maryland | 1987 |
| Brown, Gary | (RB) | Penn St. | 1998 |
| Brown, Otto | (DB) | Praine View | 1970-73 |
| Brown, Roger | (DB) | Virginia Tech. | 1990-91 |
| Brown, Rosie | (T) | Morgan St. | 1953-65 |
| Browning, Greg | (E) | Denver | 1947 |
| Brunner, Scott | (QB) | Delaware | 1980-83 |
| Bryant, Bill | (DB) | Grambling | 1976-78 |
| Buckley, Curtis | (S) | East Texas St. | 1998 |
| Buckley, Marcus | (LB) | Texas A&M | 1993-98 |
| Bucklin, Tom | (B) | Idaho | 1931 |
| Buetow, Bart | (G) | Minnesota | 1973 |
| Buffington, Harry | (G) | Oklahoma A&M | 1942 |
| Buford, Maury | (P) | Texas Tech | 1988 |
| Buggs, Danny | (WR) | W. Virginia | 1975-76 |
| Bunch, Jarrod | (RB) | Michigan | 1991-93 |
| Bundra, Mike | (DT) | USC | 1965 |
| Burgess, Charlie | (LB) | Carson-Newman | 1987 |
| Burkhardt, Art | (G) | Rutgers | 1928 |
| Burnett, Dale. | (B) | Kansas Teachers | 1930-39 |
| Burnine, Hal | (E) | Missouri | 1956 |
| Burt, Jim | (DT) | Miami | 1981-88 |
| Busch, Mike | (QB) | S. Dakota St. | 1987 |
| Butkus, Carl | (T) | George Wash. | 1949 |
| Butler, Skip | (K) | Texas, Arlington | 1971 |
| Buzin, Dick | (T) | Penn St. | 1969-70 |
| Byers, Ken | (G) | Cincinnati | 1962-64 |
| Byler, Joe | (T) | Nebraska | 1946 |
| Byrd, Boris | (CB) | Austin, Peay | 1987 |
| **C** | | | |
| Cagle, Chris | (B) | Army | 1930-1932 |
| Caldwell, Alan | (CB) | N. Carolina | 1979 |
| Caldwell, Bruce | (B) | Yale | 1928 |
| Calligaro, Len | (B) | Wisconsin | 1944-45 |
| Calloway, Chris | (WR) | Michigan | 1992-98 |
| Campbell, Carter | (LB) | Weber St. | 1972-73 |
| Campbell, Glen | (E) | Kansas Teachers | 1929-33 |
| Campbell, Jesse | (S) | N. Carolina St. | 1992-96 |
| Campfield, Billy | (RB) | Kansas | 1983 |
| Cancik, Phil | (LB) | N. Anzona | 1980 |
| Cannady, John | (B) | Indiana | 1947-54 |
| Cannella, John | (T) | Fordham | 1933-34 |
| Cantor, Leo | (B) | UCLA | 1942 |
| Capps, Wilbur | (B) | Okla. St. Central | 1929 |
| Caranci, Roland | (T) | Colorado | 1944 |
| Carney, Art | (G) | Navy | 1925-26 |
| Carpenter, Brian | (DB) | Michigan | 1982 |
| Carpenter, Rob | (RB) | Miami, Ohio | 1981-85 |
| Carr, Henry | (DB) | Arizona St. | 1965-67 |
| Carr, Reggie | (DE) | Jackson St. | 1987 |
| Carrocio, Russ | (G) | Virginia | 1954-55 |
| Carroll, Jim | (LB) | Notre Dame | 1965-66 |
| Carroll, Vic | (T) | Nevada | 1943-47 |
| Carson, Harry | (LB) | S. Carolina St. | 1976-88 |
| Carthon, Maurice | (RB) | Arkansas St. | 1985-91 |
| Case, Pete | (G) | Georgia | 1965-70 |
| Cavanaugh, Matt | (QB) | Pittsburgh | 1990-91 |
| Cephous, Frank | (RB) | UCLA | 1984 |
| Ceppetelli, Gene | (C) | Villanova | 1969 |
| Chandler, Don | (K) | Flonda | 1956-64 |
| Chandler, Karl | (C) | Princeton | 1974-77 |
| Chatman, Cliff | (RB) | Central St.(Okla) | 1982 |
| Chemerko, George | (B) | Fordham | 1947-48 |
| Cherry, Mike | (QB) | Murray St. | 1997-98 |
| Chickerneo, John | (B) | Pittsburgh | 1942 |
| Childs, Clarence | (DB) | Flonda A&M | 1964-67 |
| Christensen, Todd | (RB) | Brigham Young | 1979 |
| Cicolella, Mike | (LB) | Dayton | 1966-68 |
| Clack, Jim | (C) | Wake Forest | 1978-81 |
| Clancy, Stuart | (B) | Holy Cross | 1933-35 |
| Clatterbuck, Bob | (QB) | Houston | 1954-57 |
| Clay, Randy | (B) | Texas | 1950-53 |
| Clay, Roy | (B) | Colorado | 1944 |
| Clayton, Harvey | (CB) | Florida St. | 1987 |
| Clements, Vin | (RB) | Connecticut | 1972-73 |
| Clune, Don | (WR) | Penn | 1974-75 |
| Coates, Ray | (B) | LSU | 1948-49 |
| Coffey, Junior | (RB) | Washington | 1969-71 |
| Coffield, Randy | (LB) | Florida St. | 1978-79 |
| Colbert, Rondy | (DB) | Lamar U. | 1974-76 |
| Cole, Pete | (G) | Trinity (Texas) | 1937-40 |
| Coleman, Charles | (TE) | Alcorn St. | 1987 |
| Colhouer, Jake | (G) | Oklahoma | 1949 |
| Collier, Jim | (E) | Arkansas | 1962-63 |
| Collins, Mark | (CB) | CSU Fullerton | 1986-93 |
| Collins, Ray | (T) | LSU | 1954 |
| Colman, Doug | (LB) | Nebraska | 1996-98 |
| Colvin, Jim | (DT) | Houston | 1967 |
| Comella, Greg | (FB) | Stanford | 1998 |

| Player | Pos. | School | Years |
|---|---|---|---|
| Comstock, Rudy | (G) | Georgetown | 1930 |
| Condren, Glen | (DE) | Oklahoma | 1965-67 |
| Conerly, Charlie | (QB) | Mississippi | 1948-61 |
| Contoulis, John | (DT) | Connecticut | 1964 |
| Cook, Charles | (DT) | Miami | 1983 |
| Cooks, Johnie | (LB) | Mississippi St. | 1988-90 |
| Cope Frank | (T) | Santa Clara | 1938-47 |
| Coppens, Gus | (T) | UCLA | 1979 |
| Cooper, Joe | (K) | California | 1986 |
| Cordileone, Lou | (G) | Clemson | 1960 |
| Corgan, Charles | (E) | Arkansas | 1927 |
| Corzine, Lester | (B) | Davis-Elkins | 1934-37 |
| Coulter, Dewitt | (T) | Army | 1946-52 |
| Council, Keith | (DT) | Hampton | 1998 |
| Costello, Tom | (LB) | Dayton | 1964-65 |
| Costello, Vince | (LB) | Ohio U. | 1967 |
| Counts, John | (B) | Illinois | 1962-63 |
| Cousino, Brad | (LB) | Miami (Ohio) | 1976 |
| Covington, Jamie | (RB) | Syracuse | 1987 |
| Cox, Greg | (S) | San Jose St. | 1989 |
| Crane, Dennis | (T) | USC | 1970 |
| Crawford, Bill | (G) | British Columbia | 1960 |
| Crawford, Ed | (B) | Mississippi | 1957 |
| Crawford, Keith | (WR) | Howard Payne | 1993 |
| Crespino, Bob | (E) | Mississippi | 1964-68 |
| Crist, Chuck | (DB) | Penn St. | 1972-74 |
| Crocicchia, Jim | (QB) | Pennsylvania | 1987 |
| Croel, Mike | (LB) | Nebraska | 1995 |
| Crosby, Steve | (RB) | Fort Hays | 1974-75 |
| Cross, Howard | (TE) | Alabama | 1989-98 |
| Crow, Lindon | (B) | USC | 1958-60 |
| Crutcher, Tommy | (LB) | TCU | 1968-69 |
| Csonka, Larry | (RB) | Syracuse | 1976-78 |
| Cuff, Ward | (B) | Marquette | 1937-45 |
| Culwell, Val | (G) | Oregon | 1942 |
| Culbreath, Jim | (RB) | Oklahoma | 1980 |
| Cummings, Mack | (WR) | Estrn Tenn. St. | 1987 |
| Curcio, Mike | (LB) | Temple | 1982 |
| Currier, Bill | (S) | S. Carolina | 1981-85 |
| **D** | | | |
| Daluiso, Brad | (PK) | UCLA | 1993-98 |
| Damiani, Francis | (T) | Manhattan | 1944 |
| Danelo, Joe | (K) | Wash. St. | 1976-82 |
| Daniel, Kenny | (DB) | San Jose St. | 1984 |
| Danowski, Ed | (QB) | Fordham | 1934-41 |
| Davis, Chris | (LB) | San Diego St. | 1987 |
| Davis, Don | (DT) | L.A. St. | 1966-67 |
| Davis, Gains | (G) | Texas Tech | 1936 |
| Davis, Henry | (LB) | Grambling | 1968-69 |
| Davis, Kelvin | (G) | Johnson Smith | 1987 |
| Davis, Paul | (LB) | N. Carolina | 1983 |
| Davis, Roger | (T) | Syracuse | 1965-66 |
| Davis, Roosevelt | (DE) | Tennessee A&T | 1965-67 |
| Davis, Scott | (G) | Iowa | 1993-96 |
| Davis, Tyrone | (CB) | Clemson | 1985-86 |
| Dawkins, Joe | (RB) | Wisconsin | 1974-75 |
| Dawsey, Lawrence | (WR) | Florida St. | 1996 |
| Dean, Randy | (QB) | Northwestern | 1977-79 |
| DeFilippo, Lou | (C) | Fordham | 1941, 45-48 |
| DelGaizo, Jim | (QB) | Tampa | 1974 |
| Dell Isola, John | (C) | Fordham | 1934-40 |
| Dennerlien, Gerry | (T) | St. Mary's | 1937-40 |
| Dennery, Vince | (E) | Fordham | 1941 |
| Dennis, Mike | (CB) | Wyoming | 1980-83 |
| Dent, Burnell | (LB) | Tulane | 1993 |
| DeOssie, Steve | (LB) | Boston Coll. | 1989-93 |
| DeRogatis, Al | (T) | Duke | 1949-52 |
| DeRose, Dan | (LB) | Sthrn. Colorado | 1987 |
| Dess, Darrell | (G) | N. Carolina St. | 1959-64 ,66-69 |
| Dillard, Stacey | (DE | Oklahoma | 1992-95 |
| DiRenzo, Fred | (RB) | New Haven | 1987 |
| DiRico, Bob | (RB) | Kutztown St. | 1987 |
| Dixon, Al | (TE) | Iowa St. | 1977-78 |
| Dixon, Zach | (RB) | Temple | 1979 |
| Dobelstein, Bob | (G) | Tennessee | 1946-48 |
| Doggert, Keith | (T) | Wichita | 1942 |
| Doolan, John | (B) | Georgetown | 1945-46 |
| Doornink, Dan | (RB) | Wash. St. | 1978 |
| Dorsey, Eric | (DE) | Notre Dame | 1986-92 |
| Douglas, Everett | (T) | Florida | 1953 |
| Douglas, John | (LB) | Missouri | 1970-73 |
| Douglas, Omar | (WR) | Minnesota | 1994-97 |
| Douglass, Maurice | (S) | Kentucky | 1995-96 |
| Douglass, Paul | (DB) | Illinois | 1953 |
| Dove, Eddie | (DB) | Colorado | 1963 |
| Downs, Gary | (RB) | N. Carolina St. | 1994,1996 |
| Dryer, Fred | (DE) | San Diego St. | 1969-71 |
| Dubinski, Tom | (QB) | Utah | 1958 |
| Dubinski, Walt | (G) | Boston Coll. | 1943 |
| Dubzinsky, Maurice | (G) | Georgetown | 1932 |
| Duckens, Mark | (DE) | Arizona St. | 1989 |
| Duden, Dick | (E) | Navy | 1949 |
| Dudley, Paul | (B) | Arkansas | 1962 |
| Duerson, Dave . | (DB) | Notre Dame | 1990 |
| Duff, Jamal | (DE) | San Diego St. | 1995-96 |
| Dugan, Bill | (G) | Penn St.. | 1987 |
| Dugan, Leonard | (C) | Wichita | 1936 |
| Duggan, Gill | (T) | Oklahoma | 1940 |
| Duhon, Bobby | (B) | Tulane | 1968-72 |
| Dunaway, Dave | (WR) | Duke | 1969 |
| Duncan, Jim | (E) | Wake Forest | 1950-53 |
| Dunlap, Bob | (B) | Oklahoma | 1936 |
| Dvorak, Rick | (LB) | Wichita St. | 1974-76 |
| **E** | | | |
| Eakin, Kay | (B) | Arkansas | 1940-41 |
| Eaton, Lou | (T) | California | 1945 |
| Eaton, Scott | (DB) | Oregon St. | 1967-71 |
| Echhardt, Oscar | (B) | Texas | 1928 |
| Eck, Keith | (C) | UCLA | 1979 |
| Eddings, Floyd | (WR) | California | 1982-83 |
| Edwards, Antonio | (DE) | Valdosta St. | 1997 |
| Edwards, Bill | (G) | Baylor | 1941-42, 46 |
| Elias, Keith | (RB) | Princeton | 1994-96 |
| Ellenbogen, Bill | (G) | Virginia Tech | 1976-77 |
| Elliott, John | (T) | Michigan | 1988-95 |
| Ellison, Mark | (G) | Dayton | 1972-73 |
| Ellsworth, Percy | (S) | Virginia | 1996-98 |
| Enderle, Dick | (G) | Minnesota | 1972-74 |
| Engler, Derek | (C) | Wisconsin | 1997-98 |
| Epps, Bobby | (B) | Pittsburgh | 1954-55, 57 |
| Erickson, Bill | (G) | Mississippi | 1948 |
| Eshmont, Len | (B) | Fordham | 1940-41 |
| Estes, Charles | (DE) | Army | 1997-98 |
| Ettinger, Don | (G) | Kansas | 1948-50 |
| Evans, Charlie | (RB) | USC | 1971-73 |
| **F** | | | |
| Faircloth, Art | (B) | N. Carolina | 1947-48 |
| Falaschi, Nello | (B) | Santa Clara | 1938-41 |
| Falcon, Terry | (G) | Montana | 1980 |
| Feather, Erwin | (B) | Kansas St. | 1929-30, 32-33 |
| Felton, Eric | (DB) | Texas Tech | 1980 |
| Fennema, Carl | (C) | Washington | 1948-49 |
| Fields, Joe | (C) | Widener | 1988 |
| Filchock, Frank | (QB) | Indiana | 1946 |
| Files, Jim | (LB) | Oklahoma | 1970-73 |
| Filipowicz, Steve | (B) | Fordham | 1945-46 |
| Filipski, Gene | (B) | Villanova | 1956-57 |
| Fischer, Cletus | (B) | Nebraska | 1949 |
| Fitzgerald, Mike | (DB) | Iowa St. | 1967 |
| Flaherty, Ray | (E) | Gonzaga | 1928-35 |
| Flenniken, Max | (B) | Geneva | 1930-31 |
| Flowers, Larry | (S) | Texas Tech | 1981-85 |
| Flowers, Richmond | (DB) | Tennessee | 1971-73 |
| Flynn, Tom | (S) | Pittsburgh | 1986-88 |
| Flythe, Mark | (DE) | Penn St. | 1993 |
| Folsom, Steve | (TE) | Utah | 1982 |
| Foote, Chris | (C) | USC | 1982-83 |
| Ford, Charlie | (DB) | Houston | 1975-76 |
| Forte, Ike | (RB) | Arkansas | 1981 |
| Fox, Mike | (DE) | W. Virginia | 1990-94 |
| Fox, Samuel | (E) | Ohio St. | 1945-46 |
| Franck, George | (B) | Minnesota | 1941,45-48 |
| Franklin, George | (RB) | Texas A&M | 1979 |
| Franklin, Mal | (E) | St. Mary's | 1934-35 |
| Friede, Mike | (WR) | Indiana | 1980 |
| Friedman, Bennie. | (QB) | Michigan | 1929-31 |
| Frederickson, Tucker | (FB) | Auburn | 1965-71 |
| Freeman, Lorenzo | (DT) | Pittsburgh | 1991 |
| Frugonne, Jim | (B) | Syracuse | 1925 |
| Fuqua, John | (RB) | Morgan St. | 1969 |
| **G** | | | |
| Gaiters, Bobby | (B) | New Mexico St. | 1961-62 |
| Galazian, Stan | (C) | Villanova | 1937-39 |
| Galbreath, Tony | (RB) | Missouri | 1984-87 |
| Galiffa, Arnold | (QB) | Army | 1953 |
| Gallagher, Dave | (DE) | Michigan | 1975-76 |
| Gallagher, Ed | (T) | Wash. & Jeff. | 1928 |
| Galyon, Scott | (LB) | Tennessee | 1996-98 |
| Garcia, Jim | (DE) | Purdue | 1966 |
| Garner, Bob | (G) | *No College* | 1945 |
| Garnes, Sam | (S) | Cincinnati | 1997-98 |
| Garrett, Alvin | (RB) | Angelo St. | 1980-81 |
| Garrett, Curtis | (DE) | Illinois St. | 1987 |
| Garvey, Art | (G) | Notre Dame | 1927-28 |
| Garzoni, Mike | (G) | USC | 1948 |
| Gatewood, Tom | (WR) | Notre Dame | 1972-73 |
| Gehrke, Bruce | (E) | Columbia | 1948 |
| Gehrke, Fred | (B) | Utah | 1948 |
| Gelatka, Charles | (E) | Mississippi St. | 1937-40 |
| Gibbons, Mike | (T) | S.W. Okla. St. | 1976-77 |
| Giblin, Robert | (S) | Houston | 1975-76 |
| Gifford, Frank | (B-E) | USC | 1952-60, 62-64 |
| Gigson, Denver | (G) | Grove City | 1930-34 |
| Gildea, John | (B) | St. Bonaventure | 1938 |
| Gillard, Larry | (DE) | Mississippi St. | 1978 |
| Gillette Walker | (WR) | Richmond | 1974-76 |
| Gladchuk Chet | (C) | Boston Coll. | 1941,46-47 |
| Glass, Chip | (TE) | Florida St. | 1974 |
| Glenn, Vencie | (S) | Indiana St. | 1995 |
| Glover, Rich | (DT) | Nebraska | 1973 |
| Godfrey, Chris | (G) | Michigan | 1984-87 |
| Gogolak, Pete | (K) | Cornell | 1966-74 |
| Goich, Dan | (DT) | California | 1972-73 |
| Golsteyn, Jerry | (QB) | N. Illinois | 1976-78 |
| Goode, Conrad | (T) | Missouri | 1984-85 |
| Goodwin, Tod | (E) | W. Virginia | 1935-36 |
| Gorgone, Pete | (B) | Muhlenberg | 1946 |
| Gossage, Gene | (T) | Northwestern | 1963 |
| Governali, Paul | (QB) | Columbia | 1947-48 |
| Gragg, Scott | (T) | Montana | 1995-98 |
| Graham, Kent | (QB) | Ohio St. | 1992-94, 98 |
| Grandelius, Ev | (B) | Michigan St. | 1953 |
| Grant, Len. | (T) | NYU | 1930-37 |
| Grate, Carl | (C) | Georgia | 1945 |
| Gravelle, Gordon | (T) | Brigham Young | 1977-78 |
| Gray, Carlton | (CB) | UCLA | 1998 |
| Gray, Earnest | (WR) | Memphis St. | 1979-84 |
| Green, Joe | (DB) | Bowling Green | 1970-71 |
| Green, Tony | (RB) | Florida | 1979 |
| Greene, A J. | (DB) | Wake Forest | 1991 |
| Greenhalgh, Bob | (B) | San Francisco | 1949 |
| Gregory, Jack | (DE) | Delta St. | 1972-78 |
| Grier, Rosey | (DT) | Penn St. | 1955-56, 58-62 |
| Griffing, Glynn | (QB) | Mississippi | 1963 |
| Griffith, Forrest | (B) | Kansas | 1950-51 |

| Player | Pos. | School | Years |
|---|---|---|---|
| Grigg, Cecil | (B) | Austin | 1926 |
| Grim, Bob | (WR) | Oregon St. | 1972-74 |
| Gross, Andy | (G) | Auburn | 1967-68 |
| Grosscup, Lee | (QB) | Utah | 1960-62 |
| Guggemos, Neal | (S) | St. Thomas (Mn) | 1988 |
| Guglielmi, Ralph | (QB) | Notre Dame | 1962-63 |
| Gunn, Jimmy | (LB) | Sthrn. California | 1975 |
| Gursky, Al | (LB) | Penn St. | 1963 |
| Gutowsky, Leroy | (B) | Oklahoma City | 1931 |
| Guy, Lou | (B) | Mississippi | 1963 |
| Guy, Melwood | (T) | Duke | 1958 |
| Guyon, Joe | (B) | Carlisle | 1927 |
| Guyton, Myron | (S) | Estrn. Kentucky | 1989-93 |
| | | | |
| **H** | | | |
| Haase, Andy | (TE) | Nrthrn Colorado | 1998 |
| Hachten, Bill | (G) | Stanford | 1947 |
| Haden, John | (T) | Arkansas | 1936-38 |
| Haddix, Wayne | (CB) | Liberty Baptist | 1987-88 |
| Hagerty, John | (B) | Georgetown | 1926-30 |
| Haines, Henry | (B) | Penn St. | 1925-28 |
| Haji-Sheikh, Ali | (PK) | Michigan | 1983-85 |
| Hall, H. | (C) | No College | 1942 |
| Hall, John | (E) | Iowa | 1955 |
| Hall, Pete | (E) | Marquette | 1961-62 |
| Hamilton, Conrad | (CB) | Estrn. New Mex. | 1996-98 |
| Hamilton, Keith | (DT) | Pittsburgh | 1992-98 |
| Hammond, Bob | (RB) | Morgan St. | 1976-79 |
| Hampton, Rodney | (RB) | Georgia | 1990-97 |
| Hanken, Ray | (E) | Geo. Wash. | 1937-38 |
| Hannah, Herb | (T) | Alabama | 1951 |
| Hanson, Dick | (T) | N. Dakota St. | 1971 |
| Hapes, Merle | (B) | Mississippi | 1942-46 |
| Hardison, Dee | (DE) | N. Carolina | 1981-85 |
| Hare, Cecil | (B) | Gonzaga | 1946 |
| Harms, Art | (T) | Vermont | 1927 |
| Harper, Charlie | (G) | Oklahoma St. | 1966-72 |
| Harper, LaSalle | (LB) | Arkansas | 1989 |
| Harris, Don | (S) | Rutgers | 1980 |
| Harrell, Gary | (WR) | Howard | 1995 |
| Harris, Oliver | (E) | Geneva | 1926 |
| Harris, Phil . | (DB) | Texas | 1966 |
| Harris, Robert | (DT) | Southern | 1995-98 |
| Harris, Wendell | (DB) | LSU | 1966-67 |
| Harrison, Ed | (E) | Boston Coll. | 1928 |
| Harrison, Granville | (E) | Mississippi St. | 1941 |
| Harrison, Max | (E) | Auburn | 1940 |
| Hart, Harold | (HB) | Texas Sthrn. | 1977 |
| Hasselbeck, Don | (TE) | Colorado | 1985 |
| Hathcock, Dave | (DB) | Memphis St. | 1967 |
| Hartzog, Howard | (T) | Baylor | 1928 |
| Hasenohrl, George | (DT) | Ohio St. | 1974 |
| Hauser, Art | (T) | Xavier | 1959 |
| Hayes, Larry | (LB) | Vanderbilt | 1961 |
| Haynes, Mark | (CB) | Colorado | 1980-85 |
| Hazeltine, Man | (LB) | California | 1970 |
| Headen, Andy | (LB) | Clemson | 1983-88 |
| Heap, Joe | (B) | Notre Dame | 1955 |
| Heater, Larry | (RB) | Arizona | 1980-83 |
| Hebert, Bud | (S) | Oklahoma | 1980 |
| Heck, Ralph | (LB) | Colorado | 1969-71 |
| Hein, Mel | (C) | Washington St. | 1931-45 |
| Heinrich, Don | (QB) | Washington | 1954-59 |
| Hendnan, Warren | (B) | Pittsburgh | 1925 |
| Henry, Steve | (DB) | Emporia State | 1980 |
| Henry, Wilbur | (T) | Wash. & Jeff. | 1927 |
| Hensley, Dick | (E) | Kentucky | 1949 |
| Herber, Arnie | (QB) | Regis | 1944-45 |
| Hermann, John | (B) | UCLA | 1956 |
| Hernon, Don | (B) | Ohio St. | 1960 |
| Herrmann, Don | (WR) | Waynesburg | 1969-74 |
| Hickl, Ray | (LB) | Texas A&M | 1969-70 |
| Hicks, Eddie | (RB) | East Carolina | 1979-80 |

| Player | Pos. | School | Years |
|---|---|---|---|
| Hicks, John | (G) | Ohio Stm | 1974-77 |
| Hienstra, Ed | (C) | Sterling | 1942 |
| Hilert, Hal | (B) | Oklahoma City | 1930 |
| Hill, Charles | (B) | No College | 1926 |
| Hill, John | (B) | Amherst | 1926 |
| Hill, Kenny | (DB) | Yale | 1984-88 |
| Hill, John | (T) | Lehigh | 1972-74 |
| Hill, Ralph | (C) | Florida A&M | 1976-77 |
| Hillebrand, Jerry | (LB) | Colorado | 1963-66 |
| Hilliard, Ike | (WR) | Florida | 1997-98 |
| Hilton, Roy | (DE) | Jackson St. | 1974 |
| Hinton, Chuck | (C) | Mississippi | 1967-69 |
| Hobgood-Chittick, N. | (DT) | N. Carolina | 1998 |
| Hodel, Merwin | (B) | Colorado | 1953 |
| Hogan, Mike | (RB) | Chananooga | 1980 |
| Hogan, Paul | (B) | Wash. & Jeff. | 1926 |
| Holland, Vern | (T) | Tennessee | 1980 |
| Holifield, Jimmy | (DB) | Jackson St. | 1968-69 |
| Holsey, Bernard | (DE) | Duke | 1996-98 |
| Horan, Mike | (P) | Long Beach St. | 1993-96 |
| Horne, Richard | (G) | Oregon | 1941 |
| Horner, Sam | (B) | VMI | 1962-63 |
| Hornsby, Ron | (LB) | S. E. Louisiana | 1971-74 |
| Hostetler, Jeff | (QB) | W. Virginia | 1984-92 |
| Houston, Dick | (WR) | E. Texas St. | 1969-73 |
| Hovious, John | (B) | Mississippi | 1945 |
| Howard, Erik | (DT) | Wash. St. | 1986-94 |
| Howard, Bob | (G) | Marietta | 1929-30 |
| Howell, Jim Lee | (E) | Arkansas | 1937-42, 46-48 |
| Howell, Lane | (T) | Grambling | 1963-64 |
| Hubbard, Cal | (T) | Geneva | 1927-29, 36 |
| Hudson, Bob | (E) | Clemson | 1951-52 |
| Huff, Sam | (LB) | W. Virginia | 1956-63 |
| Hugger, Keith | (WR) | Connecticut | 1983 |
| Hughes, Ed | (B) | Tulsa | 1956-58 |
| Hughes, Ernie | (C) | Notre Dame | 1981-83 |
| Hughes, Pat | (LB) | Boston U. | 1970-76 |
| Hunt, Byron | (LB) | SMU | 1981-88 |
| Hunt, George | (K) | Tennessee | 1975 |
| Hutchinson, Bill | (B) | Dartmouth | 1942 |
| Hutchinson, R. | (T) | Chattanooga | 1949 |
| Huth, Gerry | (G) | Wake Forest | 1956 |
| Hyland, Bob | (G) | Boston Coll. | 1971-75 |
| | | | |
| **I** | | | |
| Imlay, Talma | (B) | California | 1927 |
| Ingram, Mark | (WR) | Michigan St. | 1987-92 |
| Irvin, Cecil | (T) | Davis-Elkins | 1932-35 |
| Iverson, Chris | (B) | Oregon | 1947 |
| | | | |
| **J** | | | |
| Jackson, Bob | (B) | N. Carolina A&T | 1950-51 |
| Jackson, Cleveland | (TE) | UNLV | 1979 |
| Jackson, Greg | (S) | LSU | 1989-93 |
| Jackson, Honor | (DB) | Pacific | 1973-74 |
| Jackson, Louis | (RB) | Cal Poly (SLO) | 1981 |
| Jackson, Mark | (WR) | Purdue | 1993-94 |
| Jackson, Terry | (CB) | San Diego St. | 1978-83 |
| Jacobs, Allen | (FB) | Utah | 1966-67 |
| Jacobs, Proverb | (T) | California | 1960 |
| Jacobson, Larry | (DT) | Nebraska | 1972-74 |
| James, Dick | (B) | Oregon | 1964 |
| Janarette, Charlie | (T) | Penn St. | 1961-62 |
| Jappe, Paul | (E) | Syracuse | 1925, 27-28 |
| Jelacic, Jon | (E) | Minnesota | 1958 |
| Jenkins, Eddie | (RB) | Holy Cross | 1974 |
| Jenkins, Izel | (CB) | N. Carolina St. | 1993 |
| Jennings, Dave | (P) | St. Lawrence | 1974-84 |
| Jessie, Brandon | (TE) | Utah | 1997 |
| Jeter, Gary | (DT) | USC | 1977-82 |
| Jiles, Dwayne | (LB) | Texas Tech | 1989 |
| Johnson, Bill | (P) | Livingston | 1970 |
| Johnson, Bob | (WR) | Kansas | 1984-86 |

| Player | Pos. | School | Years |
|---|---|---|---|
| Johnson, Curley | (K) | Houston | 1969 |
| Johnson, Damian | (G) | Kansas St. | 1986-89 |
| Johnson, Dennis | (TE) | Mississippi St. | 1980 |
| Johnson, Gene | (DB) | Cincinnati | 1961-62 |
| Johnson, Herb | (B) | No College | 1954 |
| Johnson, Jon | (B) | Mississippi | 1948 |
| Johnson, Ken | (RB) | Miami | 1979 |
| Johnson, Larry | (C) | Haskell | 1936-39 |
| Johnson, Len | (G) | St. Cloud | 1970 |
| Johnson, LeShon | (RB) | Nrthrn. Illinois | 1998 |
| Johnson, Nate | (WR) | Hillsdale | 1980 |
| Johnson, Pepper | (LB) | Ohio St. | 1986-92 |
| Johnson, Randy | (QB) | Texas A&M | 1971-73 |
| Johnson, Ron | (RB) | Michigan | 1970-75 |
| Johnston, Brian | (C) | North Carolina | 1986-87 |
| Jones, Cedric | (DE) | Oklahoma | 1996-98 |
| Jones, Chris | (C) | Delaware State | 1987 |
| Jones, Clarence | (T) | Maryland | 1991-93 |
| Jones, Ernie | (DB) | Miami | 1977-79 |
| Jones, Homer | (E) | Texas Southern | 1964-69 |
| Jones, James | (DE) | N. Carolina A&T | 1987 |
| Jones, Robbie | (LB) | Alabama | 1984-87 |
| Jones, Tom | (G) | Bucknell | 1932-36 |
| Jordan, David | (G) | Auburn | 1984-86 |
| Jurevicius, Joe | (WR) | Penn St. | 1998 |
| | | | |
| **K** | | | |
| Kab, Vyto | (TE) | Penn St. | 1985 |
| Kane, Herb | (T) | Okla.Teachers | 1944-45 |
| Kanell, Danny | (QB) | Florida St. | 1996-98 |
| Kanicki, Jim | (DT) | Michigan St. | 1970-71 |
| Kaplan, Bernie | (G) | West Maryland | 1935-36 |
| Karcis, John | (B) | Carnegie Tech | 1938-39, 43 |
| Karilivacz, Carl | (DB) | Syracuse | 1958 |
| Katcavage, Jim | (DE) | Dayton | 1956-68 |
| Keahy, Eulis | (G) | George Wash. | 1942 |
| Kearns, Tom | (T) | Miami | 1945 |
| Kelley, Brian | (LB) | Cal. Lutheran | 1973-83 |
| Kelly, Ellison | (G) | Michigan St. | 1959 |
| Kelly, John S. | (B) | Kentucky | 1932 |
| Kelly, Paul | (QB) | New Haven | 1987 |
| Kemp, Jackie | (QB) | Occidental | 1958 |
| Kendricks, Jim | (T) | Texas A&M | 1927 |
| Kennard, George | (G) | Kansas | 1952-55 |
| Kennedy, Tom | (QB) | L. A. St. | 1966-67 |
| Kenyon, Bill | (B) | Georgetown | 1925 |
| Kerrigan, Tom | (G) | Columbia | 1930 |
| Kershaw, George | (E) | Colgate | 1949 |
| Ketzko, Alex | (T) | Michigan St. | 1942 |
| Keuper, Ken | (B) | Georgia | 1948 |
| Killenger, Glenn | (B) | Penn St. | 1926 |
| Killett, Charlie | (B) | Memphis St. | 1963 |
| Kimball, Bruce | (G) | Massachusetts | 1982 |
| Kimber, Bill | (E) | Florida St. | 1959-60 |
| Kimmel, Jerry | (LB) | Syracuse | 1987 |
| Kinard, Terry | (S) | Clemson | 1983-89 |
| King, Gordon | (T) | Stanford | 1978-85 |
| King, Jerome | (DB) | Purdue | 1980 |
| King, Phil | (B) | Vanderbilt | 1958-63 |
| Kinscherf, Carl | (B) | Colgate | 1943-44 |
| Kirby, John | (LB) | Nebraska | 1969-70 |
| Kirouac, Lou | (G) | Boston Coll. | 1963 |
| Kitzmiller, John | (B) | Oregon | 1931 |
| Klasoskus, Al | (T) | Holy Cross | 1941-42 |
| Kline, Harry | (E) | Kansas Teachers | 1939-41 |
| Klotovich, Mike | (B) | St. Mary's | 1945 |
| Knight, Pat | (B) | SMU | 1952, 54-55 |
| Kobrosky, Milt | (B) | Trinity (Conn.) | 1937 |
| Kolman, Ed | (T) | Temple | 1949 |
| Koontz, Joe | (E) | San Francisco St. | 1968 |
| Koppisch, Walter | (B) | Columbia | 1925-26 |
| Kotar, Doug | (RB) | Kentucky | 1974-81 |
| Kotite, Rich | (TE) | Wagner | 1967, 69-72 |

| Player | Pos. | School | Years | Player | Pos. | School | Years | Player | Pos. | School | Years |
|---|---|---|---|---|---|---|---|---|---|---|---|
| Koy, Ernie | (B) | Texas | 1965-70 | Markham. Dale | (DE) | N. Dakota | 1980 | Miller, Solomon | (WR) | Utah St. | 1986 |
| Kozlowski, Brian | (HB) | Connecticut | 1994-96 | Marker. Cliff | (B) | Washington St. | 1927 | Milling, James | (WR) | Maryland | 1991 |
| Krahl, Jim | (DT) | Texas Tech | 1978 | Marsh, Dick | (G) | Oklahoma | 1933 | Mills, Jeff | (LB) | Nebraska | 1994 |
| Kratch, Bob | (G) | Iowa | 1989-93 | Marshall, Arthur | (WR) | Georgia | 1994-96 | Milner, Bill | (G) | Duke | 1950 |
| Krause, Max | (RB) | Gonzaga | 1933-36 | Marshall, Ed | (WR) | Cameron St. | 1976-77 | Milstead, Century | (T) | Yale | 1925, 27-28 |
| Krause, Ray | (T) | Maryland | 1951-55 | Marshall, Leonard | (DE) | LSU | 1983-92 | Minisi, Tony | (B) | Penn | 1948 |
| Kyles, Troy | (WR) | Howard | 1990 | Martin, Frank | (B) | Alabama | 1945 | Minniear, Randy | (RB) | Purdue | 1967-69 |
|  |  |  |  | Martin, George | (DE) | Oregon | 1975-88 | Mischak, Bob | (G) | Army | 1958 |
|  |  |  |  | Martinkovich, J. | (E) | Xavier | 1957 | Mistler, John | (WR) | Arizona St. | 1981-84 |
| **L** |  |  |  | Massey, Robert | (CB) | N.C. Central | 1997 | Mitchell, Grandville | (E) | Davis-Elkins | 1935 |
| Lacey, Bob | (E) | N. Carolina | 1965 | Mastrangelo, John | (G) | Notre Dame | 1950 | Mitchell, Harold | (T) | UCLA | 1952 |
| Lagod, Chester | (G) | Chattanooga | 1953 | Matthews, Bo | (RB) | Colorado | 1980 | Mitchell, Russell | (C) | Mississippi | 1987 |
| Ladlaw, Scott | (RB) | Stanford | 1980 | Matan, Bill | (DE) | Kansas St. | 1966 | Modzelewski, D | (DT) | Maryland | 1956-63 |
| Lakes, Roland | (DT) | Wichita | 1971 | Maumalanga, Chris | (DT) | Kansas | 1994 | Molden, Frank | (DT) | Jackson St. | 1969 |
| Lalonde, Roger | (DT) | Muskingum | 1965 | Maynard, Brad | (P) | Ball St. | 1997-98 | Molenda, John | (B) | Michigan | 1932-35 |
| Landeta, Sean | (P) | Towson St. | 1985-93 | Maynard, Don | (B) | Texas Western | 1958 | Monty, Pete | (LB) | Wisconsin | 1997-98 |
| Landry, Tom | (DB) | Texas | 1950-55 | Mayock, Mike | (DB) | Boston Coll. | 1982-83 | Moore, Dana | (P) | S. Mississippi | 1987 |
| Landshell, Granville | (B) | USC | 1940 | Maxon, Alvin | (RB) | SMU | 1978 | Moore, Eric | (G) | Indiana | 1988-93 |
| Lane, Eric | (FB) | Tennessee | 1997 | Mazurek, Ed | (B) | Xavier | 1960 | Moore, Henry | (B) | Arkansas | 1956 |
| Lane, Gary | (QB) | Missouri | 1968 | McBride, John | (B) | Syracuse | 1925-28, 32-33 | Moore, Ken | (C) | W. Va. Wesleyan | 1940 |
| Lapka, Myron | (DT) | USC | 1980 | McCafferty, Don | (E) | Ohio St. | 1946 | Moorehead, Emery | (WR) | Colorado | 1977-79 |
| Larson, Greg | (C) | Minnesota | 1961-73 | McCaffrey, Ed | (WR) | Stanford | 1991-93 | Moran, Dale (Hap) | (B) | Carnegie Tech | 1928-34 |
| Lascari, John | (E) | Georgetown | 1942 | McCann, Jim | (P) | Arizona St. | 1973 | Moran, Jim | (T) | Idaho | 1964-67 |
| Lasker, Greg | (S) | Arkansas | 1986-88 | McCann, Tim | (DT) | Princeton | 1969 | Morgan, Bill | (T) | Oregon | 1933-36 |
| Lasky, Frank | (T) | Florida | 1964-65 | McConkey Phil | (WR) | Navy | 1984-88 | Morgan, Dan | (G) | Penn State | 1987 |
| Lasse, Dick | (LB) | Syracuse | 1962-63 | McCoy, Mike | (DT) | Notre Dame | 1979 | Morrall, Earl | (QB) | Michigan St. | 1965-67 |
| Lechner, Edgar | (T) | Minnesota | 1942 | McChesney, Bob | (E) | Hardon-Simmons | 1950 | Morris, Joe | (RB) | Syracuse | 1982-89 |
| Leemans, Tuffy | (B) | George Wash. | 1936-43 | McClain, Clint | (B) | SMU | 1941 | Morrison, Joe | (B-E) | Cincinnati | 1959-72 |
| Leo, Jim | (LB) | Cincinnati | 1960 | McCreary, Loaird | (TE) | Tennessee St. | 1979 | Morrison, Pat | (DB) | S. Connecticut St. | 1987 |
| Levy, Harvey | (G) | Syracuse | 1928 | McDaniel, LeCharls | (CB) | Cal-Poly | 1983-84 | Morrow, Bob | (B) | Ill. Wesleyan | 1945 |
| Lewis, Art | (T) | Ohio | 1936 | McDowell, John | (T) | St. John's (Minn ) | 1965 | Morton, Craig | (QB) | California | 1974-76 |
| Lewis, Danny | (B) | Wisconsin | 1966 | McElhenny, Hugh | (B) | Washington | 1963 | Mote, Kelly | (E) | Duke | 1950-52 |
| Lewis, Thomas | (WR) | Indiana | 1994-97 | McFadden, Paul | (PK) | Youngstown | 1988 | Mowatt, Zeke | (TE) | Florida St. | 1983-89,91 |
| Lieberum, Don | (B) | Manchester | 1942 | McGee, Ed | (T) | Temple | 1940 | Mrosko, Bob | (TE) | Penn St. | 1990 |
| Liebel, Frank | (E) | Norwich | 1942-47 | McGhee, Kanavis | (LB) | Colorado | 1991-93 | Mullady, Tom | (TE) | Rhodes Coll. | 1979-84 |
| Lincoln, Jeremy | (CB) | Tennessee | 1998 | McGlasson, Ed | (C) | Youngstown St. | 1981 | Mullen, Tom | (G) | SW Mo. St. | 1974-77 |
| Linnin, Chris | (DE) | Washington | 1980 | McGriff, Curtis | (DT) | Alabama | 1980-86 | Mulleaneaux, Lee | (B) | Arizona | 1932 |
| Lindahl, Virgil | (G) | Nebraska St. | 1945 | McGinley, Ed | (T) | Penn | 1925 | Mullins, Noah | (B) | Kentucky | 1949 |
| Little, Jim | (T) | Kentucky | 1945 | McGowan, Reggie | (WR) | Abilene Christian | 1987 | Munday, George | (T) | Kansas Teachers | 1931-32 |
| Livingston, Cliff | (LB) | UCLA | 1954-61 | McGrew, Lawrence | (LB) | USC | 1990 | Munn, Lyle | (E) | Kansas St. | 1929 |
| Livingston, Howard | (B) | No College | 1944-47 | McGriggs, Lamar | (DB) | Wstrn. Illinois | 1991-92 | Murdock, Les | (K) | Florida St. | 1967 |
| Lloyd, Dan | (LB) | Washington | 1976-79 | McKinney, Odis | (DB) | Colorado | 1978-79 | Murray, Earl | (G) | Purdue | 1951 |
| Lockhart, Carl | (DB) | N. Texas St. | 1965-75 | McLaughlin, Joe | (LB) | Massachusetts | 1980-84 | Murtaugh, George | (C) | Georgetown | 1926-32 |
| Long, Bufford | (B) | Florida | 1953-55 | McLaughry, John | (B) | Brown | 1940 | Myers, Tom | (B) | Fordham | 1925-26 |
| Longo, Tom | (DB) | Notre Dame | 1969-70 | McLean, Ron | (DE) | CSU-Fullerton | 1988 | Myles, Toby | (T) | Jackson St. | 1998 |
| Lott, Billy | (B) | Mississippi | 1958 | McMullen, Dan | (G) | Nebraska | 1929 |  |  |  |  |
| Love, Walter | (WR) | Westminster | 1973 | McMullen, Typail | (S) | Middle Tennessee | 1997 | **N** |  |  |  |
| Lovelady, Edwin | (WR) | Memphis St. | 1987 | McNeil, Clifton | (WR) | Grambling | 1970-71 | Nash, Bob | (T) | Rutgers | 1925 |
| LoVetere, John | (DT) | Compton | 1963-65 | McQuay. Leon | (RB) | Tampa | 1974 | Neill, Bill | (DT) | Pittsburgh | 1981-83 |
| Lovuolo, Frank | (E) | St. Bonaventure | 1949 | McRae, Bennie | (DB) | Michigan | 1971 | Neill, Jim | (B) | Texas Tech | 1937 |
| Lummus, John | (E) | Baylor | 1941 | Mead, John | (E) | Wisconsin | 1946-47 | Nelson, Andy | (DB) | Memphis St. | 1964 |
| Lumpkin, Ron | (DB) | Arizona St. | 1973 | Meggett, David | (RB) | Towson St. | 1989-94 | Nelson, Karl | (T) | Iowa State | 1984-88 |
| Lunday, Ken | (C) | Arkansas | 1937-41, 46-47 | Meisner, Greg | (DT) | Pittsburgh | 1991 | Nesser, AL | (E) | No College | 1926-28 |
| Lurtsema, Bob | (DT) | W. Michigan | 1967-71 | Mellus, John | (T) | Villanova | 1938-41 | Nettles, Doug | (DB) | Vanderbilt | 1980 |
| Lynch, Dick | (DB) | Notre Dame | 1959-66 | Menasco, Don | (B) | Texas | 1952-53 | Neville, Tom | (T) | Mississippi St. | 1979 |
| Lyons, George | (T) | Kansas St. | 1929 | Menefee, Hartwell | (E) | New Mexico St. | 1966 | Newman, Harry | (QB) | Michigan | 1933-35 |
|  |  |  |  | Mendenhall, John | (DT) | Grambling | 1972-79 | Nicholson, Frank | (LB) | Delaware St. | 1987 |
| **M** |  |  |  | Mercer, Jim | (QB) | Oregon St. | 1942-43 | Nielsen, Walter | (B) | Arizona | 1940 |
| MacAfee, Ken | (E) | Alabama | 1954-58 | Mercein, Chuck | (FB) | Yale | 1965-66 | Niles, Gary | (B) | Iowa | 1946-47 |
| Mackorell, John | (B) | Davidson | 1935 | Merrill, Casey | (DE) | UC-Davis | 1983-85 | Nittmo, Bjorn | (K) | Appalachian St. | 1989 |
| Mackrides, Bill | (QB) | Nevada | 1953 | Mertes, Bernie | (B) | Iowa | 1949 | Nix, Emery | (QB) | TCU | 1943-46 |
| Maddox, Tommy | (QB) | UCLA | 1995 | Messner, Max | (L) | Cincinnati | 1964 | Nolan, Dick | (DB) | Maryland | 1954-57, 59-61 |
| Maher, Bruce | (DB) | Detroit | 1968-69 | Meuth, Kevin | (T) | SW Texas St. | 1987 | Norby, John | (B) | Idaho | 1934 |
| Maikkula, Ken | (E) | Connecticut | 1942 | Mietznier, Saul | (C) | Carnegie Tech | 1929-30 | Nordstrom, Harry | (G) | Trinity (Conn.) | 1925 |
| Mallory, Larry | (DB) | Tennessee St. | 1976-78 | Miklich, Bill | (B) | Idaho | 1947-48 | Norris, Jimmy | (CB) | Upsala | 1987 |
| Mallouf, Ray | (QB) | SMU | 1949 | Mikolajczyk, Ron | (T) | Tampa | 1976-79 | Norton, Jim | (DT) | Washington | 1970 |
| Mangum, Pete | (LB) | Mississippi | 1954 | Miles, Leo | (B) | Virginia St. | 1953 | Nutt, Richard | (B) | Texas St. | 1949 |
| Manton, Tilly | (B) | TCU | 1936-38 | Miller, Calvin | (DT) | Oklahoma St. | 1979 |  |  |  |  |
| Manuel, Lionel | (WR) | Pacific | 1984-90 | Miller, Corey | (LB) | South Carolina | 1991-98 | **O** |  |  |  |
| Marefos, Andy | (B) | St. Mary's | 1941-42 | Miller, Ed | (B) | New Mexico | 1939-40 | Oates, Bart | (C) | Brigham Young | 1985-93 |
| Marion, Frank | (LB) | Florida A&M | 1977-83 | Miller, Jim | (P) | Mississippi | 1987 | Oben, Roman | (T) | Louisville | 1996-98 |
| Marone, John | (G) | Manhattan | 1943 | Miller, Mike | (WR) | Tennessee | 1983 | O'Brien, Dave | (G) | Boston Coll. | 1965 |
| Maronic, Dusan | (G) | No College | 1951 | Miller, Nate | (T) | LSU | 1998 | Obradovich, Jim | (TE) | Sthrn. Cal. | 1975 |

| Player | Pos. | School | Years |
|---|---|---|---|
| Odom, Steve | (WR) | Utah | 1979 |
| Okoli, Ramon | (DL) | Murray St. | 1996 |
| Olander, Cliff | (DB) | New Mexico St. | 1980 |
| Oldershaw, Doug | (G) | Santa Barbara | 1939-41 |
| Oldham, Ray | (S) | Middle Tennessee | 1979 |
| Orduna, Joe | (RB) | Nebraska | 1972-73 |
| Ostendarp, Jim | (B) | Bucknell | 1950-51 |
| Owen, Alton | (B) | Mercer | 1939-41 |
| Owen, Steve | (T) | Phillips | 1926-36 |
| Owen, Tom | (QB) | Wichita St. | 1983 |
| Owen, Vilas | (QB) | Wisc. Teachers | 1942 |
| Owen, William | (T) | Oklahoma A&M | 1929-37 |
| Owens, R. C. | (E) | Idaho | 1964 |

**P**

| Player | Pos. | School | Years |
|---|---|---|---|
| Palazzi, Lou | (C) | Penn St. | 1946-47 |
| Palelei, Lonnie | (G) | UNLV | 1998 |
| Palm, Mike | (B) | Penn St. | 1925-26 |
| Park, Kaulana | (RB) | Stanford | 1987 |
| Parker, Frank | (DT) | Oklahoma St. | 1969 |
| Parker, Ken | (DB) | Fordham | 1970 |
| Parnell, Fred | (T) | Colgate | 1925-27 |
| Parry, Owen | (T) | Baylor | 1937-39 |
| Paschal, Bill | (B) | Georgia Tech | 1942-47 |
| Paschka, Gordon | (G) | Minnesota | 1947 |
| Patten, David | (WR) | Wstrn. Carolina | 1997-98 |
| Patterson, Don | (DB) | Georgia Tech | 1980 |
| Patterson, Elvis | (DB) | Kansas | 1984-87 |
| Patton, Bob | (T) | Clemson | 1952 |
| Patton, Jim | (DB) | Mississippi | 1955-66 |
| Peay, Francis | (T) | Missouri | 1966-67 |
| Pederson, Winifield | (T) | Minnesota | 1941-45 |
| Pegram, Erric | (RB) | N. Texas St. | 1997 |
| Pelfrey, Ray | (B) | Kentucky St. | 1953 |
| Perdue, Willard | (E) | Duke | 1944 |
| Perez, Mike | (QB) | San Jose St. | 1991 |
| Perkins, Johnny | (WR) | Abilene Christian | 1977-83 |
| Perretta, Ralph | (C) | Purdue | 1980 |
| Perry, Leon | (RB) | Mississippi | 1980-82 |
| Pesonen, Dick | (DB) | Minn. (Duluth) | 1962-64 |
| Peter, Christian | (DT) | Nebraska | 1997-98 |
| Peterson, Marty | (T) | Pennsylvania | 1987 |
| Petrilas, William | (E) | No College | 1944-45 |
| Petigrew, Gary | (DT) | Stanford | 1974 |
| Petty, Jack | (G) | Rutgers | 1926-28 |
| Peviani, Bob | (G) | USC | 1953 |
| Phillips, Ewell | (G) | Okla. Baptist | 1936-37 |
| Phillips, Ryan | (LB) | Idaho | 1997-98 |
| Piccolo, Bill | (C) | Canisius | 1943-45 |
| Pierce, Aaron | (TE) | Washington | 1992-97 |
| Pietrzak, Jim | (DT) | Estrn. Michigan | 1974-78 |
| Pipkin, Joyce | (E) | Arkansas | 1948 |
| Pisarcik, Joe | (QB) | New Mexico St. | 1977-79 |
| Pittman, Danny | (WR) | Wyoming | 1980-83 |
| Plansky, Tony | (B) | Georgetown | 1928-29 |
| Plum, Milt | (QB) | Penn St. | 1969 |
| Podoley, Jim | (B) | Central Mich. | 1962 |
| Poole, Barney | (E) | Mississippi | 1954-55 |
| Poole, Jim | (E) | Mississippi | 1937-41, 46 |
| Poole, Ray | (E) | Mississippi | 1947-52 |
| Porter, Rob | (DB) | Holy Cross | 1987 |
| Post, Bob | (DB) | Kings Point | 1967 |
| Potteiger, Earl | (B) | Ursinus | 1926-28 |
| Powell, Andre | (LB) | Penn St. | 1993-94 |
| Powell, Dick | (E) | Davis-Elkins | 1931 |
| Powers, Clyde | (DB) | Oklahoma | 1974-77 |
| Pough, Ernie | (WR) | Texas Southern | 1978 |
| Prestel, Jim | (DT) | Idaho | 1966 |
| Price, Eddie | (FB) | Tulane | 1950-55 |
| Principe, Dominic | (B) | Fordham | 1940-42 |
| Pritchard, Bosh | (B) | VMI | 1951 |
| Pritko, Steve | (E) | Villanova | 1943 |
| Prokop, Joe | (P) | Cal Poly Pomona | 1992 |

| Player | Pos. | School | Years |
|---|---|---|---|
| Pugh, Marion | (QB) | Texas A&M | 1941, 45 |
| Pupunu, Al | (TE) | Weber St. | 1997-98 |

**Q**

| Player | Pos. | School | Years |
|---|---|---|---|
| Quatse, Jess | (T) | Pitt | 1935 |

**R**

| Player | Pos. | School | Years |
|---|---|---|---|
| Rader, Dave | (QB) | Tulsa | 1979 |
| Ragazzo, Phil | (T) | Wstrn. Reserve | 1945-47 |
| Ramona, Joe | (G) | Santa Clara | 1953 |
| Randolph, Thomas | (CB) | Kansas St. | 1994-97 |
| Rapacz, John | (C) | Oklahoma | 1950-54 |
| Rasheed, Kenyon | (FB) | Oklahoma | 1993-94 |
| Raymond, Corey | (S) | LSU | 1992-94 |
| Reagan, Frank | (B) | Penn | 1941, 46-48 |
| Reasons, Gary | (LB) | NW Louisiana St. | 1984-91 |
| Reece, Beasley | (DB) | N. Texas St. | 1977-83 |
| Reed, Henry | (DE) | Weber St. | 1971-74 |
| Reed, Mark | (QB) | Moorehead St. | 1982 |
| Reed, Max | (C) | Bucknell | 1928 |
| Reed, Smith | (B) | Alcorn A&M | 1965-66 |
| Reese, Darren | (G) | Ohio University | 1994 |
| Reese, Henry | (C) | Temple | 1933-34 |
| Regular, Moses | (TE) | Missouri Valley | 1996 |
| Rehage, Steve | (S) | Louisiana St. | 1987 |
| Rehder, Tom | (T) | Notre Dame | 1990 |
| Reynolds, Ed | (LB) | Virginia | 1992 |
| Reynolds, Jerry | (G/T) | UNLV | 1995-98 |
| Reynolds, Owen | (E) | Georgia | 1925 |
| Rhenquist, Milt | (C) | Bethany | 1931 |
| Rhodes, Ray | (WR) | Tulsa | 1974-79 |
| Rice, J | (B) | No College | 1929 |
| Rich, Herb | (B) | Vanderbilt | 1954-56 |
| Richards, Elvin | (B) | Simpson | 1933-39 |
| Riesenberg, Doug | (T) | California | 1987-95 |
| Riley, Lee | (DB) | Detroit | 1960 |
| Rivers, Nate | (RB) | S. Carolina St. | 1980 |
| Rizzo, Jack | (RB) | Lehigh | 1973 |
| Roberson, Brian | (WR) | Fresno St. | 1997 |
| Roberts, Gene | (B) | Chattanooga | 1947-50 |
| Roberts, Tom | (T) | DePaul | 1943 |
| Roberts, William | (T) | Ohio St. | 1984-94 |
| Robinson, Jimmy | (WR) | Georgia Tech | 1976-79 |
| Robinson, Stacy | (WR) | N. Dakota St. | 1985-90 |
| Robustelli, Andy | (DE) | Arnold | 1956-64 |
| Rodriguez, Ruben | (P) | Arizona | 1992 |
| Roland, Johnny | (RB) | Missouri | 1973 |
| Roller, Dave | (DT) | Kentucky | 1971 |
| Roman, George | (T) | Wstrn. Reserve | 1950 |
| Rooney, Cobb | (B) | Colorado | 1925 |
| Rosatti, Roman | (T) | Michigan | 1928 |
| Rose, Roy | (E) | Tennessee | 1936 |
| Rote, Kyle | (E) | SMU | 1951-61 |
| Rouson, Lee | (RB) | Colorado | 1985-90 |
| Rovinski, Tony | (B) | Holy Cross | 1933 |
| Rowe, Harmon | (B) | San Francisco | 1950-52 |
| Royston, Ed | (G) | Wake Forest | 1948-49 |
| Rossell, Fay | (B) | Lafayette | 1933 |
| Rucker, Reggie | (WR) | Boston U. | 1971 |
| Rudolph, Coleman | (LB) | Georgia Tech | 1994-96 |
| Rutledge, Jeff | (QB) | Alabama | 1982-88 |

**S**

| Player | Pos. | School | Years |
|---|---|---|---|
| Saalfeld, Kelly | (C) | Nebraska | 1980 |
| Sally, Jerome | (DT) | Missouri | 1982-86 |
| Salschieder, John | (B) | St. Thomas | 1949 |
| Sanchez, John | (T) | San Francisco | 1949-50 |
| Sanders, Brandon | (S) | Arizona | 1997-98 |
| Sarausky, Tony | (B) | Fordham | 1935-37 |
| Sark, Harvey | (G) | Phillips | 1931 |
| Satenstein, Bernie | (G) | NYU | 1933 |
| Saxton, Brian | (TE) | Boston Coll. | 1996 |
| Scales, Dwight | (WR) | Grambling | 1979 |
| Schichtle, Henry | (QB) | Wichita | 1964 |

| Player | Pos. | School | Years |
|---|---|---|---|
| Schmeelk, Gary | (T) | Manhattan | 1942 |
| Schmidt, Bob | (T) | Minnesota | 1959-60 |
| Schmit, Bob | (LB) | Nebraska | 1975-76 |
| Schnelker, Bob | (E) | Bowling Green | 1954-60 |
| Schnellbacher, Otto | (B) | Kansas | 1950-51 |
| Scholtz, Bob | (C-T) | Notre Dame | 1965-66 |
| Schreiber, Adam | (C) | Texas | 1994-96 |
| Schubert, Eric | (K) | Pittsburgh | 1985 |
| Schuene, Paul | (G) | Wisconsin | 1928 |
| Schuler, Bill | (T) | Yale | 1947-48 |
| Schwab, Ray | (B) | Oklahoma City | 1931 |
| Scott, George | (B) | Miami, (Ohio) | 1959 |
| Scott, Joe | (B) | San Francisco | 1948-53 |
| Scott, Lance | (C) | Utah | 1997-98 |
| Scott, Malcolm | (TE) | LSU | 1983 |
| Scott, Tom | (LB) | Virginia | 1959-64 |
| Sczurek, Stan | (LB) | Purdue | 1966 |
| Sedbrook, Len | (B) | Oklahoma City | 1929-31 |
| Sehorn, Jason | (CB) | USC | 1994-98 |
| Seick, Earl | (G) | Manhattan | 1942-43 |
| Seitz, Warren | (WR) | Missouri | 1987 |
| Selfridge, Andy | (LB) | Virginia | 1974-77 |
| Shaffer, Leland | (QB) | Kansas St. | 1935-43, 45 |
| Shaw, Dennis | (QB) | San Diego St. | 1976 |
| Shaw, George | (QB) | Oregon | 1959-60 |
| Shaw, Pete | (DB) | Northwestern | 1982-84 |
| Shaw, Rickey | (LB) | Oklahoma St. | 1988-89 |
| Shay, Jerry | (CT) | Purdue | 1970-71 |
| Shediosky, Ed | (B) | Tulsa | 1945 |
| Sherrard, Mike | (WR) | UCLA | 1993-95 |
| Sherrod, Horace | (E) | Tennessee | 1952 |
| Sherwin, Tim | (TE) | Boston Coll. | 1988 |
| Shiner, Dick | (QB) | Maryland | 1970 |
| Shipp, Bill | (T) | Alabama | 1954 |
| Shirk, Gary | (TE) | Morehead St. | 1976-82 |
| Shufelt, Pete | (LB) | Texas El Paso | 1994 |
| Shofner, Del | (E) | Baylor | 1961-67 |
| Shy, Les | (RB) | Long Beach St. | 1970 |
| Siegel, Jules | (B) | Northwestern | 1948 |
| Silas, Sam | (DT) | S. Illinois | 1968 |
| Simmons, Roy | (G) | Georgia Tech | 1977-80 |
| Simms, Bob | (E) | Rutgers | 1960-62 |
| Simms, Phil | (QB) | Morehead St. | 1979-93 |
| Simonson, Dave | (T) | U. of Minn. | 1975 |
| Simpson, Al | (T) | Colorado St. | 1975-76 |
| Singer, Walter | (E) | Syracuse | 1935-37 |
| Sinnott, John | (T) | Brown | 1980 |
| Singletary, Bill | (LB) | Temple | 1974 |
| Sisley, Brian | (NT) | S. Dakota St. | 1987 |
| Sivell, Ralph | (G) | Auburn | 1944-45 |
| Skladany, Leo | (E) | Pittsburgh | 1950 |
| Skorupan, John | (LB) | Penn St. | 1978-80 |
| Slaby, Lou | (LB) | Pittsburgh | 1964-65 |
| Small, Eldridge | (DB) | Texas A&M | 1972-74 |
| Small, George | (DT) | N. Carolina A&T | 1980 |
| Smith, Doug | (S) | Ohio St. | 1987 |
| Smith, Jeff | (LB) | USC | 1966-67 |
| Smith, Jeff | (TE) | Tennessee | 1987 |
| Smith, Joey | (WR) | Louisville | 1991-92 |
| Smith, Lance | (G) | LSU | 1994-96 |
| Smith, Richard | (G) | Notre Dame | 1930-31 |
| Smith, Torin | (DE) | Hampton U. | 1987 |
| Smith, Willis | (B) | Idaho | 1934-35 |
| Smith, Zeke | (G) | Auburn | 1961-62 |
| Snead, Norm | (QB) | Wake Forest | 1972-74, 76 |
| Snyder, Gerry | (B) | Maryland | 1929 |
| Soar, Hank | (B) | Providence | 1937-44, 46 |
| Sohn, Ben | (G) | USC | 1941 |
| Sparks, Phillippi | (CB) | Arizona St. | 1992-98 |
| Spencer, Willie | (RB) | No College | 1977-78 |
| Spinks, Jack | (G) | Alcorn A&M | 1956-57 |
| Springer, Harold | (E) | Oklahoma St. | 1945 |
| Stafford, Harrison | (B) | Texas | 1934 |

| Player | Pos. | School | Years | Player | Pos. | School | Years | Player | Pos. | School | Years |
|---|---|---|---|---|---|---|---|---|---|---|---|
| Stahlman, Dick | (E) | DePaul | 1927 | Triplett, Bill | (HB) | Miami (Ohio) | 1967 | White, Freeman | (E-LB) | Nebraska | 1966-69 |
| Staten, Randy | (DE) | Minnesota | 1967 | Triplett, Mel | (FB) | Toledo | 1955-60 | White, Marsh | (RB) | Arkansas | 1975-77 |
| Stein, Sam | (E) | No College | 1931 | Trocolor. Bob | (B) | Alabama | 1942-44 | White, Phil | (E) | Oklahoma | 1925-27 |
| Steinfeld, Al | (C) | C W Post | 1983 | Tucker, Bob | (TE) | Bloomsburg St. | 1970-77 | White, Robb | (DE) | South Dakota | 1988-89 |
| Stenn, Paul | (T) | Villanova | 1942 | Tuggle, John | (RB) | California | 1983-85 | White, Sheldon | (CB) | Miami (Ohio) | 1988-89 |
| Stevens, Ted | (C) | Brown | 1926 | Tunnell, Emlen | (DB) | Iowa/Toledo | 1948-58 | White, Stan | (QB) | Auburn | 1994-97 |
| Stienke, Jim | (DB) | SW Texas St. | 1974-77 | Turbert, Francis | (B) | Morris Harvey | 1943 | Whittington, Mike | (LB) | Notre Dame | 1980-83 |
| Stits, Billy | (DB) | UCLA | 1959-61 | Turner, Kevin | (LB) | Pacific | 1980 | Whittle, Jason | (T) | S.W. Missouri St. | 1998 |
| Stokes, Tm | (T) | Oregon | 1981 | Turner, J. T. | (DT) | Duke | 1977-83 | Whitmore, David | (DB) | Stephen Austin | 1990 |
| Stoltenberg, Bryan | (C) | Colorado | 1997 | Turner, Odessa | (WR) | NW LouisianaSt. | 1987-91 | Wilberg, Oscar | (B) | Neb. Wesleyan | 1930 |
| Stone, Ron | (G) | Boston Coll. | 1996-98 | Tuttle, Orville | (G) | Oklahoma City | 1937-41 | Widmer, Corey | (LB) | Montana St. | 1992-98 |
| Strada, John | (TE) | William Jewell | 1974 | Tyler, Maurice | (DB) | Morgan St. | 1978 | Widseth, Ed | (T) | Minnesota | 1937-40 |
| Strahan, Michael | (DE) | Texas Southern | 1993-98 | Tyler, Pete | (B) | Hardin-Simmons | 1938 | Wietecha, Ray | (C) | Northwestern | 1953-62 |
| Stribling, Bill | (E) | Mississippi | 1951-53 | | | | | Wilkins, Dick | (E) | Oregon | 1954 |
| Strong, Ken | (B) | NYU | 1933-35, 39-47 | **U** | | | | Wilkinson, Bob | (E) | UCLA | 1951-52 |
| Stroud, Jack | (G-T) | Tennessee | 1953-64 | Umont, Frank | (T) | No College | 1943-45 | Williams, Brian | (C) | Minnesota | 1989-98 |
| Stuckey, Henry | (DB) | Missouri | 1975-76 | Umphrey, Rich | (C) | Colorado | 1982-84 | Williams, Byron | (WR) | Texas-Arlington | 1983-85 |
| Stynchula, Andy | (D-E) | Penn St. | 1964-65 | Underwood, Olen | (LB) | Texas | 1965 | Williams, Ellery | (E) | Santa Clara | 1950 |
| Sulaitis, Joe | (B) | No College | 1943-53 | Urch, Scott | (T) | Virginia | 1987 | Williams, Frank | (B) | Utah St. | 1948 |
| Summerall, Pat | (D-E) | Arkansas | 1958-61 | | | | | Williams, George | (DE) | N. Carolina St. | 1998 |
| Summerell, Carl | (QB) | E. Carolina | 1974-75 | **V** | | | | Williams, Jarvis | (S) | Florida | 1994 |
| Sutherin, Don | (B) | Ohio St. | 1959 | Van Horn, Doug | (G) | Ohio St. | 1968-79 | Williams, Joe | (G) | Lafayette | 1925-26 |
| Sutton Ed | (B) | N. Carolina | 1960-61 | Vanoy, Vernon | (DT) | Kansas | 1971 | Williams, Perry | (DB) | N. Carolina St. | 1984-93 |
| Sutton Frank | (T) | Jackson St. | 1987 | Van Pelt, Brad | (LB) | Michigan St. | 1973-83 | Williams, Shaun | (S) | UCLA | 1998 |
| Svare, Harland | (LB) | Washington St. | 1955-60 | Varajon, Mike | (FB) | Toledo | 1987 | Williams, Van | (RB) | E. Tenn. St. | 1987 |
| Svoboda, Bill | (LB) | Tulane | 1954-59 | Vargo, Larry | (LB) | Detroit | 1966-67 | Williams, Willie | (DB) | Grambling | 1965, 67-73 |
| Swain, Bill | (LB) | Oregon St. | 1965-67 | Visnic, Larry | (G) | St. Benedict | 1943-45 | Williamson, Ernie | (T) | N. Carolina | 1948 |
| Swiacki, Bill | (E) | Columbia | 1948-50 | Vokaty, Otto | (B) | Heidelberg | 1932 | Willis, Ken | (K) | Kentucky | 1992 |
| Swartwoudt, Gregg | (T) | N. Dakota | 1987 | Volk, Rich | (DB) | Michigan | 1976 | Wilson, Butch | (E) | Alabama | 1968-69 |
| Szczecko, Joe | (DT) | Northwestern | 1969 | Vosberg, Don | (E) | Marquette | 1941 | Wilson, Fay | (B) | Texas A&M | 1927-32 |
| | | | | Voss, Walter | (E) | Detroit | 1926 | Windauer, Bill | (DT) | Iowa | 1975 |
| **T** | | | | | | | | Winrow, Jason | (G) | Ohio St. | 1994 |
| Tabor, Phil | (DT) | Oklahoma | 1979-82 | **W** | | | | Winter, Bill | (LB) | St. Olaf | 1962-64 |
| Taibi, Joe | (DE) | Idaho | 1987 | Wafer, Carl | (DT) | Tennessee St. | 1974 | Winters, Frank | (C) | Western Illinois | 1989 |
| Taffoni, Joe | (T) | Tennessee-Martin | 1972-73 | Walbridge, Lymen | (G) | Fordham | 1925 | Wolfe, Hugh | (B) | Texas | 1938 |
| Talley, Ben | (LB) | Tennessee | 1995-96 | Walker, Herschel | (RB) | Georgia | 1995 | Wood, Gary | (QB) | Cornell | 1964-66, 68-69 |
| Tarkenton, Fran | (QB) | Georgia | 1967-71 | Walker, Mickey | (G) | Michigan St. | 1961-65 | Woodward, Dick | (C) | Iowa | 1950-51, 53 |
| Tarrant, Bob | (E) | Kan. St. Teachers | 1936 | Walker, Robert | (RB) | West Virginia | 1996 | Woolfolk, Butch | (RB) | Michigan | 1982-84 |
| Tate, David | (S) | Colorado | 1993 | Wallace, Roger | (WR) | Bowling Green | 1976 | Woolford, Gary | (S) | Florida State | 1980 |
| Tate, John | (LB) | Jackson St. | 1976 | Walls, Bill | (E) | TCU | 1937-43 | Wooten, Tito | (S) | N.E. Louisiana | 1994-98 |
| Tautolo, John | (OG) | UCLA | 1982-83 | Walls, Everson | (DB) | Grambling | 1990-92 | Word, Roscoe | (DB) | Jackson St. | 1976 |
| Taylor, Billy | (RB) | Texas Tech | 1978-81 | Walton, Joe | (E) | Pittsburgh | 1961-63 | Wright, Mike | (CB) | Washington St. | 1992 |
| Taylor, Bob | (DE) | Maryland St. | 1963-64 | Walton, Wayne | (G) | Abilene Christian | 1971 | Wright, Steve | (T) | Alabama | 1968-69 |
| Taylor, Lawrence | (LB) | N. Carolina | 1981-93 | Walton, Whip | (LB) | San Diego St. | 1980 | Wyan Kervin | (LB) | Maryland | 1980 |
| Thigpen, Tommy | (LB) | N. Carolina | 1993 | Warren, Vince | (WR) | San Diego St. | 1986 | Wycoff, Doug | (B) | Georgia Tech | 1927-31 |
| Thomas, Aaron | (E) | Oregon St. | 1962-70 | Watkins, Larry | (RB) | Alcorn A&M | 1975-77 | Wynne, Harry | (E) | Arkansas | 1945 |
| Thomas, Bob | (K) | Notre Dame | 1986 | Watson, Tim | (S) | Howard | 1995 | | | | |
| Thomas, George | (B) | Oklahoma | 1952 | Watts, Ted | (CB) | Texas Tech | 1985 | **Y** | | | |
| Thome, Chris | (C) | Minnesota | 1992 | Washington, Gene | (WR) | Georgia | 1979 | Yarbrough, James | (S) | Murray St. | 1987 |
| Thompson, James | (WR) | Memphis St. | 1978 | Washington, John | (DE) | Oklahoma St. | 1986-92 | Yeager, Howard | (B) | Santa Barbara | 1940-41 |
| Thompson, Reyna | (CB) | Baylor | 1989-92 | Way, Charles | (FB) | Virginia | 1995-98 | Yelvington, Dick | (T) | Georgia | 1952-57 |
| Thompson, Rocky | (RB) | West Texas St. | 1971-73 | Weaver, Larry | (B) | Fullerton | 1955 | Younce, Len | (G) | Oregon St. | 1941-48 |
| Thompson, Warren | (LB) | Oklahoma St. | 1987 | Webb, Allen | (DB) | Arnold | 1961-65 | Young, Dave | (TE) | Purdue | 1981 |
| Thornton, George | (DE) | Alabama | 1993 | Webber, Howard | (E) | Kansas St. | 1926 | Young, Rodney | (S) | LSU | 1995-98 |
| Thorpe, Jim | (B) | Carlisle | 1925 | Webster, Alex | (B) | N. Carolina St | 1955-64 | Young, Willie | (T) | Grambling | 1966-75 |
| Thurlow, Steve | (B) | Stanford | 1964-66 | Weinmeister, Arnie | (T) | Washington | 1950-53 | Youso, Frank | (T) | Minnesota | 1958-60 |
| Tidwell, Travis | (QB) | Auburn | 1950-51 | Weisacosky, Ed | (LB) | Miami (Fla.) | 1967 | Yowarsky, Walt | (E) | Kentucky | 1955-57 |
| Tierney, Leo | (C) | Georgia Tech | 1978 | Weiss, John | (E) | No College | 1944-47 | | | | |
| Tillman, Lewis | (RB) | Jackson St. | 1989-93 | Welch, Herb | (S) | UCLA | 1985-88 | **Z** | | | |
| Timberlake, Bob | (QB) | Michigan | 1965 | Wells, Harold | (LB) | Purdue | 1969 | Zapustas, Joe | (E) | Fordham | 1933 |
| Tipton, Dave | (DE) | Stanford | 1971-73 | Wells, Joel | (B) | Clemson | 1961 | Zatechka, Rob | (G) | Nebraska | 1995-98 |
| Tittle, Y A | (QB) | LSU | 1961-64 | Wells, Kent | (DT) | Nebraska | 1990 | Zeno, Coleman | (WR) | Grambling | 1971 |
| Tobin, George | (G) | Notre Dame | 1947 | Wells, Mike | (QB) | Illinois | 1975 | Zofko, Mickey | (RB) | Auburn | 1974 |
| Tobin, Steve | (C) | Minnesota | 1980 | Wellborn, Joe | (C) | Texas A&M | 1966-67 | Zyntell, Jim | (G) | Holy Cross | 1933 |
| Tomaini, Army | (T) | Catawba | 1945 | Wesley, Cecil | (C) | Alabama | 1928 | | | | |
| Tomlin, Tom | (G) | Syracuse | 1925 | West, Stan | (G) | Oklahoma | 1955 | | | | |
| Toogood, Charlie | (DT) | Nebraska | 1958 | Weston, Jeff | (DT) | Notre Dame | 1979-82 | | | | |
| Toomer, Amani | (WR) | Michigan | 1996-98 | Westoupal, Joe | (C) | Nebraska | 1929-30 | | | | |
| Tootie, Jeff | (LB) | San Francisco St. | 1987 | Wheatley, Tyrone | (RB) | Miichigan | 1995-98 | | | | |
| Topp, Bob | (E) | Michigan | 1954-56 | Wheelwright, Ernie | (B) | So. Illinois | 1964-65 | | | | |
| Torrey, Bob | (RB) | Penn State | 1979 | White, Adrian | (S) | Florida | 1987-89 | | | | |
| Treadaway, John | (T) | Hardon-Simmons | 1947-48 | White, Art | (G) | Alabama | 1937-39, 45 | | | | |
| Treadwell, David | (PK) | Clemson | 1993-94 | White, Jim | (T) | Notre Dame | 1945-50 | | | | |

**The Pro Football Hall of Fame**
21, 23a, 25b, 26b, 28a-f, 29a-b, 32, 34b, 47, 52b, 56b, 61a-c, 63, 70a-b, 73a, 79b, 83a-b, 86b, 88, 98a, 99b, 104a-b, 105a-b,107a, 108a, 110a, 113b, 114, 118a-c, 119a-c, 120a-d, 121a-b,121d-e, 129, 131b, 133a-b,134a, 138b, 144a, 165

**Dan Rubin**
6-7, 17, 18, 19, 30, 34a, 35, 36, 38, 39a, 39b, 40-41, 44, 45, 46-47, 56a, 57, 58-59, 62a-c, 84, 85b, 86a, 87, 96, 97, 102-103, 107b, 108b, 109, 110b, 111, 123, 134b, 135, 138a, 140-141, 142

**NFL Properties, Inc.**

**© NFL Photos**
26a, 54, 99a, 124, 131a, 137

**© Hof/ NFL Photos**
37, 50-, 51, 94, 98b, 106, 112, 122, 125

**© UPI/ NFL Photos**
52a, 53, 113a, 130

**© Morris Berman/ NFL Photos**
139

**© George Gellatly/ NFL Photos**
95

**© HY Peskin/ NFL Photos**
60

**© Dan Rubin/ NFL Photos**
61d

**© Wide World Photo/ NFL Photos**
115

**© Michael Zagaris/ NFL Photos**
68

**Jerry Pinkus**
10-11, 33, 48, 49, 75a-b, 77, 79a, 80, 81, 85a, 92, 93b, 134c, 143, 146, 148, 149, 151, 153, 155, 182

**Larry French**
2-3, 4-5, 14-15, 78-79, 90-91, 93a, 100a-b, 101, 126-127, 147, 156-157, 158, 160-161, 162, 163

**Jim Turner**
65b, 65d, 66-67, 71, 72-73, 73b, 74, 152, 154, 159

**Bill Cummings**
12-13, 64, 65a, 65c, 69, 89, 116, 117, 150

**George Tiedemann**
8-9, 144b, 145

**The Collection of Wellington Mara**
24-25, 27

**The Moran Family Collection**
23b, 128

**The New York Football Giants**
22, 31

**© 1959 Time Inc. Reprinted by Permission**
86c

**Kevin Halle**
1

**Boldface** indicates pages with photos.